To Ted,

Thanks for ' '
over the years!

Steve

School, Reform and Society in the New Russia

Studies in Russian and East European History and Society

General Editors: **R. W. Davies**, Emeritus Professor of Soviet Economic Studies, and **E. A. Rees**, Senior Lecturer in Soviet History, both at the Centre for Russian and East European Studies, University of Birmingham

Recent titles include:

Lynne Attwood
CREATING THE NEW SOVIET WOMAN

John Barber and Mark Harrison (*editors*)
THE SOVIET DEFENCE-INDUSTRY COMPLEX FROM STALIN TO KHRUSHCHEV

Vincent Barnett
KONDRATIEV AND THE DYNAMICS OF ECONOMIC DEVELOPMENT

R. W. Davies
SOVIET HISTORY IN THE YELTSIN ERA

James Hughes
STALINISM IN A RUSSIAN PROVINCE

Melanie Ilič
WOMEN WORKERS IN THE SOVIET INTERWAR ECONOMY

Peter Kirkow
RUSSIA'S PROVINCES

E. A. Rees (*editor*)
DECISION-MAKING IN THE STALINIST COMMAND ECONOMY

Lennart Samuelson
PLANS FOR STALIN'S WAR MACHINE
Tukhachevskii and Military-Economic Planning, 1925–1941

Vera Tolz
RUSSIAN ACADEMICIANS AND THE REVOLUTION

Studies in Russian and East European History and Society
Series Standing Order ISBN 0–333–71239–0
(*outside North America only*)

You can receive future titles in this series as they are published by placing a standing order. Please contact your bookseller or, in case of difficulty, write to us at the address below with your name and address, the title of the series and the ISBN quoted above.

Customer Services Department, Macmillan Distribution Ltd, Houndmills, Basingstoke, Hampshire RG21 6XS, England

School, Reform and Society in the New Russia

Stephen L. Webber
Lecturer
University of Birmingham

Foreword by Anthony Jones

in association with
CENTRE FOR RUSSIAN AND EAST EUROPEAN STUDIES
UNIVERSITY OF BIRMINGHAM

First published in Great Britain 2000 by
MACMILLAN PRESS LTD
Houndmills, Basingstoke, Hampshire RG21 6XS and London
Companies and representatives throughout the world

A catalogue record for this book is available from the British Library.

ISBN 0–333–73396–7

First published in the United States of America 2000 by
ST. MARTIN'S PRESS, INC.,
Scholarly and Reference Division,
175 Fifth Avenue, New York, N.Y. 10010

ISBN 0–312–22413–3

Library of Congress Cataloging-in-Publication Data
Webber, Stephen L., 1967–
School, reform, and society in the new Russia / Stephen L. Webber.
p. cm. — (Studies in Russian and East European history and society)
Includes bibliographical references and index.
ISBN 0–312–22413–3
1. Educational change—Russia (Federation) 2. Education and state—Russia (Federation) 3. Education—Russia (Federation)
I. Title. II. Series.
LA839.2.W4 1999
370'.947—dc21 99–12894
CIP

This book is printed on paper suitable for recycling and made from fully managed and sustained forest sources.

10 9 8 7 6 5 4 3 2 1
09 08 07 06 05 04 03 02 01 00

Printed and bound in Great Britain by
Antony Rowe Ltd, Chippenham, Wiltshire

For Sasha
May he enjoy the best of Russian and English educational traditions

Contents

List of Tables and Figure

Tables

Figure

Foreword

Russian society has been in a state of chronic crisis for at least a decade, and nowhere is the long-term damage that has been inflicted greater than in the areas of education and health. The human capital of a nation is its most precious resource, and investment in people is arguably the wisest investment any society can make. There is now a firm consensus among researchers that an effective system of education that is accessible to all is essential for long-term economic survival and growth. Central to this endeavour is the teaching profession, without whose energy, skills, knowledge and entrepreneurism education will not prepare new generations to live and work in the conditions of a global economy. This is as true in Russia as in any other country, and that nation's future is highly dependent on what is happening in the schools of today. The question to be asked, of course, is how well are Russia's schools doing, and how able is the teaching profession to deliver what is needed? Stephen Webber has done a remarkable job of helping us to make that judgement.

In the rush of the daily media to cover the latest, most bizarre, or most frightening news coming out of Russia, much of the real story of the state of that nation is missed. High on the list of those items that are ignored is the fate of the schools and the devastation of the teaching profession. Official policies of the 1990s have made a bad situation worse by continuing the Soviet tradition of constant tinkering and interfering with education, but given the economic bankruptcy of the State the results have been even more damaging than in earlier years. Unable to pay the salaries due to teachers or to provide the money to maintain the fabric of the schools, the central authorities have pursued a campaign of moving responsibility for education to the local level, without providing the means to meet these obligations. At the same time, education is being increasingly privatized, without much concern for the ability of an impoverished population to pay for this, or for the necessity to enforce high standards of performance in the burgeoning private system. The result is a teaching profession that is demoralized, schools that are in increasingly poor repair and lacking in essential equipment, and a growing number of school-age children who are not receiving any form of education (more than a million by recent, official estimates). There is evidence that the educational level of today's young Russians is lower than that of their parents, a situation that does not bode well for the long-term recovery of the nation. Moreover, the number of young people who are turning to anti-social activities is seen as alarming by many Russian observers, who now speak openly of 'the lost generation'.

Those of us who are concerned about the implications of this for Russia's future (and for the ways in which that future will affect the rest of the world) are fortunate to have been provided by Stephen Webber with an in-depth, informed, clear-eyed, and fair assessment of education in today's Russia. Central to his account is the role of teachers, of their ability to prepare students for life in a new society, and of the ability of this profession to survive the current crisis. As he points out, teachers have gone on strike during the last ten years more than any other occupational group, and have become increasingly vocal in their condemnation of the harm that is being done to a generation of young people. And yet, there is no evidence that it has had any effect on official actions, nor that teachers by themselves can stem the further decline of what was once considered one of Soviet Russia's proudest achievements – a stable and quite successful system of public education.

Free of jargon or ideology, and written in a style that is accessible to all, *School, Reform and Society in the New Russia* is both thoughtful and informative. It is the definitive account of this topic, and is likely to remain so for years to come.

ANTHONY JONES
Associate Director, the Gorbachev Foundation of North America and Editor of 'Russian Education and Society'

Acknowledgements

I would not have been able to complete this study without the support of a large number of people and organisations, in England, Russia and elsewhere. The following list must, necessarily, exclude many of those who gave their support, but I would like them to know that their help was always most appreciated.

I would like to thank, in the first instance, the staff of the Department of Russian at the University of Exeter, and in particular Mr Michael Pursglove, for his tireless encouragement and invaluable advice. Mr George Avis, Dr James Muckle, Mr Jim Norman and Lady Jeanne Sutherland of the Study Group on Education in Russia, the Independent States and Eastern Europe all offered useful advice and information throughout the research, as did Mr Ted Neather, of the School of Education at the University of Exeter. In the Centre for Russian and East European Studies, University of Birmingham, my colleagues Dr John Dunstan, Ms Moya Flynn and Dr Hilary Pilkington all provided detailed critiques of my ideas, thus helping to improve the text, and I am grateful for the careful editing and constructive comments and suggestions of Dr Arfon Rees and Professor Bob Davies, editors of the CREES–Macmillan series. Dr Chris Williams of the Institute of Education, University of London, also gave helpful comments, as did (another) Dr Chris Williams, of the University of Central Lancashire. I very much appreciated the support and encouragement given by colleagues from the United States, in particular from Professors Ben Eklof, Larry Holmes, Anthony Jones, Mark Johnson, Steve Kerr and Howard Mehlinger. As ever, the responsibility for omissions, shortcomings and errors of fact and opinion lies with me alone.

I am extremely grateful to the Ford Foundation and to the Research and Development Committee of the British Association for Slavonic and East European Studies (BASEES), which funded two of my research visits to Russia.

The field research in Russia would not have been possible without the willing cooperation of the many teachers, pupils, administrators and others who have allowed me to study their school system and offered their support and their views. Special thanks are due to

Larisa Aleksandrovna Chernushkina and her colleagues, and to Vladimir Il'ich Chuprov, Vladimir Abramovich Karakovskii, Tat'yana Ivanovna Kasatkina, Inna Vladimirovna Ravich-Shcherbo, Irina Fedorovna Romanovich, Lyudmila Mikhailovna Smirnova and Yuliya Al'bertovna Zubok.

My wife Tanya has been an untiring source of encouragement and understanding, and has also provided invaluable critical appraisal of my work, in her capacity as a professional educationalist who knows, much better than I, what it means to work in the Russian and English school systems. Finally, I should thank both our families for making everything possible, and Sasha – for being such a charming distraction from academic toil!

List of Terms and Abbreviations

APN SSSR (*Akademiya pedagogicheskikh nauk*)	Academy of Pedagogical Sciences of the USSR
akkreditatsiya	accreditation (of schools)
aspirantura	postgraduate study
attestat zrelosti	school-leaving certificate
attestatsiya	appraisal (teacher); attestation (school)
avtorskaya shkola	school in which experimental work is conducted (term used in late 1980s, early 1990s)
bakalavr	Bachelor's degree
BUP (*bazisnyi uchebnyi plan*)	core curriculum
CPSU	Communist Party of the Soviet Union
diplom	qualification gained on completion of higher education (approx. equiv. to UK degree)
DOBRO (*Dvizhenie 'Obrazovanie – Budushchee Rossii'*)	Socio-political movement 'Education is the Future of Russia'
doshkol'noe obrazovanie	pre-school education
deideologizatsiya	'deideologisation'
depolitizatsiya	'depoliticisation'
detskii sad (pl. *detskie sady*)	kindergarten
dogovornaya/kontraktnaya sistema	agreement/contract system (of graduate employment)
doktorantura	doctoral studies
dotsent	Russian academic position (approx. equiv. to British 'Reader')
Duma (Gosudarstvennaya duma)	State parliament (Russian Federation)
ETS *(edinaya tarifnaya setka*)	common salary network

edinoe obrazovatel'noe prostranstvo	common educational space
eksperimental'naya ploshchadka	experimental site (school used as centre for testing innovations)
Evrika	('Eureka'). Non-state educational organisation which provides INSET services
FPRO *(Federal'naya programma razvitiya obrazovaniya)*	Federal Programme for the Development of Education
gimnaziya (pl. *gimnazii*)	gymnasium
GORUNO *(Gorodskoe upravlenie narodnogo obrazovaniya)*	municipal educational authority
Goskomimushchestvo	State Committee on Property
Gosudarstvennyi komitet po vysshemu obrazovaniyu (Goskomvuz)	State Committee on Higher Education
grazhdanovedenie	civics education
gumanitarizatsiya	humanitarisation
gumanizatsiya	humanisation
INSET	in-service education for teachers
Institut povysheniya kvalifikatsii (IPK)	INSET centre
Institut usovershenstvovaniya uchitelei (IUU)	INSET centre
klassicheskaya gimnaziya	classical gymnasium
klassnyi rukovoditel' (pl. *klasnnye rukovoditeli*)	form tutor
Komsomol (VLKSM)	All-Union Leninist Communist Union of Youth
lichnost'	personality, character, the individual
litsei (pl. *litsei*)	lycée
magistratura	Master's degree
malokomplektnaya shkola	small-enrolment school (in rural areas)
MARO (*Moskovskaya akademiya razvitiya obrazovaniya*)	Moscow Academy for the Development of Education
massovaya shkola	'mass' school

metodicheskii den'	methodology day
metodicheskii tsentr	teachers' centre
metodist (pl. *metodisty*)	advisory teacher / senior teacher
MIROS (*Moskovskii institut razvitiya obrazovatel'nykh sistem*)	Moscow Institute for the Development of Educational Systems
nachal'naya voennaya podgotovka	preliminary military training
nachal'noe obrazovanie	primary education
nachal'noe professional'noe obrazovanie	preliminary vocational education
Narodnyi uchitel' SSSR	People's Teacher of the USSR
NQT	newly qualified teacher
oblast'	region (of the Russian Federation)
OBLUNO (*Oblastnoe upravlenie narodnogo obrazovaniya*)	regional educational authority
obrazovatel'nye standarty	educational standards
obshcheobrazovatel'naya shkola	comprehensive school
obshchestvennyi dolg	social duty (of Soviet citizen)
ostatochnyi printsip	'leftover principle' (educational financing)
otsev	a) reference to pupils who leave school by choice after the 9th grade b) reference to phenomenon of expulsion of considerable numbers of pupils, for various reasons, in the post-Soviet period
pedagogicheskaya gimnaziya/ pedagogicheskii litsei	pedagogical gymnasium / lycée
pedagogicheskii institut (*pedinstitut*, pl. *pedinstituty*)	pedagogical institute
pedagogicheskii klass (*pedklass*)	pedagogical class
pedagogicheskii kolledzh (*pedkolledzh*)	pedagogical college
pedagogicheskii sovet (*pedsovet*)	school committee

Pedagogicheskoe obshchestvo	'The Pedagogical Society'
pedagogicheskoe uchilishche (*peduchilishche*) (pl. *pedagogicheskie uchilishcha*)	pedagogical college
pedagogicheskii universitet (*peduniversitet*)	pedagogical university
Pedagogika sotrudnichestva	'Pedagogy of Cooperation' (banner of reform movement from mid-1980s)
perestroika	policy of economic and social 'restructuring' introduced by M.S. Gorbachev after 1985
PTU (*Professional'no-tekhnicheskoe uchilishche*)	vocational-technical college
proforientatsiya	vocational orientation (career guidance)
Profsoyuz rabotnikov narodnogo obrazovaniya i nauki	Trade Union of Educationalists and Scientists
protsentomaniya	'percentage mania' (grade inflation)
RAO (*Rossiiskaya akademiya obrazovaniya*)	Russian Academy of Education
raspredelenie	'distribution' system (under which graduates were allocated, during the Soviet era, to a work placement for up to three years, upon completion of their studies)
razgosudarstvlenie	'destatisation' (of the education system)
razvivayushchee obuchenie	'developmental education' – an approach to teaching and learning developed by Soviet educational psychologists from the 1970s
Rossiiskii pedagogicheskii parlament	'Russian pedagogical parliament'
RUNO (*Raionnoe upravlenie narodnogo*	district educational

obrazovaniya)	authority
spetsializirovannaya shkola (spetsskhola)	specialised school for intensive study of a particular subject (e.g. foreign language)
srednee professional'noe obrazovanie	secondary specialised education
stavka	a) salary grade b) number of contact hours of teaching staff
stazher	newly qualified teacher (NQT)
tekhnikum (pl. *tekhnikumy*)	technical college
uchitel'–ispolnitel'	'teacher–fulfiller'
Universitet pedagogicheskogo masterstva (UPM)	university of pedagogical mastery
uravnilovka	'levelling' of students in Soviet system
ustav shkoly	school statute
vechernyaya srednyaya shkola	evening school (for those who left school before completing 11 grades)
VNIK – *Shkola (Vremennyi nauchno-issledovatel'skii kollektiv*)	Ad hoc Research Group on the School
vospitanie	upbringing
vseobuch	universal education
vysshee uchebnoe zavedenie (VUZ, pl. VUZy)	higher-education establishment
yasli	crèche
Zasluzhennyi uchitel' RSFSR	Honoured Teacher of the RSFSR
zavuch (*zaveduyushchii uchebnoi chast'yu*)	deputy headteacher
ZUNy (*Znaniya, umeniya, navyki*)	Knowledge, skills, habits (supposed emphasis of Soviet curriculum)

Introduction

The Russian school system is undergoing a process of comprehensive reform, which is intended, according to its declared aims, to support the processes of democratisation and the development of a market economy in Russia, and address the long-overdue need to engage in the thorough revision of the content and nature of schooling itself. In trying to attain these ambitious goals, however, the schools have to contend not only with the usual problems which accompany such processes of reform in any country, but also with a funding crisis that has denied the system the resources it desperately requires, causing fears over its very survival as a viable entity, and with the fall-out from the social crises which have afflicted Russia in recent years.

Accordingly, while the focus of this book is on the *internal* experience of change within the school system, the importance of the *external* factor – the school–society relationship – is stressed throughout, permeating each chapter, and providing, in Parts I and III, an evaluation of society's attitude towards its schools. This all-embracing format has proved necessary because of the relative neglect of the subject of Russian education in recent years by the academic community in English-speaking countries, which has preferred to concentrate on matters of politics and economic reform in Russia (a brief survey of the abundant literature on the Russian 'transition' will reveal that the words 'education' and 'school' appear all too infrequently in the indexes of these works).[1] Although a small number of books on Russian school reform have been published in English (e.g. Eklof and Dneprov (eds), 1993,[2] Holmes, Read and Voskresenskaya, 1995;[3] Jones (ed.), 1994[4]), providing a useful foundation of analysis and information on the reforms, only the last-named book includes substantial analysis of the process of implementation, and this is based on early impressions (the contributions were written in 1992–93).

The current volume seeks to fill this gap in the literature, with an examination of the state of the school system and its response to reform by the late 1990s. The holistic nature of the study, dictated by the dearth of material on this subject, inevitably means that my treatment of the issues raised will be relatively brief. The book concentrates only on the school system, for instance, and does not cover pre-school, vocational or higher education. Further important issues which deserve fuller treatment include the subject of personal and social education, syllabus content, gender and ethnicity as factors in education, the position of rural schools, and so on. It is hoped, therefore, that this work, by setting out the parameters of school development in post-Soviet Russia, will act as a foundation for future studies of change at the micro-level, in which certain hypotheses generated here (e.g. concerning the positive effects of inertia in the system, or on pupil attitudes towards the education they receive) can be examined in more detail.

In general, though, this represents a task for Russian educational sociologists, rather than for foreign observers. While an impressive amount of work has been conducted in educational research in recent years, making up for the stifling neglect of the Soviet period, the domestic research base on education in Russia remains weak, in comparison with, for example, the amount of attention given to the English education system by researchers in the United Kingdom. Further, despite the absence of officially imposed ideological constraints on the field of educational sociology, the nature of the approaches adopted still appears to be limited by the traits of the old system, both with regard to conceptual paradigms and the methodology of research. However, the adoption of innovative approaches and methods is held back by the level of decay and contraction in Russia's research base in the field of sociology in general: resources are scarce, barely sufficient to provide a skeleton framework of analysis.[5] While progress may prove possible in pockets, therefore, comprehensive treatment of school–society relations, which could include evaluation of such notions as the 'hidden curriculum', well developed in the West yet hardly discussed in Russia, may only be achievable some years hence.

Organisation

In Part I, the societal and educational contexts of the current reform programme are examined. In Chapter 1 the question of the importance of a 'vision' of societal development is raised. Does Russia know what it wants from its school system? Is it possible to define the needs of any country, especially one embroiled in social upheaval? An analysis of the nature of participation in policy-making is given in Chapter 2, followed, in Chapter 3, by a review of the reform agenda itself. Does the programme for change represent a realistic and appropriate response to the needs of the country?

Part II provides an evaluation of the experience of implementation, beginning with a review, in Chapter 4, of the impact of change in educational administration at federal, regional and school levels. A framework for devolution has been installed, and many administrators and teachers report early satisfaction with the new freedoms they enjoy, yet some ask whether, in the rush to dismantle the old system, the centre divested itself of control too rapidly. Alongside the benefits that devolution can bring, the danger of loss of cohesion is a major concern. Chapters 5 and 6 focus on the course of change in the schools themselves.[6] The little-studied issue of the culture of the Russian school is addressed, and an assessment made of the extent to which this culture is conducive to the implementation of reform. I search for signs of change in the system, and argue that, while examples of positive and negative experience can be identified in many cases, most schools are still adopting a 'coping' approach to change, with relatively little real reform having yet taken place. In order to carry change forward, there is a pressing need for effective mechanisms of cohesion and support. As is shown in Chapter 7, positive developments in this area are hindered by a lack of resources, a feature too of the teacher–education network, which is examined in Chapter 8, and which is struggling to effect revision of its content and structure in order to meet new demands.

Following a progress report on the internal condition of the school system, Part III gives an overview of the school–society relationship. The weakness of the societal safety net is demonstrated, and it is suggested that while the school has managed to survive 'attempts' on its life in recent years, it remains vulnerable. Can the new Russia really hope to build a democratic society and thriving economy if it continues to ignore the problems of the schools, and therefore of the young, in this way?

Studying Russia's schools: lessons for the individual and the system

For Western students of the Soviet school system in the pre-*perestroika* era, the difficulties were considerable, with severe limitations placed by the Soviet authorities on the degree of access to statistical data, documents, and the schools themselves. Such problems have diminished considerably over recent years, and I have enjoyed a far greater amount of access than would previously have been the case. Nevertheless, studying Russian education still poses a sizeable challenge to the observer – Russian, as well as foreign. The problems encountered by the individual researcher, however, reflect difficulties faced by the system as a whole, as I now explain.

Approach

Providing an analysis of the experience of change across a school system is a task which would be difficult enough even in one's own country, examining a system in which one grew up; in the case of a foreign system the matter is complicated by a range of factors – cultural insight, familiarity with the traditions and practices of that system, the foreign language itself – which combine to make comparative education a challenging field for those who venture into it.[7] Further, an attempt to generalise from limited research findings and provide a system-wide analysis is problematic, of course. In the Soviet system at least one could rely on the degree of commonality which the unified curriculum and other measures imposed. Now, with decentralisation in full swing, it is becoming increasingly difficult to talk of the Russian system as a single, identifiable entity.

Nevertheless, beneath the superficial appearance of change, the amount of true diversification in the system is still limited, and the common traditions of the Soviet school are still very much present from Karelia to Kamchatka. For the time being, therefore, a degree of generalisation should still be seen as acceptable. The intention here, after all, is to obtain an *impression* of the patterns of development in the schools. In order to achieve this goal, the research has drawn on available documentary evidence and the findings of field research conducted between 1990 and 1997. This included the use of expert interviews with subjects who were qualified to respond to questions on developments at a country-wide level, along with interview and questionnaire data gathered in a range of educational establishments.

Access issues

The Russian education system comprises the following levels:

- pre-school (*doshkol'noe obrazovanie*) (birth to 6 years)
- primary level (*nachal'noe obrazovanie*) (6–11 years)
- basic secondary (*bazovoe*, or *nepolnoe srednee obrazovanie*) (11–15)

- general secondary (*obshchee*, or *polnoe srednee obrazovanie*) (11–17)
- preliminary vocational (*nachal'noe professional'noe obrazovanie*) (from 15)
- secondary-specialised education (*srednee spetsial'noe obrazovanie*) (from 15)
- higher education (*vysshee obrazovanie*) (from 17).

During the course of the research, schools and other establishments in the cities of Yaroslavl' (located some 300 kilometres north-east of Moscow), Moscow and St Petersburg were visited. While the more favourable economic and social conditions found in the latter two cities, in comparison with other Russian cities and regions, render their experience somewhat distinct and unrepresentative of Russia as a whole, their inclusion here was seen as valuable, as these centres have acted as testbeds for the innovations in Russian education, with these ideas then tending to filter down into the system as a whole. Yaroslavl', in contrast, does not enjoy the privileges of the two 'capitals' (although its proximity to Moscow can be an advantage in terms of access to centres of innovation and policy-making), but is a relatively poor city, where the material state of the schools, at least, is more typical of those in the country in general. Contact was also maintained with educationalists in the cities and regions of Novgorod, Penza, Perm', Petrozavodsk and Vladimir.

A summary of the establishments covered by the research follows, with the figure in the left column indicating the number actually visited, and the number in brackets showing the number of additional establishments with which indirect contact was made. (An outline of the structure of educational provision for the 6–17 age-band in the Russian education system is given in Appendix 1.)

Establishments visited / contacted:

1 Schools and colleges			
• 'Comprehensive schools'[8]	(*Obshcheobrazovatel'nye shkoly*)	12	(23)
• Specialised schools[9]	(*Spetsializirovannye shkoly*)	6	(12)
• State gymnasia/lycées	(*Gimnazii* and *litsei*)	7	(9)
• Non-state schools	(*Negosudarstvennye / chastnye shkoly*)	4	(4)
2 Higher and secondary-specialised education			
• Pedagogical institutes/ universities	(*Pedagogicheskie instituty/ universitety*)	3	(4)
• Universities	(*Universitety*)	3	(2)
• Pedagogical colleges	(*Pedagogicheskie uchilishcha*)	2	(3)

3 In-service education

- In-service training establishments (*Instituty povysheniya kvalifikatsii*) 3 (1)
- District methodology centre (*Raionnyi metodicheskii tsentr*) 1

4 Other establishments

- Centre for Pedagogical Innovation (Moscow)
- Centre for Psychological Rehabilitation of Children 1
- Centre for the Sociology of Education
- Institute of General and Educational Psychology
- Ministry of Education of the Russian Federation.

I owe a debt of gratitude to the many educationalists and administrators who afforded me access to their establishments and arranged for interviews and the questionnaire survey to be conducted. Schools in any system can be difficult to 'penetrate' for the researcher,[10] and while the Soviet legacy of uneasiness in dealing with foreigners has decreased considerably, it somewhat goes against the nature of teachers to welcome outsiders into their 'secret garden'. I attempted to overcome such reticence, when it occurred, by asking to be accepted as a fellow professional (who had once worked in the English school system), and also by making it clear that I was not in Russia merely to find faults with their system (a perception about foreigners which I have discovered among a considerable number of Russian teachers, and one which is not without foundation), but wished instead to share information and experience. On a number of occasions I chose to spend the first ten minutes of encounters by delivering a critique of the English school system, to prove that the issues faced by teachers in both countries have much in common.

For the most part, teachers responded positively to this approach, and many proved more than willing to enter into a frank and profound discussion. Lesson observations, however, were less useful for the purposes of the research, as the classes tended to be 'show lessons', with prepared (sometimes rehearsed) dynamics of question and answer interchange between teacher and pupils, which taught me little about the nature of change in the learning process. This practice, of showing one's 'best side' to a visitor, is something found in any school system, of course (indeed, the current format of school inspection in England positively encourages it), but it has a particularly long tradition in Russia.

The fact that I was a foreigner also influenced the behaviour of teachers (and, perhaps, their pupils), for another ingrained feature of Soviet/Russian life, and one which is, fortunately, now disappearing, concerns the perceived need to give preferential treatment to foreign guests, who have tended often to enjoy a better reception than Russians themselves. It is difficult to imagine, for instance, that a young Russian researcher would be able to walk into the Department for Education and Employment in London and obtain an immediate interview with a senior minister, as I did in the Russian Ministry of Education in Moscow. The task for the researcher is not to abuse such treatment, despite the temptations, and to retain a sense of perspective: while it may be easier to gather evidence from well-informed contacts in Moscow, the view of teachers at the chalk face, far from the ministry, is likely to be quite different.

Statistical data

The extent of the problem of access to data on the Russian system may surprise Western scholars who are used, now, to the immediate access to comprehensive and accurate data offered by electronic databases. As the director of the Centre for the Sociology of Education (Russian Academy of Education) mentioned to me following my complaints about such problems, Russian administrators and researchers do not possess some 75 per cent of the statistics they need to provide a full analysis of the system. Even when data are collected, their validity may be suspect, as several leading educationalists whom I interviewed on the matter suggested, while further difficulties arise with the dissemination of statistical information.

Awareness of macro- vs micro-level issues

Many teachers tend to concentrate on their immediate professional and social surroundings, and often do not have a well-developed awareness of 'systemic' issues. This can hinder the work of the independent researcher (I sometimes found that I had a better understanding of system-wide developments than my interviewees), and it also has important implications for the work of the schools, influencing the extent to which effective professional communication can take place between educationalists in various parts of the country. This is an issue to which I will return later in the book.[11]

Interviews

Over the period of research, some 346 interviews (unstructured and semi-structured) were conducted with a range of subjects, as follows:

Administrators	7	Parents	22
Business people	5	Pupils	38
Deputy Minister of Education	1	Teachers	148
Educational journalists	6	Teacher-educators	33
Headteachers	14	Trainee teachers	41
Higher education lecturers	17	Researchers	22
Ministerial officials (federal)	4	Total	346

Headteachers and teachers sub-sample

In the combined teachers and headteachers' sample of 162 interviewees, the female:male ratio of interviewees was 83.3 per cent to 16.7 per cent (135 and 27 respectively), a figure which is close, in fact, to the distribution in the Russian system as a whole (84.7 per cent and 15.3 per cent respectively).[12] The over-representation of women in the teaching profession is referred to as part of a process of *feminizatsiya*, or the 'feminisation' of the schools, and is held to reflect the poor level of material reward associated with teaching careers, which acts as a disincentive for potential male recruits. Some 13.0 per cent (21) of this sub-sample of 160 were based in non-state schools, 26.5 per cent (43) were from state gynmasia or lycées, and the remaining 60.5 per cent (98) worked in ordinary state comprehensives. (This weighting towards 'new' establishments reflected my desire to examine the part which they, in particular, were playing in the change process.) With regard to geographical location, some 45.1 per cent (73) worked in Yaroslavl', 32.1 per cent (52) worked in Moscow, 17.3 per cent (28) in Petersburg, and 5.5 per cent (9) came from other cities across Russia.

Direct comparison of interview evidence is difficult, as there is considerable variation in the length of interviews, the number of subjects present, the questions which it was possible to ask, and so on. I was not in a position to impose a strictly ordered interview regime, but had, instead, to adapt to the demands and circumstances of my interviewees (many, for example, had only a limited amount of time available). Although some interviews were recorded on cassette, the dictaphone was used infrequently, as it was perceived by some early respondents as threatening. I considered it to be more important to hold open conversations, rather than restricted discussions, and thus abandoned the use of cassettes in favour of recording in note form. This was seen as acceptable, given that interviews were not the focal point of the research, but another means of achieving the montage of impressions of change to which the larger study aspired.

Problems were encountered in maintaining contact with interviewees and their schools over the period of the research (in one case, for instance, a change of headteacher meant that I was no longer able to visit a school which had provided extremely valuable interviews on a previous visit, while in general, the increased staff turnover in the schools disrupted my access to interviewees). This affected the nature of interviewing, since it proved very difficult to employ standard questions over a length of time, given the interrupted and broken nature of contact. The sample of interviewees is not presented as representative, although an attempt was made to interview a wide cross-section of the teaching community, with regard to gender, age, subject taught, seniority, type of school in which the interviewee worked.

Questionnaire survey

To supplement the qualitative evidence, a small-scale questionnaire survey of teachers' attitudes was conducted in December 1995 in schools in Moscow and St Petersburg, with further copies distributed in April 1996 to teachers in Yaroslavl', Perm' and Moscow. In all, 132 usable replies were obtained. A copy of the questionnaire (translated into English) is provided in Appendix 2. Because of its small size this sample should not be seen as representative, of course, although I will refer at times during the book to some of the findings, for the purpose of illustration of developments observed during my field-work.

Part I

The Aims of Reform

1
What Does Russia Need from its Schools?

The need for change

It was clear, following the dissolution of the Soviet Union in December 1991, that the school system of the New Russia would have to undergo fundamental change of some kind. The question was, what kind of change, and how much? As will be shown in Chapter 3, wide-ranging change activities had already emerged some time before 1991, and work was well underway, in the newly independent Russian Ministry of Education, on the preparation of educational legislation to address, as its authors stated, the 'crisis' in Russia's schools. The most striking evidence that something was wrong in the system was produced by the publication of statistical data on the material difficulties of the schools, which were the result of decades of neglect under the leftover principle (*ostatochnyi printsip*) of financing, with education, in common with the other parts of the welfare sector, being given much lower priority in state budgets than other sectors such as defence, a trend which had become increasingly pronounced in the course of Brezhnev's period in office. The lack of investment was felt particularly by rural communities, with teacher shortages and under-supply of teaching resources adding to rural Russia's general state of marked inferiority in comparison with urban centres. With regard to the content of education, reform-minded educationalists had come increasingly to question the nature of teaching and learning in the schools. Their criticism was aimed not so much at the level of academic achievement (the data provided by Soviet authorities had indicated impressive levels of knowledge, in international comparative reports, in subjects such as mathematics and physics, although the value of such data and such comparisons is, in fact, rather limited and superficial), but rather at the actual philosophy of education which underpinned the, ostensibly, communist school system of the USSR.

The extent to which talk of crisis, and the need for change, were justified or exaggerated, will be discussed later in this study. For the present, it is sufficient to say that the educational community, politicians, the mass media and the public at large seemed to have been convinced, according to the research findings of Soviet and Western analysts, that the problems of the schools were extensive, and fundamental reform was required.[1] If the schools were to be asked to engage in change, though, they would require a sense of direction to be given by policy-makers and society at large. Was this forthcoming?

The problem of defining society's educational needs

The study of educational change in the West has devoted considerable attention to the question of 'vision', of knowing what change is supposed to achieve, in order to clarify goals and the means of achieving those goals.[2] Building a shared vision is no easy task, of course, even in the case of relatively small-scale change which concerns only the micro-environment of one school. When educational change efforts are explicitly allocated goals linking them to societal change, the question of a shared vision becomes even more difficult to define and implement, for, as White argues, achieving consensus on society's needs is problematic:

> Some say that education should promote the growth of understanding (or knowledge, or reason, or the mind) for its own sake; others, that it should help each pupil to develop his potentials to the full. Some see 'individuality' or 'personal autonomy' as of first importance. Some believe in all-round development, in a balance between intellectual and practical achievements or between the arts and the sciences; others put more emphasis on excellence within specialisms. Others, again, speak of the needs of society, of ensuring a literate and numerate work-force, or an intelligent or participatory democracy. Some stress art and culture, others moral character: the list of aims is almost endless.[3]

As Jonathan points out, talk of the 'needs' of society belies a rather simplistic approach, in which the fact that we do not live in homogenous societies is ignored in favour of providing misleading clarity of aims.[4] Thus, while the most influential sources of declarations of the aims of education, given their power to direct policy, are the various levels of government (with the weighting of power decided by the level of distribution of power within the system), these will probably reflect the needs only of a proportion of the population, even in a liberal democracy. Conflict theorists such as Bourdieu[5] and Willis,[6] feminist writers and others have demonstrated convincingly that certain groups (e.g. women, ethnic minorities,[7] people with special educational needs) have tended to be disenfranchised from having significant influence on educational policy. The matter is further complicated by the fact that beneath official policy may lie hidden agendas of educational aims, as Davies suggests in her evaluation of the apparent eagerness of many governments around the world in recent years to support schemes for 'school improvement':

> The myth is that everyone from the government downwards would like school effectiveness, but that there are just too many material or attitudinal constraints on its implementation. In fact, governments do not want effective schools in the academic or even vocational sense. The last thing a government wants is too many articulate, well-qualified students.[8]

The notion of setting 'national' aims of education, therefore, is rather illusory, as policies will inevitably reflect the political and ideological beliefs and goals of the policy-makers. The change of direction which elections at national and local levels can bring, however, along with diversity of development, interpretation and application of policy from national through local to school levels (especially in decentralised systems), and other factors, do lend a certain dynamism to the nature of the organisation of schooling, something which is more noticeable in liberal democracies, and less developed (and possibly actively suppressed) in centralised, one-party systems such as the Soviet Union. In a well-established democracy, furthermore, there are, in principle, a range of social, political, legal and economic checks and balances (e.g. through mass media coverage of the issue of education, strike action by teachers), which add to this dynamic tension, ensuring that some kind of debate (albeit often ill-informed) takes place in society over the content and nature of education.[9] In the case of the New Russia, the country is in the process of an uncertain transition towards democratic governance, with a population which has little experience of (and, many would suggest, relatively little trust to date in) democratic traditions, and in which the scope for engaging in debates on issues such as education is limited by the fact that attention is often focussed on the more visible aspects of political, economic and social change. The danger arises, accordingly, that the development of educational policy is, as I will argue in Chapter 10, being informed only by a shallow societal debate, a situation which holds serious implications both for the schools, and for Russian society as a whole.

The new Russia: a crisis of identity

The root cause of the shallowness of this debate can be found in the broader context of the crisis of identity with which the new Russia has struggled in the 1990s. The end of the Soviet Union marked the end of an era, but, as Rigby summarises succinctly, uncertainly still hangs over the question of which path of development Russia is to choose now:

> Does Russia need a period of conservative or transformative authoritarianism? If not, should it be a presidential or a parliamentary democracy? . . . How much freedom is consonant with social and political peace? Should as much 'socialism' as possible be retained? If marketisation is desirable and/or inevitable, what should be the rôle and extent of state involvement? Should market reforms go the 'shock therapy' Polish road, the authoritarian Chinese road, or some other? . . . All this suggests a near chaos defying analysis.[10]

One might argue that it does not really matter if Russia cannot decide what it wants to be, and that the results of the 1993 and 1995 elections to the state parliament (*Duma*) show that a democratic tradition is being nurtured, no matter how unwelcome the outcome of those elections may have been to the 'democrats' and Western observers. The difficulty lies, of course, in the extent of the disagreement and uncertainty over the course that Russia is to take, and the lengths to which Russia's leaders and potential leaders are prepared to go in pursuit of their particular vision of Russia's future. So long as armed force is seen as a legitimate recourse for solving political problems, as we saw in October 1993 when President Boris Yeltsin ended the executive–legislature dispute by sending in the tanks to attack the parliament building, Russian society and its institutions will continue to suffer from a lack of stability that could lead to severe disruption, even disintegration of the nation, a backdrop against which the enormous problems of the school system must be placed. While society needs to pay attention to the part that the schools must play in shaping Russia's future course of development, however, similar attention should be paid to the needs of the schools themselves. The following section introduces a number of the principal themes to be covered in this study.

What does the school need from Russia?

Any school system needs a certain degree of societal stability in order to be able to function effectively; the upheaval in Russia's social fabric, however, is taking its toll on the school, which must deal with the fall-out from the rising unemployment level, soaring crime rates, destitution, and many other problems which are reflected in the attitudes and behaviour of the pupils. The school's greatest need for stability, though, is financial: can the country guarantee its schools, its teachers, its pupils that they will receive adequate material support during this difficult period of transition?

The school is still waiting for a tangible commitment to education on the part of its government and its society. Early hopes that the new Russian government would display a greater interest in education than the Soviet state had quickly turned to disillusionment. Yeltsin's first decree on becoming President of the Russian Federation in June 1991 was devoted to education, in the form of the notorious Decree No. 1, in which it was promised, for instance, that the average salary for teachers would be no lower than the average salary in the industrial sector.[11] Russia's teachers have long since given up on this and other promises.

Finally, in this chapter we have seen that the last of the school's needs, for clarity regarding the desired direction for societal development, is currently far from being answered. For the time being, perhaps, this will not be that great a problem. After 70 years of pretending to be marching in one direction, which seemed to be so clear at the start, but which soon saw various detours, dead ends, and abrupt reversals on the way, there are some who might be glad of a rest from 'knowing' where they are heading. Certain members of society, as we shall see, have taken advantage of the confusion to set out their own personal agenda, ignoring the effect that this might have on those around them. This can be tolerated for a while, for the inertia of the old system will continue to keep things more or less together, but the longer that society takes to reach a sufficient level of consensus on what it wants to be, the longer the school will have to wait to find out what is required of it, in order to be able to make an appropriate evaluation of its capability (and, perhaps, desire) to respond.

2
The Development of the Reform Agenda

To what extent did the debate on education, and the development of the reform agenda, involve Russia's politicians, representatives of the business community, industry, ethnic minorities, the wider public, and, indeed, the teaching profession itself? Identifying actors and the nature of their influence in the development of reforms is not an easy task, but even an approximate answer to this question will help in an evaluation of the reform agenda.

Direct participation in educational policy-making is limited in most countries, of course and, as was shown in the previous chapter, certain groups may find that their ability to influence policy is severely limited. Nevertheless, in Western liberal democracies the opportunities provided to discuss policy openly, and for groups to lobby freely for their own interests, have increased in recent decades, on the whole, and lend a dynamism to the development of the education system, affording some possibility at least for educationalists, political parties, business organisations, parent groups, religious organisations and others to attempt to bring some influence to bear on the course of policy.

In the Soviet Union, as will be demonstrated in this chapter, there was a limited amount of indirect participation in the formation of educational policy by, for example, the industrial sector and the military, and by the pubic at large. In contrast with democratic states, however, the degree of accountability of the agencies responsible for deciding educational policy (ultimately the Soviet government and the Communist Party of the Soviet Union (CPSU)) was extremely limited. Using Archer's typology of political manipulation of education systems, the USSR can be characterised as having an 'impenetrable' political centre, in which 'power' in decision-making was enjoyed by a small number of actors within the dominant group.[1] The restriction on negotiation[2] which this situation engendered denied the school the dialogue that it needed with its society, and acted as a brake on the development of both.

Policy-making before *perestroika*: the centre's monopoly?

As the reforms were being developed in the late 1980s and early 1990s, it was fashionable for those involved to describe their task as a struggle against the 'totalitarian' nature of the Soviet system, thus establishing, as they saw it, the pressing need for fundamental change. Dneprov, for instance, portrayed the State's control over education as draconian:

> The root evil of the existing system of educational governance is its bureaucratic nature, which precludes any changes for the population to play a rôle in running the schools. The present structure of governance . . . stands for the absolute tyranny of the educational bureaucracy over more than sixty million 'enserfed' schoolchildren and their parents, who share the unfortunate fate of their own offspring.[3]

Perhaps such descriptions were influenced by scarred memories of the Stalinist years, but was this doom-laden picture appropriate? If such assertions are sound, then this should mean that the population had been excluded from the decision-making process – was this the case? It is true that the CPSU did try to keep the system under tight control, and that the net effect was to stifle creative pedagogical thought and practice. Indeed, sanctions were brought to bear on those who did not conform to what the central authorities saw as the 'right' line,[4] while direct participation in policy-formation was kept to a minimum. This is not to say, though, that the people and the teaching community did not have their say:

> It has never been true that Soviet teachers sat around waiting to be told what to do, and previous reforms of the system have either emerged from movements of opinion in the profession and society, or else have failed because they did not have support among educators.[5]

The degree of audibility of the grassroots' voice varied considerably during the Soviet era. In the first decade of Soviet rule, with school system and society in flux, the resistance of teachers and parents to the introduction of the Unified Labour School contributed significantly to its eventual abandonment by the authorities.[6] In Stalin's dumbstruck society, parental discontent with the partial imposition of paid education after 1940[7] was certainly more muted, and the opportunity to influence its repeal more limited as the CPSU asserted its position during this period, although there is nevertheless evidence of some amount of pressure exerted by the public on the centre.[8] Under Khrushchev's thaw, the chance to cold-shoulder state policy reappeared, as the ambitious but poorly conceptualised reforms of 1958 foundered.[9] Similar problems were encountered by the last 'Soviet' reform of 1984:

> In spite of much talk, and constant exhortations to make the reforms a reality, the resistance of the educational establishment (backed by a public that was unenthusiastic about the provisions of the reform) managed essentially to sabotage them.[10]

Policy, then, was subject to the influence of the population. However, that influence was reactive in nature. The CPSU introduced a measure, and the people passed judgment on it; if it was not accepted, the State would have to respond, sooner or later, but it was the centre which retained almost absolute control over the formation and initiation of policy. This is not to say that it was impossible for certain groups in society to affect decision-making. The industrial and agricultural sectors had some influence, and powerful interest groups were able at times to exert considerable pressure in order to achieve their aims. In the late 1960s, for instance, the armed forces were successful in their attempt to have 'Basic Military Training' (*Nachal'naya voennaya podgotovka*) reintroduced into the schools, as compensation for the loss of one year in the length of conscript service.[11] The education system, in contrast, was not in a position to demand such attention and concessions from the centre. The teaching profession did not enjoy the economic muscle of industry or the privileged position of the armed forces, and thus had no real means of presenting its views in a collective and effective manner. Furthermore, the trade union and other organisations which, ostensibly, represented the pedagogical community were firmly under the control of the authorities. Parents and pupils acted on individual initiative, based principally on their perceptions of how policies affected them, and not on the implications for their society. On the whole therefore, the field of educational policy-making was largely the domain of the CPSU, acting through the various ministries responsible for the education system, advised by the Academy of Pedagogical Sciences (*Akademiya Pedagogicheskikh Nauk* – APN).

The Soviet state's jealously guarded control over education in the USSR, and the limited opportunities provided for the airing of public opinion, meant that the centre could mislead itself into believing that it was in charge of the system; yet through its suppression of critical debate it failed to see the problems that such debate could have revealed. The fact that the educational community – apart from the conservative and politically loyal APN – was divorced to a great extent from the policy-making process contributed to the problems that ensued.

Soviet citizens were not accustomed to being in charge of the destiny of their society, but by the 1980s an air of frustration was apparent, a growing sense that things could not continue as they were for much longer. As far as teachers were concerned, the denial of participatory rights in policy matters limited significantly the extent to which they were likely to perceive a degree of 'ownership' of school policy. Although the last 'Soviet' school reform of 1984 included a limited amount of indirect participation by the teaching force, for instance, it was still largely a top-down affair.[12] Under *perestroika*, however, the situation was to undergo a substantial transformation.

Soviet education post-1984: a new paradigm of policy-making?

The significance of the momentum of change in the second half of the 1980s lies in the part played by grassroots' activity. However, bottom-up initiative by itself was not enough to exert profound change. There had, after all, been such activity throughout the Soviet period, as some teachers developed their own methodological approaches, even created teaching materials themselves, despite the restrictions imposed by the authorities. Some worked away quietly for the benefit of their own pupils and perhaps their immediate colleagues, with little recognition; a few, such as V.A. Sukhomlinskii,[13] received attention from the wider teaching community, and enjoyed something approaching tolerance from the authorities; while others ran into problems with the bureaucracy when their work strayed beyond the bounds of the officially acceptable. It was the advent of *perestroika* that was to allow real change: the grassroots' activity of the late 1980s was able to make the impact it did because of the parallel, revolutionary developments in Soviet society itself. This period of Soviet education, from 1985 to 1991, has been documented in previous studies and publications, in Russian and English,[14] so the following summary can, accordingly, be brief.

The innovators and the 'Pedagogy of Cooperation'

From the mid-1980s, the work of a number of 'teacher-innovators', who were practising educationalists developing methodological approaches independently of the APN (often based on a more child-centred approach than that promoted by the official curriculum), attracted a good deal of attention from both within and outside the teaching profession. They included, notably, V.F. Shatalov, whose books *Pedagogicheskaya proza*[15] (Pedagogical Prose) and *Kuda i kak ischezli troiki*[16] (Where and How the Threes Disappeared)[17] struck a chord among many teachers, and the Georgian teacher Shalva Amonashvili, whose works *Zdravstvuite deti!*[18] (Hello Chidren!) and *Kak zhivete deti?*[19] (How Are You, Children?) provided what appeared to be an attractive alternative to existing Soviet approaches to the teaching of primary-age pupils. The innovators' work was publicised by the teachers' newspaper *Uchitel'skaya gazeta*, which sponsored a series of meetings of the group, at which the manifesto of the *Pedagogika sotrudnichestva* (Pedagogy of Cooperation) was put forward.[20] As Dunstan and Suddaby write:

> The substance of the Pedagogy of Cooperation was that Soviet education needed new methods and relationships based on cooperation and trust between all participants – teachers, pupils and parents. Instead of the old methods based on compulsion, pupils should be freed from the fear of failure, and conditions should be created whereby successful learning is assured.[21]

The ideas contained within these manifestos were nothing new in international terms, and they tended to be rather vague, lacking concrete suggestions for implementation. As Grant notes, the innovators seemed to have achieved success partly through their charismatic approach, but:

> The trouble with this kind of approach, as many other systems have found in the past, is that most teachers are not charismatic. Also, however refreshing this 'progressive' approach must have seemed, methodology (however excellent) cannot solve problems of structure, content and direction, and these were far from clear.[22]

At that time, however, the ideas produced an impetus for a wider discussion on the school, as first the teaching profession, and then the Soviet public itself took a closer interest.

The energetic promotion of the movement for change by *Uchitel'skaya gazeta* was supplemented by coverage in the mass media, which appeared to attract considerable interest, not just from the teaching profession but also from wider society. This level of curiosity aroused was probably due not so much to the topic of the school itself, as to the chance afforded to observe and participate in a critique of a Soviet social institution, a process of societal self-analysis that had long been denied the Soviet public, to this degree at least. Nevertheless, while the public's motives for following the debate may not have been directly related to the school, the very fact that the debate had focused on education served to raise awareness of the state of the school system, and of the alternatives being put forward, thus adding further momentum to the development of reform ideas and helping to foster the school's much-needed dialogue with its society.

The tempo and scope of the discussion within the educational community developed quickly, with publications reflecting a clear break with the staid approach of the past, as issues were treated in an increasingly probing and unrestricted manner.[23] Further, alongside the printed dialogue, a growing number of teachers were also taking part in more active manifestations of the change momentum, with the emergence, for instance, of the idea of the *avtorskaya shkola* ('author school'), which established experimental approaches to teaching based on the premises of the Pedagogy of Cooperation, and by the setting up of the *Evrika klub tvorcheskoi pedagogiki* (Eureka Club of Creative Pedagogy), promoted by *Uchitel'skaya gazeta*, which provided a forum for teachers to discuss various pedagogical approaches.[24] Such developments led in turn to the establishment of the *Tvorcheskii soyuz uchitelei SSSR* (The Creative Union of Teachers of the USSR), involving many of the original innovators, which held its first congress in May 1989.[25]

The scene by the late 1980s, then, was quite different from that which had existed only a short time before. Teachers could criticise state policy and put forward their own alternatives, without such an overriding fear of sanctions that had previously hung over the profession. Furthermore, events at the centre had begun to follow, rather than dictate, the mood emerging at the grassroots' level, indicating that, perhaps, the reformers would, after all, be rewarded with a real chance to change the direction of Soviet education.

The centre's transformation

The education debate attracted the attention of senior politicians from both 'radical' and 'conservative' wings of the CPSU. Boris Yeltsin, for instance, added his contribution,[26] and Gorbachev referred to education at times as part of his overall promotion of *perestroika*.[27] It was Egor Ligachev, however, a senior member of Gorbachev's Politburo, who took the most prominent stance on education among the USSR's political élite, speaking out in favour of the democratisation of the school, and of paying more attention to the needs of the individual. At the 1988 February Plenum of the Central Committee of the CPSU it was Ligachev's speech which appeared to make the biggest impact, as he criticised openly some of the faults of the existing system, and in particular the perceived failure of the 1984 reform, thus lending official credence of a sort to the message being put forward by the reformers.[28]

The political leadership's support for change opened the path to comprehensive revision of the ministerial structure and of the rôle of the APN.[29] In 1988 the three existing ministries responsible for the governance of education – the USSR Ministry of Education (*Ministerstvo prosveshcheniya SSSR*), the USSR Ministry of Higher and Secondary-Specialised Education (*Ministerstvo vysshego i srednego spetsial'nogo obrazovaniya SSSR*) and the USSR State Committee for Vocational-Technical Education (*Gosudarstvennyi komitet SSSR po professional'no-tekhnicheskomu obrazovaniyu*) were merged to form a single State Public Education Committee of the USSR (*Gosudarstvennyi komitet SSSR po narodnomu obrazovaniyu*), a process that was repeated at republican level.

Gennadii Alekseevich Yagodin was named head of the new State Committee, with Vladimir Dmitrievich Shadrikov as his deputy. Both ministers were respected academics with extensive practical experience of working in and administering the education system, and both had been working towards reform in their previous roles in, respectively, the higher and secondary education sectors.[30] While they were seen as more cautious than the 'radical' reformers, their goals appeared to coincide largely with those being put forward at the time by the more active members of the reform movement.[31]

The conversion of the centre was not as simple as that, of course. As Jones points out, the bureaucratic 'reshuffles' left the same people in the same posts as before, thus reinforcing the effect of inertia.[32] This was to be expected. However, Yagodin did seek to inject an element of dynamism into the affair with the establishment of *VNIK–Shkola: Vremennyi Nauchno-Issledovatel'skii Kollektiv – Shkola* (the Ad hoc Research Group on the School), under the direction of an educational historian from the APN, Eduard Dneprov, and comprising several prominent educationalists, psychologists and sociologists, many working within the APN. This group produced a large array of reports over the next three years on a wide range of topics on the theme of school reform, work that would form the basis of the Russian reform agenda.[33]

VNIK–Shkola's activities drew opposition from conservative elements in the APN. The APN was under fire itself, though, and a fierce battle was fought over the need for its reorganisation,[34] thus weakening the academy's position. The struggle between the two factions culminated in 1988 in the publication, almost simultaneously, of two views of the development of the school under the title of 'Concept of the Secondary School', one from the APN,[35] the other produced by VNIK–Shkola.[36] The teaching community was thus given the chance to compare the two, and for many, VNIK–Shkola's offering was seen to be: 'More radical, less jargon-ridden, more impatient with the past and less concerned to please its opponents.'[37] The State Committee adopted the VNIK version later in 1988.[38]

Between 1988 and 1990 the reformers complained of the stalling of reform as the old guard regrouped, and of the dilution of the proposals put forward in the VNIK–Shkola concept. Nevertheless, the education debate had been prised open, wrested away from the APN after so many years, and there were signs of real plurality in the process of policy-formation. As the Soviet Union headed towards its demise, there seemed, alongside the many problems facing the school, to be at least a glimmer of hope that the reforms would be able to gather further momentum.

The birth of the Russian reforms: opportunities and dangers

This hope appeared to be justified when, in June 1990, Dneprov was appointed Minister of Education of the RSFSR. By the summer of 1991 a draft of a proposed law on education was published just after Yeltsin issued his first presidential decree, which was devoted to the subject of education.[39] Within six months the dissolution of the USSR added to the momentum. The reform movement had now completed its takeover of the centre – or so it seemed. As Marinicheva notes with a mixture of hope and foreboding:

> Intellectuals in power ... what a catastrophe! ... It seems as if all at once they have assumed charge of governments ... all with an unprecedented, unique societal mission: to dismantle totalitarianism, this cancerous tumour of the twentieth century. They have an unenviable fate.[40]

The Law on Education of the Russian Federation was passed, after a period of review and considerable rewriting of the drafts, on July 10, 1992.[41] This represents a remarkably short space of time, given that the law was prepared amid the confusion of the transition from USSR to independent Russia. More important, the early appearance of the law meant that Russia's schools were given a tangible indication of the intentions of their ministry and their government, and provided with a legal and administrative framework within which they could shape their response.

There was a price to pay for the rapidity with which the law was drawn up, however, as subsequent analysis of the legislation was to highlight a considerable number of technical difficulties, internal contradictions, ambiguities and other faults. This was, perhaps, inevitable, given the complexity of the legislation and immaturity of the Russian legal process. The effect which such problems have had on implementation will be examined in Part II.

With regard to the question of participation in drawing up the law, were the reformers able to build on and continue the new tradition of consultation that had emerged in the late 1980s? According to the following account, the tradition was, indeed, carried on:

> The Committee for Science and National Education of the Supreme Soviet of the Russian Federation decided to organise a wide-ranging

> consultation procedure with, among others, the Russian Academy of Sciences and its institutions, the Academy of Pedagogical Sciences and leading research centres connected with different branches of the economy, with national educational and science trade union committees, social organisations, representatives of the scientific and teaching sectors, readers of *Uchitelskaya gazeta*, etc.[42]

At the international level, the Ministry of Education took advantage of new-found opportunities for collaboration by signing a bilateral agreement between the Russian Federation and Belgium, under the auspices of which an international committee was established to provide advice on the preparation of the law.[43] While such cooperation can be seen to have had positive outcomes, not least in bringing Russian educationalists and administrators into closer contact with their Western counterparts, the ultimate value of Western 'assistance' to the education system of Russia (and, indeed, other countries of the region) has subsequently come under critical scrutiny.[44] This issue will be addressed in more detail in Part III.

Returning to the domestic scene, however, assessing the nature and extent of participation is problematic. It is very difficult to say with certainty which groups, bodies and organisations took part, which commanded most influence, which were excluded from the consultations; we can, though, draw some conclusions using knowledge of developments in broader society and in the teaching profession at that time. It is safe to say that society at large played less part in the final formation of the reform agenda than might have been wished for. That this was so is due largely to the nature of the period that Russians were living through. The interest that appeared to have been shown towards the education debate quickly declined as the end of empire drew closer, and as the myriad crises in the USSR acquired a tangible reality for most of the population. The fledgling political movements, too, were in no hurry to discuss education. Instead, their priority was survival and securing a position in the fluid and unpredictable new world of democratic politics.

Little input could have been expected from the underdeveloped business community, and while the industrial community was able to draw on a stronger foundation, it was also too busy following events in political and economic affairs to be too concerned about the schools. Other elements of what must be loosely termed civil society were just finding or refinding their identity (e.g. the Orthodox Church), or were virtually non-existent (e.g. parent groups). Even the education community seemed to be in no fit state to make a meaningful contribution: the official educationalists' union was still an ineffectual body that had not adjusted to changing times, while the Creative Union of Teachers, which had appeared to be so full of promise, had lost its way since 1989.[45]

This combination of factors meant that the neglect of the education policy debate was almost inevitable. This was unfortunate, since this was the very time that society should have been most vigilant, most concerned about what was happening in its schools. As will be argued in Part III, this lack of interest was to continue well past the transition from Soviet Union to Russia, and is still a negative factor in the schools' development.

The reformers thus had to operate in something of a vacuum, although they were able to refer to the considerable amount of discussion that had occurred in the mid- to late 1980s, which may be seen to have offset this disadvantage somewhat. Some of the reformers may even have felt that they had something of a mandate from society to proceed with change. As for the teaching force, it could also be argued that this appeared to be an educationalist's reform, since the teaching profession had its own people in charge of the ministry, with ideas that had, ostensibly, come from the grassroots. Further, the transition from one form of government and society to a very different model opened up opportunities afforded only rarely, if ever, to the architects of educational change, a *carte blanche* to engage in profound revision of the existing system.

Meanwhile, in the absence of a healthy civil society and the safety net that this provides to the school system, it was demonstrated to the Russian school system just how vulnerable its position was, as the Ministry of Education entered into a bitter struggle for control of the reform agenda with the legislature.[46] The battle progressed up to and beyond the publication of the Law on Education, with Vladimir Shorin (the Speaker) and others in the Russian Supreme Soviet trying to secure Dneprov's resignation.

Such battles appeared, at times, to lead the reformers to view the 'struggle' in black and white terms, a tendency which reflected the spirit of the times: the transition period was full of uncertainty, of threats of a conservative takeover, of fears of a descent into civil war and a black hole of economic and social chaos. Many Russians, and for that matter Western observers, came to see the situation in Russian society in the form of straightforward choices, between conservative and democrat, state socialism and the free market, choice and state control. The school system, however, needed stability, not uncertainty, for it was likely to suffer from polarisation in the policy sphere.

At times it appeared that the Ministry of Education was determined to push through change as quickly as possible, despite the risks. In 1992, for example, Dneprov outlined the huge programme of change that the reformers had prepared and stated that: 'We have two years. If we do not complete our programme within this period we will all resign.'[47] The desire to prevent any reversal of the 'achievements' of reform was also stressed by Dneprov's successor, Evgenii Viktorovich Tkachenko, who was appointed after Dneprov's dismissal in late 1992: 'The main thing in the education system today is to ensure the irreversibility of the process of reform.'[48] To expect results in two years is folly – school reform will take years, decades to implement properly. Making such demands on the schools placed an unfair burden on them, at a time when they needed support and guidance more than ever.

3
The Programme for Change

Crisis in the schools?

As we have seen, senior figures in the CPSU had expressed considerable disquiet with regard to the lack of progress in implementing the 1984 reforms. Dneprov went further, labelling these measures 'pseudo-reforms', which had only exacerbated the problems facing the schools.[1] One might argue that it was not so much in the substance of those reforms that the problems lay, for they did introduce a number of positive measures, such as an increase in teachers' salaries;[2] rather, they suffered from poor planning and implementation. However, there was a widespread sense of dissatisfaction apparent with regard to the state of the schools, which the 1984 reforms could not adequately address.

The innovators challenged the school's reputation for academic success, for instance, drawing attention to the drawbacks associated with the concentration on the so-called ZUNy (*Znaniya, Umeniya, Navyki*), the triad of knowledge, skills and habits, in the Soviet curriculum. They claimed that this bias neglected the cognitive and social development of the child, and criticised the heavily teacher-centred approach and emphasis on the acquisition of knowledge through rote-learning,[3] their comments echoed by similar observations from Western analysts.[4]

These and other factors, so the reform camp claimed, had brought the school system to a situation of deep crisis, a perception shared by many Soviet educationalists and a significant number of parents, as shown by surveys conducted in the late 1980s and early 1990s. In a 1989 survey of 1000 teachers across the Soviet Union, for example:

> Of [those] surveyed, 72.6 per cent believe that the school system is now in serious crisis and in need of fundamental reorganisation. Around 23 per cent of teachers thought that the school needs some changes and only 1 per cent felt that the school completely meets the demands of society . . . About 1300 parents were also interviewed and their reactions were less critical, though 42.8 per cent of men and 55.8 per cent of women replied that they did not like their children's schools.[5]

The evidence of other studies which came to similar conclusions seemed to confirm the existence of a widespread perception of crisis in education.[6] Just what the nature of this crisis was believed to be was relatively little discussed, although reference was made to falling standards, the increasing material problems of the schools, and the perennial teacher shortage issue. To some extent, the detail may be seen as less significant than the impression of crisis: such surveys were probably influenced by the general mood in society, that the Soviet Union as a whole was falling deeper into a state of crisis. Indeed, one might argue that the belief that a crisis exists is just as meaningful as the provision of proof; if the majority, according to such surveys, felt that change was required, then this can be taken as a legitimate premise for pursuing reform, although embarking on reform without having clearly defined the parameters of discontent with the existing system, and setting out the scope and goals of desired changes, does carry inherent risks, as will be demonstrated.

The reform agenda

The response adopted by Dneprov's ministry in the 1992 Law on Education drew on the ideas that had been circulating in the reform movement in the late 1980s.[7] The programme can be summarised as follows:

- **Decentralisation and regionalisation** – the devolution of responsibility for administration to regional (and republican) levels, municipal and district councils and the schools themselves (see Articles 28–40 of the Law on Education).
- **Democratisation** – the introduction of greater public accountability; granting parents and the local community a greater say in the running of the schools (see Articles 50–52), including the provision of educational opportunities for ethnic minorities.

- **Deideologisation** – removing the possibility of promoting one ideological viewpoint to the exclusion of others (see Article 14).
- **Differentiation/diversification** – breaking the State's 'monopoly' control of education, with, for example, the introduction of 'choice' in the provision of schooling, including the establishment of non-state schools and home-schooling (see Articles 36 and 39).
- **Humanisation** – e.g. giving greater emphasis to the needs of the individual; improving teacher–pupil relations (see Articles 2 and 14).
- **Humanitarisation** – giving greater emphasis to the humanities subjects in the curriculum.

The programme was well received in many quarters, with one Russian observer going so far as to say that Russia had become one of: 'the most democratic nations on earth in the sphere of education'.[8] Praise also came from Western analysts, one seeing the law as: 'a majestic piece of statecraft'.[9] Indeed, the content of the legislation, at least in appearance, resembled closely the nature of educational policies followed by many liberal democracies, thus giving rise to hopes with regard to the potential effect that the agenda might have on social change in Russia, particularly on the issue of democratisation. While it aspired to influence the process of transformation, however, the legislation could not help but be affected by the nature of societal change itself, and reflect many of the tensions, uncertainties and contradictions apparent in Russia in the early 1990s. The result was a piece of legislation which appears to be forward-looking and progressive, yet which at the same time displays a strong undertone of backward-looking, remedial measures designed to deal with the perceived legacy of the past. Given such factors, would the centre, and the system, be able to adapt the agenda for implementation in the fast-changing atmosphere of the Russia of the mid- to late 1990s, in which the conditions which shaped the 1992 law might no longer be so relevant? In the following sections a critique is given of the premises on which the reform policies were based, which will set the context for the evaluation of the course of change provided in Part II.

Removing ideology from the schools?

Deideologisation is a clumsy concept, and a policy which is almost impossible to implement, for the school cannot be divorced from the reality of the world around it. Of course, some effort was required to address the legacy of the Soviet era, through the fundamental revision of the content of curricula and course materials, the nature of pedagogical approaches recommended in teacher-training programmes, and many other aspects of school life. The scale of the problem, however, was not as great as was portrayed by some reformers. The extent to which Soviet pupils (and their teachers) paid lip-service to the faith, as opposed to supporting it actively and with conviction, had grown in the 1970s and 1980s, reflecting wider trends in society, a process which progressed further still during the ideological upheavals of the Gorbachev era, which saw the 'communist' faith and its legacy discredited and eventually abandoned as the official state creed. The task facing the reformers in 1991 was akin to removing a dead or dying weed from the ground – while care was still needed to ensure the weed would not take root again, the remnants of the growth were mainly superficial, lying on the surface (in the form of portraits of Lenin, textbooks, etc.), rather than deep in the school's essence. This is borne out by the ease with which the trappings of the communist legacy were removed from the classroom, continuing a process which had been underway for some time (e.g. with the cancellation of history examinations in 1990, etc.). If the ideology had been so deeply ingrained, such processes would surely have involved far greater effort.

As has been the case with other areas of the reforms, decisions to remove the legacy of the past were acted upon before the system had time to assess fully the potential impact of such moves, and to introduce new structures and mechanisms that would be better suited to the goals of democratisation. The Komsomol and Pioneer organisations were banned from the schools, for instance, as part of the overall policy to prevent the Communist Party, or any other political or social movement, from enjoying a direct influence in state institutions. However, for the majority of young people the ideological trappings of the Pioneer organisation were not of great importance; rather, its main function was as an umbrella organisation for a wide range of leisure and educational activities, including the summer camps of which the Soviet system was rightly proud. Since the demise of the Pioneers, alternative groups have failed to take their place and the network of extra-curricular centres available to children has crumbled.[10]

Alongside the process of dismantling the Pioneer organisation and the system of *vospitanie* ('upbringing'), with the consequences that this has brought, a number of more positive developments have appeared as part of the process of democratisation. Programmes in civic studies (*grazhdanovedenie*) have been established and textbooks prepared,[11] and the issue of civics education discussed widely by the Ministry of Education[12] and the pedagogical press. In addition, some establishments and organisations are actively involved in running courses and arranging workshops and conferences on these matters, including the 'Association for Civics Education' (*Assotsiatsiya za grazhdanskoe obrazovanie*).

Nevertheless, such advances have been accompanied by more destructive, remedial approaches resulting from the attempt to rid the curriculum of 'Soviet morality', as the reformers have added to the development of a moral vacuum in the schools. Of course, the reformers cannot be blamed for failing to provide rapid solutions to the values crisis felt by Russian society in the flux of transition. Rather, it is the fact that insufficient attention was paid to the need to revise the nature of the *vospitanie* area of the curriculum, and to provide guidance to the teaching force on how to approach such issues, which has been criticised by some in the Russian education system.[13]

Taking the state out of education

In the population at large, the level of confidence in and respect towards the CPSU and the Soviet state had fallen dramatically towards the end of the 1980s, and this sceptical attitude towards government and issues of authority and accountability has continued to affect the stance taken by many in Russia in the 1990s towards the rôle of the State:

> We have changed our views on private property, on political pluralism, become used to the freedom of speech and of the press, and so on . . . But one myth has remained – that of the state school. We remain convinced that the education and upbringing of a child is the State's prerogative. Until we free ourselves from this myth, we will not see any real change.[14]

A similar line was promoted by other senior figures within the Ministry of Education. Deputy Minister Viktor Aleksandrovich Bolotov, for instance, writing in 1994, noted:

> State educational policy is in search of a balance between two seemingly contradictory functions. The sphere of education has

> to be an instrument of state policy and serve to secure the national interests of Russia. The sphere of education has to perform a service function, securing the interests of the child, family, community, etc. The latter function has been non-existent during the last 70 years of Russian history.[15]

Was such criticism justified? The Soviet school was, admittedly, administered through a hyper-centralised system of control, and variation within the system, the involvement of the local community in school affairs, the concept of public accountability and other issues were subject to considerable constraints, while the idea that non-state educational establishments might be allowed to exist alongside the state sector was unthinkable before 1987. Yet, as was shown in Chapter 1, one can contest the view that the Soviet school served only the needs of the State, that pupils were destined only to be cogs within the system. Soviet citizens did, indeed, have a limited amount of freedom in comparison with citizens in the Western 'democracies', but this does not mean that they did not seek to adapt circumstances to meet their own needs, to follow their own agendas. The local community, too, was not totally excluded from the life of the school, as Bolotov appears to claim, but had a voice, albeit muted, through parental involvement, through links with local industry or farms. Much work was, indeed, required in these areas after 1991 to establish greater involvement and to bring the school closer to the individual and the community – indeed, calls for democratisation, for increased accountability, for the involvement of parents and others in the school's affairs must be seen as positive – but the picture was not as bleak as the reformers painted it.

There was a need for society to be given more of a say in the running of its schools, in order that the balance which Bolotov spoke of might be achieved. The Law on Education removed the state 'monopoly' on education which had existed under the Soviet system, extending the right to manage educational establishments to state, municipal and private organisations, thus bringing the Russian system broadly into line with the practices found in most Western democracies. However, some of the more radical supporters of reform appeared to believe that the State's role in education should be reduced to a minimum – a demand which may be received sympathetically in some quarters in certain Western countries, but which ignores the fact that the State must inevitably, in an age when education and other social welfare systems are becoming increasingly complex and expensive to run, have a major part to play in educational provision. While such opposition to the State's position appeared to diminish in the early 1990s (as the reform camp itself was institutionalised into the centre), as will be shown in Part III, *razgosudarstvlenie* would re-emerge as an issue of great controversy in the mid-1990s, albeit with a subtle change in emphasis.

Restructuring the system

Moves towards decentralisation had actually been underway for some time, through initiatives undertaken both by the centre, under Yagodin as Minister of Education of the USSR, and by the regions, cities and schools themselves.[16] Indeed, one could say that by 1991 the Russian reformers were left with little option but to decentralise, so great was the apparent clamour of the regions to gain responsibility for managing the schools in their area, although such enthusiasm was matched by the centre's willingness to relinquish control. Yet was rapid decentralisation sensible, given the risk it carries of losing cohesion, even fragmentation? Perhaps, again, the reformers were guided at least partly by a desire to deal with the perceived legacy of the past, and to render their reforms irreversible, which affected their judgment on the potential consequences for the school system of relaxing central control to the degree they proposed. In the atmosphere of 1990–92, with Russia's course of transition still far from clear and the 'democrats' fearful of a takeover by the 'hardline' communists, it was, perhaps, understandable that the reformers should wish to increase the prospects of the irreversibility of change by decentralising quickly. From the reformers' point of view, given the context of transition, maybe rapid decentralisation was justified after all, whatever the long-term consequences for system-wide cohesion.

As the process of decentralisation gathered momentum, so too did the amount of diversity in educational provision, as so-called 'alternative' schools, including non-state establishments, were established alongside the standard Soviet comprehensive school (*obshcheobrazovatel'naya shkola*). The first private schools had appeared in 1987, and their numbers grew rapidly, with particularly strong representation in Moscow and St Petersburg.[17] An increasing number of state schools – often, although not exclusively, those which already had a 'specialised' status[18] – joined the trend of renaming themselves as gymnasia (*gimnazii*) or lycées (*litsei*), the traditional pre-revolutionary titles, either as a whole school or with gymnasium classes in the 10th and 11th forms.[19] Such schools often offer educational programmes which are very similar to those in the traditional Soviet school, although with a stronger academic bias and the addition, in some, of subjects such as Latin, an extra foreign language or business studies. Some establishments have attempted a more radical departure from the Soviet pattern by promoting the ideas of Montessori or Steiner (Waldorf), or using approaches developed by Russian educationalists and philosophers, an example being Bibler's 'dialogue of cultures' method.[20]

Such developments were welcomed and encouraged by the reformers, who saw this as part of the drive towards the 'liberalisation' of the educational environment in Russia that would bring the country into line with the practice of democracies in the West. Together with the extended 'choice' for parents and pupils that such schools were seen to provide, the reformers also hoped that the alternative and non-state network would be able to act as 'beacons of change' for the system as a whole, taking advantage of their liberation from the legacy of the Soviet school, and thus, so it was felt, able to engage more energetically in innovation.

The appearance of alternative schools and the increase in the practice of selective entrance procedures has, relatively, received a good deal of attention in the mass media;[21] indeed, a short series was even run on the 'Russian Television' channel under the title 'Private school: for and against.'[22] In this larger debate, both the implications of selective entrance, parental choice, and fee-paying for the country's educational and social fabric have been addressed, although the discussion has been influenced, naturally, by the limited experience of Russia in these matters (the alternative network is, after all, trying to achieve in the space of a few years what has taken many decades in Western systems), and by the philosophical atmosphere prevailing in the transformation period, in which discussion of such issues as élitism and equality, money and privilege has been rather distorted and vacuous.

The new ideas being introduced into the school system often appeared exciting and attractive, and it became fashionable among some parents to turn to the alternative sector. The centre showed its support for such schools in material terms as well, preparing arrangements for them to receive state funding.[23] These initiatives would seem to be perfectly reasonable, for the new establishments would be likely to encounter difficulties in the early period of their existence, yet enthusiasm for the alternative schools needed to be accompanied by a similar level of support for the 'mass' school. The impression received by some educationalists, at least, was that the needs of the traditional Soviet school were not given due attention by the reformers. The question of the part played by alternative schools in the reform process will be addressed in Part II.

The learning experience: reform and the curriculum

The debate over diversification is interconnected with much of the discussion concerning the reform proposals for the curriculum, in particular the issue of so-called *uravnilovka*, or 'levelling', and the consequent need, as seen by the reformers, to introduce a more differentiated approach to education. The Soviet approach of treating all children as equal, and thus offering them a unitary curriculum to be followed at the same pace as their peers, with no 'streaming', or separation of pupils by ability, had, the reformers claimed, led to pupils' achievement in school being held down to an imposed 'average', which disadvantaged all.[24] The task now was to introduce differentiation to offset this legacy, and provide a learning experience more suited to the needs of the individual and various ability levels. This appears to be perfectly in order – but were the claims of *uravnilovka* completely justified, or was there a danger of overstating this case, as with other aspects of the reforms?

Within limits, the debate over so-called egalitarian and differentiated approaches had actually been conducted for many years in the USSR.[25] The introduction of specialised schools was one outcome of the debate, a concession to the argument that greater provision was needed for the more able pupils. Such establishments catered for a minority, of course, but even with regard to the ordinary Soviet school, we can contest the view that the problem of *uravnilovka* was absolute. The degree of variation in educational provision and quality between urban and rural areas, for instance, has always been an issue in Russian and Soviet education,[26] while similar disparities can be observed between smaller towns in the provinces and more affluent regional centres, not to mention Moscow and St Petersburg, which have traditionally been seen almost as a country apart from what is derogatively termed the 'periphery'.

Further, it would be wrong to assume that the Soviet curriculum was delivered in a uniform manner by all teachers, in complete accordance with the methodological and ideological guidelines on non-differentiation. While there was much that needed to be done to the curriculum and to the approach to teaching in order to render them suitable for the purposes of a child-centred, differentiated environment, the reformers did not have to start from nothing, for teachers had, consciously or unconsciously, been practising differentiation throughout the Soviet era. Some teachers were effective at preparing students for entrance to higher education, others worked successfully with lower-ability pupils, some responded well, others not so well to the task of mixed-ability teaching – but all brought their own individual approach to bear within what seemed at first sight to be a very tight set of pedagogical parameters imposed by the authorities.

Nevertheless, while there was a considerable amount of such 'hidden' differentiation in the Soviet system, there was clearly considerable scope for introducing a more 'open' form of differentiation, in which these issues could be addressed in a wide-ranging debate on the issue, informed by detailed research and, if possible, comparative studies to examine the experience of other systems in operating a differentiated approach. Indeed, there was a great deal of discussion of this topic in the pedagogical press, with some articles presenting rational, scientific arguments which promised to allow the system to develop a reasoned response to the matter.[27] At the same time, however, the debate over differentiation and egalitarianism in the early 1990s also seemed to be overshadowed by the rejection by some of the perceived legacy of the past, and of the supposed influence of communist ideology on pedagogical practice. As in society as a whole, in the education system a reaction has been observed against the supposedly collectivist nature of Soviet interpersonal relations, and a shift towards a greater concentration on the individual, and thus the expression and pursuit of individual sentiments and desires.

It became fashionable among some educationalists and psychologists to talk of the need to cater for 'gifted' (*odarennye*) children, who, it was said, had been disadvantaged by the Soviet school's practice of levelling, and who should now be afforded special attention in order to offset this problem.[28] Many alternative schools, accordingly, were set up with the specific purpose of educating an 'élite.' Amid the rush to cater for the gifted, it seemed for a time that the average and below-average ability children were to be neglected, at least by the more fashion-conscious elements of the reform movement. Yet one might argue that it was these ability groups, particularly those in the lower bands, who had in fact been most disadvantaged by the unitary Soviet curriculum, for they had not been seen as a priority either by the authorities or by the teaching staff, in a system which measured its success often by the grades pupils were awarded and the number of pupils who gained entrance to higher education. Indeed, in many ways the Soviet curriculum was geared to the more academically orientated children, carrying on the traditions of the pre-revolutionary Tsarist school to which the Soviet system owed so much of its heritage.

While this imbalance of attention to the various ability groups has been redressed somewhat in subsequent years, it serves to highlight the manner in which the issue of differentiation tended to lead to a certain polarisation of views, between those who were seen to cling to 'Soviet' beliefs on equality, and those for whom the Soviet curriculum represented an infringement of the rights of the individual. As Dunstan notes astutely:

> This contempt for the Soviet curriculum is relevant to the redrawing of the battle lines between the differentiators and the egalitarians. The latter have lost massive ground, almost to the point of becoming marginalised . . . But to write off the egalitarians as yesterday's men and women, who think in outmoded categories and occasionally preach an outworn creed, simply will not do. Here also some differentiation is needed![29]

The Law on Education declared in Article 2 ('Principles of State Policy with Regard to Education') the Russian state's commitment to the principles of:

> The humanist character of education, the priority of universal humanitarian values, the life and health of citizens, the free development of personality.[30]

The so-called humanisation of education, which had been promoted by the innovators in the 1980s, was therefore enshrined as the foremost principle of education policy. But what did this mean in practice? The term humanisation is rather vague, and, as will be shown later, open to a wide variety of interpretations. In the literature of the reform movement, however, while a precise definition of humanisation is not provided, the consensus of opinion shows that it is used to denote the perceived need to counter the emphasis in the Soviet school on the acquisition of knowledge and the priority on academic achievement, in favour of devoting more attention to the needs of the individual pupil. From the late 1980s onwards, the notion of 'child-centred learning,' and the importance of the individuality, or personality of the child (*lichnost'*), came increasingly to be promoted by senior figures in the reform camp and in the upper echelons of the State Committee on Education,[31] and the policy of humanisation apparently received widespread support among educationalists in general.[32] Apart from seeking comparisons with models in foreign systems, such moves were seen to be building on the foundations laid by the innovators' 'pedagogy of cooperation', and before that by Soviet educationalists such as Sukhomlinskii, Makarenko and Blonskii,[33] with some teachers going back even further, to see what lessons might be taken from the experience and views of Lev Tolstoi, the nineteenth-century educationalist Konstantin Ushinskii and other Russian writers and educationalists with regard to child-centred learning. In recent years, the importance of emphasising the needs of the individual pupil, by concentrating on the *lichnost'*, or the personality of the individual, has been stressed, and the phrase 'humanisation' has come to be a 'buzz phrase' in Russian education, as teachers and administrators across the system have adopted the slogan.

The recognition of the need to address the question of teacher–pupil relations, and to increase the amount of attention paid to the pupil as individual, as opposed to the pupil as recipient of knowledge, was a welcome development in the Russian system. However, as a number of foreign and Russian observers have noted, the arguments put forward in support of humanisation have tended to be rather imprecise, and those advocating the policy have often shown only a partial awareness of the implications of introducing it.[34] Again, the call for humanisation was based at least to some degree on a desire to tackle perceived problems of the Soviet system, but without having 'decontextualised' these problems to compare them objectively with those encountered in Western education systems. The articles, documents and speeches presented by the reform camp during the late 1980s and early 1990s, for instance, contained frequent references to the 'authoritarian' nature of the Soviet school, along with claims that the school had suppressed the individuality of its pupils. Dneprov went as far as to compare the Soviet school to a 'prison-like institution,'[35] while others suggested that in place of the strict Soviet establishment, the school should be transformed into a 'temple of good' (*khram dobra*),[36] in order to offset the authoritarian tradition. Further, it was argued by some in the reform movement that the 'authoritarian' Soviet school had played a key rôle in the maintenance of the 'totalitarian' Soviet state, and that now, in order to create a democratic society, the need for the humanisation of the school must be seen as a priority. To what extent was such criticism of the Soviet school justified?

A considerable amount of evidence has been put forward in Russia in recent years, in questionnaire surveys and qualitative studies, as well as anecdotal accounts in the pedagogical press, to support claims of the need to improve teacher–pupil relations.[37] Indeed, from conversations with Russian pupils, parents and adults in general, and to a lesser extent, with teachers, there does appear to be a degree of consensus that such developments are necessary, to counter patterns of teacher-dominated relations which, in the worst cases, allowed teaching staff to abuse the power they wielded by humiliating pupils, with the latter having little opportunity to protect themselves from such treatment. To an observer from, say, the UK or the USA, the need for 'humanisation' may indeed seem to be pressing, for at the superficial level, relations between staff and pupils in the Russian school still appear to be overly formal and strict, yet someone from, say, France, Germany or Japan, or indeed a Briton educated in the 1950s, may well feel that the nature of relations in the Russian school differs little from their own experience of schooling.

It is somewhat misleading to pay too much attention to a supposed correlation between authoritarian schooling and the presence of an authoritarian political regime. While an authoritarian school model may suit the needs of an authoritarian government, it should be remembered that the vast majority of school systems around the world, including those in liberal democracies, can be said to be founded in authoritarian approaches. Moreover, the presence of democratic traditions in a given country owes something, of course, to the process of socialisation evident in the schools, but the strength of such traditions, and the character of that country's political system, is shaped by a complex range of factors of which educational experience is but one part. The UK has been governed by what is widely recognised to be a democratic system (albeit imperfect) for some considerable time, yet, as Davies,[38] Rogers[39] and others have pointed out convincingly, many aspects of the organisation of schooling in England and the USA (respectively) do not appear to be that conducive to the inculcation of democratic values.

There is no space here to debate in depth the relative merits of various forms of 'democratic' and 'authoritarian' education. Instead, I wish merely to highlight the need to contextualise the discussion of the Russian reformers' promotion of humanisation, and to suggest that such matters could form the basis of revealing comparative studies, from which Western educationalists might profit from acquaintance with some of the innovative practices that have been introduced in Russian in recent years.

The issue of humanitarisation, or revising and enhancing the position of humanities subjects within the curriculum, has been the subject of considerable discussion,[40] and overlaps, to a degree, with the debate on humanisation. (Indeed, the two terms are sometimes used interchangeably by Russian educationalists.) This policy was required, it was said, both because the Soviet curriculum had placed far too much emphasis on scientific and technical subjects, and because the social science and humanities disciplines had been corrupted by the inclusion of 'ideological' material. The latter point is indisputable. History syllabuses, for instance, had been particularly affected, giving the official Soviet interpretation of the past with no room for alternative viewpoints, while other subjects (e.g. geography, foreign languages) were also in need of revision. A great deal of activity has been seen in these matters, with considerable effort made to modify syllabuses and produce new textbooks.[41]

Revision of the humanities is one thing; expanding their share of the curriculum at the expense of the natural sciences and mathematics is another – care would need to be taken to ensure that this policy was not taken too far. The strength of Soviet education had been in the sciences and mathematics, yet here, too, revision was required if Russia was to retain a sound foundation in these subjects, which will surely prove of great importance in the efforts to modernise the ailing economy.

If less attention is given in the reform programme itself to the school's rôle in economic development, however, the issue has been taken up in other quarters. The World Bank, for instance, refers in its report on the state of Russian education to the presence of what it terms the 'wrong skills for a market economy,'[42] and recommends the implementation of measures to correct this. One could take issue with the World Bank over what exactly is meant by the 'wrong skills', and question the extent to which Western education systems can truly be said to provide the 'right' skills. Nevertheless, this matter has begun to receive a growing amount of attention from within the school system in Russia, with research studies conducted, and educational programmes initiated in many schools to introduce pupils to the principles of the market.[43] Further, the importance attached to the development of cognitive skills, cooperative learning, communication and interaction in the proposals for curricular change, and the encouragement of lifelong learning could be said to support the societal goals of laying foundations for democracy and the market economy.

An agenda to change society?

The concerns highlighted in this critique of the agenda should not be taken to indicate that the reforms are flawed. The core of the programme, after all, does display great similarity to policies being followed by liberal democracies around the world; whatever the intrinsic merits or drawbacks of the policies as educational goals, the Russian system might justifiably see safety in numbers. Further, it has to be remembered that the initiation of the reforms represents only one part of the change process, for reforms can only be said to exist when implementation is attempted. While the views of the centre still carry substantial authority, in the increasingly devolved atmosphere of the post-Soviet system the interpretations imposed on the aims of reform are likely to be quite diverse. As the policies pass through the *prism of change*, their progress will depend on a myriad factors: on how they are interpreted, understood or misunderstood, supported or opposed; on the extent to which sufficient resources are provided to ensure implementation, and so on. In other words, it will be the responsibility of the system itself to subject the reforms to scrutiny, to assess their applicability, and the potential of the schools to implement them.

Before looking at the course of implementation in Part II, however, a note of caution is required with regard to the apparent faith which the reform camp placed in the ability of their policies to influence the course of transformation in Russian society as a whole. Is such faith justified? Belief in the school's influence is by no means limited to Russia, of course, but is common among educationalists across the world – in contrast to the lack of attention often afforded to education from other quarters in society. In recent years an intense debate has taken place over the future shape of education, and its importance in overall social change, as we head towards the twenty-first century.[44] In many, if not all of the countries of the former 'communist' bloc, too, there has been a tendency in the education community to portray education as a panacea for society's ills. However, as Sandi warns:

> The misconception starts when education is conceived as a 'miraculous' way for changing society, or, in Eastern [European] countries, advancing democracy and making progress towards market economies.[45]

There are limits to the school's potential to exert *constructive* influence on societal development. With regard to the school's rôle as a centre for inculcating democratic values, for instance, convincing arguments have been put forward by scholars of education in established democracies to demonstrate both the unsuitability of existing practices in school systems to the inculcation of democratic values in the young,[46] and to highlight the fact that the young citizen's apprenticeship in democracy and development of attitudes towards politics stem from a far wider range of sources than the school, with the family, according to a good deal of evidence, acting as the most important influence. Various initiatives have been undertaken to give schools a more active rôle, some with successful results, but we are still some way from finding truly effective approaches.[47] If this is the case in stable countries with well-established democracies, then the challenge for Russia and other countries with a weak democratic tradition is even greater. In this, and in the matter of influencing economic development, while the school clearly does have a major part to play, the effect of policies directed towards such ends is likely to take a considerable amount of time to be seen. Destructive influence, on the other hand, can occur far more swiftly, especially in countries which are engaged in substantial social transformation.

Despite the cultural, economic and, to a growing extent, political diversity of the nations of the former 'communist' bloc in the former Soviet Union and Central and Eastern Europe, in many regards their experience of educational reform displays a number of similarities, as the following comment, made with reference to four Central European countries, shows:

> Change in the political system demanded the *elimination* of the former system of education. [my emphasis][48]

We can find echoes of the tendency of Russian reform leaders to overstate the nature of the legacy they had to contend with,[49] the urgent need perceived among reformers to move rapidly to a new model of schooling, often based on the practice of Western democracies,[50] and the priority given to the school's rôle in the democratisation process.

The flux which accompanies transformation can lead to positive outcomes of renewal, as the chance is taken to move on from certain traditional practices that have become obsolete. The population itself may be more receptive to significant change, perhaps seeing it as inevitable if the overall situation is to improve, an attitude not often found in more tranquil times. From this point of view, the task of the population, of the politicians, economists, and of those who lead change, is to take advantage of such opportunities while they last, opportunities that come only rarely in a nation's history. Alongside such positive potential, however, there are clear attendant risks and dangers. Transitions are often painful affairs, with tension arising from the struggle to revise the nation's philosophical base. Long-term planning, as we have seen, may be abandoned in favour of a more impulsive approach to policy-making, while the extent of upheaval, often accompanied by weakness in the state of civil society, can render institutions such as the school vulnerable. In such circumstances, the contrast between positive and negative influences becomes clear: to build something through education takes years, decades even; the effects of destruction, on the other hand, can be felt much more rapidly. If access to educational provision is reduced, if expenditure is cut back, if establishments are closed, then the effect on society may be observed within a few years, or even immediately.

The challenge facing those who are managing the reform of Russia's school system is how to take advantage of the rare opportunities to engage in profound change, while not creating further social problems that may well, eventually, defeat the progress of societal transformation itself. Perhaps, as some educationalists suggested to me in the period immediately after the dissolution of the USSR, the priority in a time of societal instability and continuing crises should be the preservation of existing structures and practices, rather than reform? For repairing a school system that has fallen victim to the negative aspects of transition is a process that would, without doubt, take a very long time indeed.

Part II

Patterns of Change in the School System

Introduction to Part II: the Study of Implementation

> The process [of reform] is gaining speed, even becoming irreversible, despite the many difficulties and obstacles in its path.[1]

> School reform has not, in fact, been realised. The efforts made by the pedagogical community over the past five years, towards changing the school and promoting new methods of teaching, has culminated in many cases in 'verbal innovation': teachers and administrators are unable substantially to transform their approaches or their way of thinking.[2]

At times an overly optimistic view is taken by some of the progress of reform in Russia's schools. In 1995, for instance, it was claimed that the 'developmental education' (*razvivayushchee obuchenie*) model of teaching and learning had been introduced and established in 42 per cent of all primary-level classes in Russia.[3] Such claims can be dismissed without even reviewing evidence put forward to support them. While they mirror the simplistic belief that has often accompanied the introduction of reform in Western systems, namely that implementation and continuation will necessarily follow as a matter of course, the body of research on educational change has provided increasingly detailed evidence of the complexity of the change process in general, and of the absence of any inevitability in the process of implementation in particular.[4] Major curricular reform does not occur this quickly, even when the system is relatively stable and enjoys adequate resources, and the teaching force is experienced in reform implementation.

Rather than search for elusive (and potentially illusory) proof of change, the aim in Part II is to attempt an evaluation of the *capacity* of the system to engage in reform (i.e. the extent to which existing patterns of the organisation of school life can be seen to be conducive to change), and to identify trends in the *process* of reform at all levels in the system (but avoiding the temptation to quantify this experience and draw hard conclusions). A review will also be made of the various obstacles which threaten not only to disrupt the implementation of reform, but also to bring into question the ability of the system even to survive as a viable entity.

From a more distant perspective, it should be noted that the study of educational reform has only relatively recently begun to receive a great deal of attention from the international academic community, although over the past 25 years we have seen a veritable explosion in the amount of research conducted on this subject.[5] The conclusions drawn by many experts in the field are rather sobering, for they point to a record of failure, rather than success in reform implementation.[6] It is in this context that we should judge the Russian reforms, for if reform has proved to be such a difficult matter in the relatively stable and prosperous countries of the West in their attempts to implement comparatively small-scale change, then the Russian scenario of a huge agenda calling for radical change in all aspects of the school's organisation, set against the backdrop of social upheaval and financial crisis, appears to offer rather bleak prospects. Russia's case can be considered unique in its scope, and there is no blueprint to show the 'right' way to approach reform.

Nevertheless, perhaps the Russian reformers can draw on the growing awareness of the dynamics of change acquired by the international community, and avoid some of the pitfalls associated with unsuccessful reform? Indeed, despite the self-imposed isolation of the USSR and the specific contexts of contemporary Russian reform, there are a number of similarities in the pattern of educational change seen in Russia before and after 1991 and the experience of, say, the school systems in the USA and the UK. The criticism (not wholly justified) levelled at the 1984 reforms by, among others, Dneprov and Tkachenko[7] that they were 'pseudo-reforms' which only amounted to tinkering with the system, rather than a serious attempt at change, mirrors closely the criticism made by some of the reform efforts in the USA in the same period.[8] More recently, the progression in reform-thinking in the USA from a piecemeal approach, through a school-improvement approach and, now, towards a 'fix-the-system' approach,[9] resembles the approach adopted in Russia of 'all-out' reform. In the end, it may well be the case that while the Russian system can learn much from the experience of others in the matter of implementation, if the Russian approach to change proves successful, notwithstanding the many difficulties facing the schools, then perhaps it should be the foreign education systems who look to Russia for guidance on how to conduct school reform.

4
The Challenge of Devolution

It has become fashionable in the West to speak of 'change management' in matters of educational reform, yet this term gives a somewhat misleading impression of the nature of the task facing the various levels of administration in the Russian system, for processes of educational change, in any country, are extremely complex affairs that can verge on being uncontrollable.[1] As policies move into the implementation phase, the central authorities lose ultimate control over the course of reform, even in what seems to be a highly controlled, centralised, unitary system, as individuals, groups and institutions respond to its policies and demands. The question is not one of managing, or controlling change, but of attempting to shape the environment in which it is to take place, creating conditions that are conducive to successful implementation.

In the Russian case, the policy of decentralisation has had a profound effect on the administration of the system at all levels, presenting officials and educationalists from the central ministry, through regional, municipal and district authorities, to the schools themselves with the demanding challenge of adapting to the loss of old, and acquisition of new, responsibilities.

The challenge for the centre

Eduard Dneprov was forced to resign from the post of minister in December 1992 as a result of increasingly heated disputes with other factions in the government. His aggressive style had proved controversial: necessary, perhaps, to give the Russian reforms the impetus to carry them forward, but at the same time a high-risk approach which threatened to alienate the teaching force. Indeed, by 1992, many within the upper echelons of the reform movement had begun to distance themselves from Dneprov,[2] and *Uchitel'skaya gazeta* had adopted an increasingly critical stance on Dneprov and the manner in which he was leading the reform process.[3]

Dneprov's replacement as minister, Evgenii Viktorovich Tkachenko, came, unlike Dneprov,[4] from a background in education, having held a professorship in a technical institute. The advantage of this experience showed in Tkachenko's more understanding approach to dealing with the schools and the teaching force, and his tenure in office was marked by a more conciliatory, cautious stance. Indeed, Tkachenko was accused of being too cautious at times, not strong enough, for instance, to stand up to the demands for cutbacks in expenditure on education made by the Ministry of Finance.[5] Such criticism was, perhaps, a little harsh: the relatively weak position of the Ministry of Education meant that he was often fighting a losing battle. Tkachenko's position was finally undermined, however, by the merger of the Ministry of Education with the State Committee on Higher Education (*Gosudarstvennyi komitet po vysshemu obrazovaniyu* or *Goskomvuz*) in the summer of 1996, with the post of Minister of the 'new' Ministry of General and Professional Education (*Ministerstvo obshchego i professional'nogo obrazovaniya*) given to V. Kinelev, the chairman of *Goskomvuz*.

We can note the degree of continuity present in the Ministry of Education over the period 1991–97, in which, for instance, only three ministers of education held office, notwithstanding the general air of instability in Russian political life.[6] More significantly (although not unrelated) is the fact that the overall direction of reform remained the same, with the Russian system spared the pendulum swing of policy change which has affected other systems in the past. Indeed, Tkachenko acknowledged his debt to the legacy of Dneprov and Yagodin, and both he, while in office, and Kinelev largely retained the policy rhetoric and substance which first emerged under Dneprov (although Kinelev was criticised for favouring the higher-education sector at the expense of other levels, including secondary, during his tenure in office).[7] That this was possible may reflect the fact that, as will be argued in Part III, a 'false consensus' had emerged with regard to the goals of reform, which suppressed potential differences of opinion and approach under the unifying influence of rather vague 'buzz words'. Indeed, one might argue that Dneprov's successors proved to be too prepared to follow the established line, and did not do enough to refine policies in accordance with the fast-changing developments in the system, and in society itself. Tkachenko, for instance, promoted with vigour the concept of 'choice' in educational provision,[8] but failed adequately to address the contradictions implicit in this argument over the extension of choice for some and the extent of provision for all, a factor that has become painfully evident in developments in the school system over recent years. Alongside the policy debate, though, we must also consider the effects of the ministry's efforts to redefine its rôle and its relations with the rest of the system, for this promised to pass the initiative in the policy debate to the lower levels.

The transformation of the function of the central ministry was initiated under Yagodin in the late 1980s, after the restructuring of the various education ministries to form the USSR State Committee on Education, and the effort continued in the Russian ministry under Dneprov from 1990 onwards.[9] The thrust of change has been to transform the ministry from a controlling and directing function, to one of coordination. In line with the new approach, for instance, Tkachenko frequently stated that schools should become used to acting on their own initiative, consulting with the ministry, rather than seeking permission or waiting for directives.[10] Such views stand in marked contrast to those held by the central authorities in the past, and represent, in principle, a sound commitment to the idea of democratisation and public accountability. In affecting this transformation, however, the ministry has, as one might expect, encountered delays and problems.

In a system that is undergoing the 'shock-therapy' of rapid devolution, the shock felt by the regions, schools and teachers when suddenly presented with responsibility for their sphere of activity, after so many years of central control, needed to be accompanied by the therapy of an effective framework for decentralisation, if the centre's declared aim of maintaining what is termed the 'unitary educational space' (*edinoe obrazovatel'noe prostranstvo*) of Russia was to be achieved. Such a framework was, accordingly, devised, and comprises.

- federal-level legislation on education (e.g. Law on Education of 1992)
- mechanisms for federal-level supervision of educational financing
- a Federal Programme for the Development of Education (*Federal'naya programma razvitiya obrazovaniya*), to act as an umbrella for regional and municipal programmes

- agreements on cooperation in education between the ministry and regional administrations
- a core curriculum (*bazisnyi uchebnyi plan*), with federal, regional and school components
- educational standards (*obrazovatel'nye standarty*) to serve as criteria for the new curricula
- assessment procedure for teaching staff
- accreditation systems for educational establishment.

Before examining the effect that these measures have had, and the resultant implications for the drive for system-wide improvement, we should pause to consider the nature of the challenge facing the centre in its attempts to manage devolution.

As reform policies pass through the change prism, their course is subject to what we can call the *currents of change*, as teachers and administrators adopt their own stance on reform. The degree to which reform outcomes match reform aims will depend on the level of coincidence in these currents; perhaps they will flow in the same direction at the same speed; perhaps they will be slower, even still, thus becalming reform; or perhaps they will flow in the opposite direction, thus severely disrupting the course of change; or, to extend the analogy further, perhaps, they will create a whirlpool in which change will simply disappear.

The currents of change at the grassroots level will only coincide with those envisaged by the centre if there is sufficient cohesion within the system. In the hyper-centralised Soviet model, the central educational authorities could be reasonably sure that their tight controls over each level of the system would ensure a high level of cohesion. Now, the course of change would depend much more heavily than before on the attitudes and actions of individual regions, institutions and teachers. Along with the benefits such a transition could bring in allowing grassroots initiative to flourish, the reformers also needed to be aware of the risk of fragmentation.

One major potential source of fragmentation stems from the tendency, highlighted earlier, of Russian teachers to adopt a micro-level view of their work. Many of the teachers whom I interviewed expressed relatively little interest in the activities of the Ministry of Education, or indeed in debates on education taking place at the national level. In some cases, this phenomenon was evident in a lack of awareness among certain interviewees of significant events that had taken place just before our conversations. A group of five teachers from various cities were unable to comment on the implications of the 43rd Article affair (see Part III) when questioned on the topic in May 1994, at the height of the debate over this issue; indeed, for a time they contested the validity of my question, stating that I must have been mistaken in thinking that such an article existed in the Russian constitution. Finally, one can encounter such attitudes as that expressed by the headteacher of a private school, who, when asked for her views on the recently published Federal Programme for the Development of Education, told me that she 'had no time to read all of those documents that the bureaucrats in the ministry think up' (conversation with the author, April 1995).

This is the legacy of the Soviet system, in which the tight controls which existed at each level served to condition behaviour to correspond to the demands of the immediate superior. Teachers toed the line set down by the headteachers and the school inspectors, headteachers conformed with the desires of the district administration, which followed the demands of the town administration, and so on. In the same way that ordinary citizens were divorced, to a great extent, from the political process, except as powerless spectators, so there was little incentive for teachers, or for that matter headteachers, to be too concerned with events outside of their own micro-environment. It will take a long time for teachers and administrators to adjust to the new, freer patterns now present in the system.

Perspectives on devolution

> The process of decentralisation has given us the possibility to take responsibility ourselves for the development of education in our region. While this is, indeed, a huge responsibility, and it has taken time for us to get used to it, we welcome it as a progressive and necessary step towards the democratisation of the system. (Regional administrator, interview with the author, April 1993)

> Rapid decentralisation will lead to the loss of control over education, and some clever administrator in the regions (*regional*), who has felt him or herself to be independent of higher authorities will be able to ensure that, for many years to come, the 'regional children' will be coming to terms with the consequences of his or her 'creativity.'[11]

Strong arguments can, naturally, be put forward in support of decentralisation. Under centralised systems the scope of change can be limited, for instance, with large-scale and radical innovation made more difficult.[12] Further, instead of an evolutionary, progressive pattern of change, centralised approaches tend to lead to a more uneven distribution of activity and inactivity in change processes (e.g. a 'stop–go effect').[13] In a decentralised system there may be greater possibilities for regional and local authorities, individual schools and teachers to apply their own initiative to questions of implementation, and thus respond more rapidly and more appropriately to the problem as it applies to their own particular circumstances. Further, the question of reform 'ownership' may also play a positive part, as participants in the change process see that they have more direct and meaningful influence over the direction of change.[14] Change can thus take on an evolutionary character, with system-wide development achieved through an incremental process, as schools and regions build and maintain a momentum of constant 'reform'.

From the perspective of the national-level policy-maker, however, there are important potential drawbacks associated with decentralised systems. While it may encourage a greater degree of innovation, and a more flexible approach to change, the very fact that individual regions and schools are adopting their own stances on these issues may lead to a certain loss of cohesion within the system, leading in extreme cases to a state of 'anarchy'.[15] In the case of the new Russia, the contexts within which educational reform was to be pursued suggested that such loss of control might be inevitable, at least to some extent. To reiterate the question posed in Chapter 3, then, were the reformers right to push ahead so forcefully with devolution?

Putting devolution into practice

The Law on Education of 1992 set the tone for the process of decentralisation, encouraging the various levels of the system to assume greater responsibility for managing the schools (see Articles 28–39 of the Law on Education). Thus, while the structure of the system in the late 1990s (see Table 4.1) resembles very closely that of the late Soviet system, with regard to the division of administration by federal, regional, municipal and school levels, the distribution of responsibility between these levels has undergone considerable change, with the federal 'centre' assuming, in principle, a more detached, facilitative role, in contrast to its former directive position.

Given the complexity of the law, its ambitious agenda and the conditions in which it had been drawn up, it was, perhaps, inevi-

Table 4.1 Administrative structure of the school system of the Russian Federation

Federal level
Government of the Russian Federation
Ministry of Education of the Russian Federation (from July 1996: Ministry of General and Professional Education of the Russian Federation) Collegium of the Ministry of Education
Regional level
Regional / Republican / Territorial Educational Administration (Regional = *Oblastnoe upravlenie narodnogo obrazovaniya* – OBLUNO)
Ministry of Education (e.g. Leningrad *oblast'* and autonomous republics)
Committee for Education (e.g. Krasnoyarsk *krai*)
City/town level
Municipal (City/Town) Educational Administration (*Gorodskoe upravlenie narodnogo obrazovaniya* – GORUNO)
Department of Education (e.g. Yaroslavl')
District level (within town or city)
District Educational Administration (*Raionnoe upravlenie narodnogo obrazovaniya – RUNO*)
School level (state schools)
School council + headteacher

table that certain internal contradictions and problems would arise with regard to the distribution of powers. As Glenn points out in his analysis of the legislation, while the regions are allocated certain functions according to some articles of the law, these powers are then overridden in other articles, with the responsibility to be retained by the central authorities.[16] Regional administrators began to draw attention to further technical drawbacks that were impeding the course of change.

> One very important problem stems from the almost complete absence of secondary legislation to support many aspects of the Law on Education. Although we are trying to fill such gaps by ourselves, it is not within our powers to do so adequately.[17]

Such flaws were recognised by the ministry, which set to work reasonably quickly after the adoption of the 1992 law to develop amendments to the legislation, presenting them to the State *Duma* in 1994. The passage of these amendments through the *Duma*, however, as has been the case with much legislation in general, was delayed, and the amendments were finally adopted only on January 23, 1996.[18] It remains to be seen whether the amendments, which concerned a range of issues including decentralisation, will deal effectively with the problems which stemmed from the original legislation.

The ministry invited proposals to be submitted for the programme in 1993, and received a number of plans from various teams based mainly in research institutes, such as the Institute of Pedagogical Innovation, the successor to VNIK; and the Institute of Theoretical Pedagogical and International Research in Education.[19] The proposals were published in the pedagogical press for wider discussion, and a committee was set up by the Ministry of Education to evaluate the various plans. One was duly selected in 1994, a published version appearing later that year.[20]

The ministry put a great deal of effort into promoting the programme in articles and conferences, setting out what it viewed as the benefits that would be gained from the programme in the wide range of activities that it covered, from pre-school education through teacher training to research and the development of the school system's material base.[21] However, although the programme was approved on March 31, 1994 by the federal government, its acceptance was held up in the *Duma* by the elections of December 1995 and by the presidential elections in June 1996. The Ministry of Education, frustrated by the delay, which meant that funding for the programme was held up, urged that the programme be granted the status of a presidential decree.[22]

According to one deputy, Larisa Babukh, the government was to blame for the delay, since it refused to make available the finances required to implement this and other federal-level programmes.[23] Gennadii Seleznev, a deputy of the Communist Party and former editor of *Uchitel'skaya gazeta*, while also drawing attention to the financial aspect of the programme's implementation, interpreted the matter differently, stating that he and his colleagues in the *Duma* had perceived the programme as 'simply propagandistic', and that their main motive for blocking its passage was due to shortcomings in the detail of the proposals, especially with regard to the financial basis that would be used to deliver the programme.[24] Although the ministry dismissed such criticism, Seleznev's comments do ring true to a large extent. The programme appears to be a 'shopping list' of desired results, rather than a detailed blueprint for the highly complex process of decentralisation. While one can accept the ministry's argument that the programme is intended to serve as a framework, with the precise nature of implementation to be decided by the regions themselves, the programme as presented can be seen as rather too heavily dominated by aims, rather than providing proposals for concrete measures that might be taken to achieve those aims. For instance, in the section on personnel issues, an intended outcome of the programme is said to be the 'raising of the prestige of the teaching profession,'[25] a goal which any teacher would agree with, but a target whose realisation seems further away than ever at present.

In the spring of 1997, a revised version of the programme was put forward, incorporating amendments designed to reflect the changed circumstances in education and society since the publication of the original.[26] According to Valerii Zuev, the Ministry of Education official responsible for overseeing the revisions, an effort had been made to review the nature of centre-region relations envisaged in the programme, taking into account the problems that had been seen to follow the granting of far greater freedom to the regions to decide their own policies, while an attempt was also made to lend greater clarity and practicality to the content of the programme.[27] Despite the long delay in passing the programme, however (at the time of writing it still had not acquired legal status), the very fact that the programme exists on paper, at least, should be seen as a positive sign, for while it is lacking in substance, it does serve as a tangible guideline for administrators and educationalists, who have been able to see the direction of change proposed by the centre. The initiative, accordingly, passed to the regions to develop their own programmes within this framework.

Some regions had already begun to develop their own programmes for education even before the various proposals for the federal programme had been discussed, anxious, it seemed, to begin to address their own needs without delay.[28] Others followed suit, as they realised that the Federal Programme for the Development of Education was likely to be delayed for some time,[29] and by 1995, 73 regions of the total of 89 had published programmes. The number of 'Agreements on Cooperation in the Sphere of Education' signed between the Ministry of Education and regional administrations (with the intention of clarifying the distribution of responsibilities within the system and increasing cooperation)[30] also grew rapidly, from seven in 1992 to 16 in 1993, 19 in 1994 and over 50 by 1996.[31] Alongside developments at the regional level, town and cities also began to develop their own programmes, ostensibly (although not always, it seems) in collaboration with the regional authorities.[32]

Outcomes of devolution

One key aim of the process of devolution of regionalisation is that of rendering the education system more responsive to regional needs. It would seem that in this respect progress is being made, as regional administrations have begun to develop approaches that respond to the various specific requirements of their region, from economic and manpower issues,[33] through cultural matters[34] to addressing the educational needs of ethnic groups.

While encouraging such developments the centre's first concern was to ensure that the various programmes being devised across the country coincided sufficiently with the ministry's vision of the way forward. Studying the outcomes of devolution across the 89 regions, though, is not an easy task, even for the Ministry of Education. The size of the country, the weakness of mechanisms of collection and analysis of data on the system, together with other factors such as the degree of cooperation shown by the regions in working with the central authorities, mean that the provision of a picture of educational development of the complexity and accuracy enjoyed in other federal systems such as the USA is not possible.

To a degree, therefore, the centre has to rely on the analysis of the contents of the programmes being proposed, as a rough indication of the directions being followed. Tkachenko, for instance, identified three main types of programme to have emerged by 1996:

- programmes which serve as a means of development for the region as a whole
- programmes which concentrate on the development of education in particular
- programmes which are termed 'programmes for the development of education', but which are, in fact, 'simply programmes of education'.[35]

Into the first group, which, naturally, is considered to be the preferred variant, one might place such programmes as that introduced by the Moscow Department of Education under the title 'Education of the Capital'.[36] This group, however, according to Tkachenko's estimate, contained only ten regions (along with the Moscow programme he named the Tula and Novgorod regions). The majority of the rest, apparently, fell into the second category of education-focused programmes, which did not, in the opinion of the ministry, devote sufficient attention to tackling problems in conjunction with other official bodies (such as the health authorities, employment agencies, etc.). This analysis, if accurate, reflects the difficulties in changing the culture of educational administration – breaking away from traditional practices has proved an extremely difficult task to achieve.

Devolution has placed new demands on administrators at all levels, of course.

> In the Soviet system we could blame the centre for any problems. Our only task was to look after the schools in our region on behalf of Moscow. The schools did what we told them to do, we did what the centre wanted. Now this is changing, and we have the opportunity to adapt the school system to suit our region. Having received this freedom, though, we do not always seem to know how best to take advantage of it. (Regional administrator, interview with the author, December 1995)

Judging from the amount of coverage devoted to this topic in the pedagogical press and from information supplied in interviews during my research, the question of the adaptation of administrators to the new paradigms introduced into the system has proved to be a problematic area:

> Some [administrators] are still oriented towards the theory and practice of administration espoused by . . . strictly centralised bureaucratic regulations . . . On the other hand, there is a group which interprets the democratisation of administration to mean the granting of unlimited powers, the absence of control, etc.[37]

There was a pressing need for providing administrators with retraining, to equip them with the new skills they require to adapt to the changing nature of their work. While such support was slow to materialise in the early stages of the reforms, progress has been made in this area, at least with regard to the establishment of retraining programmes and the identification of federally approved practices in the professional development of administrators.[38] Whether the system will be able to find the resources necessary to fund this retraining is another matter, yet until it is provided, the air of confusion that has accompanied devolution will continue, for even the most talented and knowledgeable of administrators and educationalists have found it difficult to cope with the fast-changing, at times contradictory nature of change in the administrative system.[39]

The real test for devolution rests on the restructuring of relations within the system, and the degree to which each level is able (and willing) to work with the others. The Ministry of Education has been stressing the need to develop *horizontal* relations between, for example, regional authorities, in order to move away from the predominantly vertical alignment of the Soviet system. To some extent this has been taking place: inter-regional conferences have been organised by the Ministry of Education on a range of issues, while many of the regions themselves have actively developed closer links with regions throughout the country. The lack of well-defined channels for such cooperation, combined with difficulties of communication and travel, research and dissemination of the results of good practice still means, however, that often the positive and negative experience that regions have gained is not passed on.[40]

Alongside the positive signs which appeared to accompany devolution, moreover, a recognition soon emerged that the process was giving rise to certain worrying problems. While some regions could be relied upon to use the new responsibilities they had received in a reasoned manner, taking into consideration the effect of their actions on those around them in the system, other regional administrations saw fit to go their own way. This is not to suggest that there was one 'right' path for the regions to follow, and that the former group of administrations have followed the ministry's line while the latter has strayed from it. Variation and divergence are perfectly acceptable, and even conflicting approaches can be tolerated to an extent; it is, rather, the threat of fragmentation that is the greater danger, as Tkachenko made clear in 1994:

> It is no secret that there are talented regional administrators who are already saying: 'My interests lie within the borders of my region, and I don't need to think about anything outside of those borders.' Such lack of understanding will lead in the end to war [between the regions and the centre]. I said as much in a letter to Viktor Stepanovich Chernomyrdin: the destruction of education will lead to the destruction of the notion of the state.[41]

There is a sense both of despair, at times, mingled with apparent regret at the way the ministry handled the issue of decentralisation from the outset, as the following comment of First Deputy Minister Bolotov, also from 1994, shows:

> It was probably decentralisation that was the most visible and quick outcome of education reform, though the depth of this process is still questionable. Yet a comparative perspective demonstrates that everywhere there is a need to establish a balance between strong state policy in education and decentralization. Unless such a balance is maintained, educational decentralization, in the context of extreme regionalization policies, might lead to chaos and disintegration.[42]

In granting them such unprecedented freedom in such a rapid manner, without giving all sides time to reflect on how to effect this transformation, the ministry placed a great deal of trust in the hands of the regions without, apparently, paying sufficient attention to the measures it could take if the actions of the regions theatened system cohesion. As a result, the centre has had to fight to regain some of the ground that it once occupied, and has at times been forced to watch helplessly as various problems have emerged. For instance, a number of cases of headteachers being dismissed by local administrators, apparently contrary to official regulations, have been publicised in the letters column of *Uchitel'skaya gazeta*, and centre-region disputes over matters of corruption highlighted.[43] In some instances, local administrations have seen fit to sell off educational establishments (such as technical colleges or kindergartens), actions that have brought the wrath of the central ministry, although the latter, again, has found it extremely difficult to succeed in reversing such moves.[44]

The picture is complicated, of course, by the nature of regional politics in Russia. While some regional administrations have decided to make education a priority, it is more common to see a picture of neglect, as regional politicians struggle to save their local economy, and maintain their own position. Given the state of flux in regional politics in Russia, any comparisons of the devolution process in education with the experience of other countries of comparable size can be of only limited use. In the 1980s the Reagan government in the USA engaged in a concerted effort to devolve greater responsibility for education to the states, with a corresponding wave of initiatives emerging at the state level.[45] However, the states were already accustomed to running the school system; the process of devolution was, therefore, an evolutionary measure, rather than the revolutionary approach seen in Russia. Further, in countries such as the USA a culture of public accountability and democracy is well-established at the regional level, a culture that is only beginning to emerge in Russia. Russian regional politicians can often be said to be following a rather narrow agenda, that focuses on the needs of their regions to the exclusion of national issues; indeed, the political allegiances of such figures with regard to national-level parties and blocs can be difficult to define. Many of the new 'democratic' politicians (and administrators) are in fact former members of the political and administrative *apparat* of the Soviet era (as is the case with the majority of federal-level politicians). As such, they may be ill-prepared for the demands of developing democratic structures in the regions.

The financing of education

In Article 40 of the Law on Education it is declared that: 'The State guarantees an annual allocation of financial means for educational needs. This allocation shall amount to no less than 10 per cent of the national income.'[46] Not surprisingly, the 10 per cent figure has never been achieved; indeed, it has proved difficult enough for the education system even to obtain a sum approaching half of that, as the legacy of underfunding of education inherited from the Soviet system has continued to plague the Russian school network.

In the Soviet era, education, as with other non-priority social institutions, was financed under the 'leftover principle' (*ostatochnyi printsip*), i.e. allocated funds once the major players in the Soviet economy, principally the military-industrial complex, had received their share. Figures for the pre-*perestroika* era were difficult to verify, but it is estimated that approximately 7 per cent of the USSR's Gross Domestic Product (GDP) was allocated to education in the early 1970s. As Gorbachev's programme of economic reform failed to alleviate, indeed, actually added to the problems of the ailing Soviet economy, so this figure declined, to 3.8 per cent in 1991. In the post-Soviet period, the figure fell again, to 3.4 per cent in 1992; after a recovery to 4.4 per cent in 1994, another fall, to 3.5 per cent, was recorded in 1995.[47]

As a point of comparison, Russia's allocations can be set against the figures found in stable countries such as the USA (5.5 per cent), the UK (5.3 per cent) or France (5.4 per cent).[48] However, one needs to bear in mind the tremendous economic decline which Russia has endured since 1991, with GDP, for instance, falling by 13 per cent in 1991, 19 per cent in 1992, 12 per cent in 1993, 15 per cent in 1994, before recovering to a fall of 2 per cent in 1995 and an estimated growth of 3 per cent in 1996.[49] An example of the effect on the schools is shown in the sharp fall in the amount of expenditure per pupil: in 1991–92 alone the decline amounted to 29 per cent per pupil in compulsory education.[50] Added to this, the Ministry of Education frequently complains that even the money that has, ostensibly, been allocated in the budget is often delayed, diverted or frozen: in 1994, for instance, only 61.3 per cent of the minimum funding requirements of the education system were met, according to the target figure of 3740.2 billion rubles set by the Ministry of Education.[51] In general, then, a bleak outlook, whose nature has been complicated by the process of regionalising responsibility for finances.

This process has been taking place in all spheres of economic activity in Russia, a process welcomed by those regions which possess a comparatively strong basis for development (in particular those with natural resources), and with misgivings by regions suffering in the transition to the 'market'. Evaluating the regionalisation of educational financing is hampered by the perennial problem of obtaining accurate information on the course of change. As the World Bank team highlights in its 1995 report, the changes introduced in the system of education as a whole have not been matched by corresponding change in the procedures for collecting statistical data; furthermore, those data that are obtained refer mainly to 'inputs' such as student numbers, rather than 'outputs' such as examination results and employment figures,[52] although some statistics are available on school graduation and youth employment.

A further problem, mentioned frequently in interviews with headteachers, concerns the confusion over the distribution of responsibility for financing among the various levels of the system. With the curriculum split into three components (federal, regional and school-defined), for example, it is not always clear which body is supposed to be in control, a situation that can be noted in a range of other issues such as teacher education, school inspection, or the provision of teaching materials. In principle, administrators and educationalists seem to be in favour of financial devolution, since it allows greater flexibility in responding to local needs, for instance with regard to teacher supply from pedagogical institutes and universities.[53] However, guarantees were required to ensure a smooth transition to a devolved model, something that in practice has not occurred, as the regionalisation of financing has proceeded apace, without waiting to ensure that all regions were in a fit position to assume this burden. By 1994, responsibility for financing had largely been passed from the federal to the regional level, the former providing only 13 per cent, the latter 87 per cent of funds for the education system from their budgets.[54] The question of establishing the pattern of multi-channel and multi-level (*mnogo-kanal'noe* and *mnogourovnevoe finansirovanie*) was left unresolved though, a situation that left the system without adequate financial protection.[55]

The picture of financing across the country is now extremely diverse, ranging from adequate, even comfortable in some areas to near collapse, according to some reports, in others. In 1994 the expenditure per 1000 population in the Koryakskii Autonomous Region was some 20 times that spent in the Tyumen' *oblast'* (1 454 100 000 rubles and 71 300 000 rubles respectively), with the vast majority of regions (66 out of 88 recorded) spending less than 200 million roubles per 1000 population.[56] Indeed, many regions continue to require subsidies from the federal budget to compensate, at least partially, for the problems they face in meeting their obligations. Ironically, the biggest spenders tend to be those regions in the far north and Siberia whose populations were, traditionally, neglected in the Soviet period, while their territory was exploited for oil and gas. In these regions, therefore, the difficulties of educational financing are far less pronounced than those faced by their counterparts in other, less well-off areas. As Zhirkov demonstrates in his analysis, a truer impression of the commitment of individual regions to education is provided by examining the percentage of their budget which is allocated to educational financing, although here again, not surprisingly, the richer regions tend to score higher.[57] This is not to deny that some regions, even those with limited resources, have not been able to make some progress towards meeting the needs of the schools, despite the difficulties:

> I should note that in those regions with which agreements [between federal and regional authorities] have been signed, where rights and duties have been distributed and set along the vertical line of administrative structure, the financing of educational estab-

> lishments is provided and is stable, and cases of dissatisfaction with conditions of work and pay arise much less frequently among the teaching staff.[58]

Yet for many regions the question of educational financing is just one part of the funding dilemma that they face, in trying to support outmoded industry, introduce reform in agriculture, cope with the growing crime rates, maintain health care, social services, the transport network and so on. It is a question of defining priorities from a list of urgent priorities: for some, such as the Penza region, which, in 1994, committed an extra 1 per cent of its budget to education after reviewing the state of the schools (information supplied by headteacher from Penza, April 1995), education is a priority; for others, different priorities are found. The Ministry of Education has struggled with the central government to release additional funds to the regions, and has had some success in this, providing welcome relief to certain hard-pressed administrations. At the same time, the ministry has become increasingly aware of attempts made by certain regions to abuse the system, and use funds allocated for education for other purposes, as Tkachenko highlighted in the case of Nakhodka, which requested, and was given, 20 billion rubles from the federal level, but spent only 6.5 billion on education, the remainder being used for foreign currency purchases and other expenses.[59] Such instances show the pressing need for tighter control over the flow of money within the system itself, for, as Tkachenko readily admitted, the ministry is often unaware of the details of funding arrangements of this kind.

Alongside their positive appraisal of some of the perceived results of devolution, therefore, the ministry had to take stock of some of the more negative implications associated with the regionalisation of financing. Bolotov, for instance, gave a strong warning that attempts to pass responsibility for financing teacher education to the regions could lead to the collapse of the entire education system,[60] while Tkachenko, who had already shown signs of misgiving *vis-à-vis* the policy of devolution as a whole, expressed disquiet over the specific consequences of the financial aspect:

> The merging of higher education establishments and their passing to the control of local budgets means going down the path of regionalisation, of the fragmentation of the education system.[61]

Thus we can see the sense of duality in the ministry's position – theoretically, ideologically even, disposed to decentralisation, but increasingly wary of its results. By this stage, however, the process of financial devolution had gone too far to reverse, at least in the short term. Could any solutions be offered?

Some slight comfort for the ministry and for the regions may be found in the fact that the birth-rate had continued to fall across the country, dropping from 16.6 per 1000 population in 1985 to 9.6 per 1000 by 1995.[62] As a result, the numbers of spaces required in schools, and the numbers of teachers needed, will fall in the years to come.[63] This, however, is false comfort, for the infrastructure is already inadequate and in desperate need of investment, even to bring it up to the level required for a smaller contingent of pupils, and there is already a significant and growing shortage of teachers.

There is no shortage of more constructive suggestions for solving the financial crisis in education, proposed in conferences and articles by Russian and Western experts.[64] Courses of action include the establishment of educational 'banks' that could provide a range of financial services to the education sector,[65] and the distribution of educational vouchers to parents, to allow them to choose the school that they wish their child to study in and deposit the voucher there. The last-named option, at least, has not received an overly warm welcome in the country as a whole, although it continues to be discussed in earnest by some at the federal level.[66] Without a full commitment on the part of federal and regional governments to providing education with at least the minimum of resources it needs, however, the crisis in financing is set to continue and to worsen in the years to come.

School administration in transition

As the administration of education from federal to district levels has undergone fundamental change, so the schools too have been coming to terms with the challenges posed by financial crisis, at the same time as attempting to transform the pattern of school administration. The process of democratisation, for instance, calls for closer links to be forged with the community, while administrative change in general is encouraged as a means of facilitating the introduction of innovation in the curriculum, all against the backdrop of severe limitations on available resources.

The legacy of neglect under the Soviet system, in which educational and other social spheres were consistently underfunded, has left the fledgling Russian state with a burden that it is in no fit shape to tackle. Meanwhile, the following problems continue to hinder school development. Many pupils in the towns, for example, find themselves in 'giant' schools (a pupil roll of 2000 is common), and around 36 per cent of schools still continue to operate in two or three 'shifts', with pupil attendance staggered throughout the day[67] (the figure in 1990 was 30 per cent).[68] According to the Ministry of Education, 33.9 per cent of schools (22 400) require urgent repairs to their buildings,[69] with 1 per cent considered to be in a dangerous condition.[70] With the cost of energy supply increasing rapidly, many schools have found themselves unable to pay their bills, and have fallen into arrears, with some, consequently, having their electricity, gas or water supply cut off.[71] Meanwhile, a considerable number of schools do not have a supply of electricity or running water, a problem that affects, principally, schools in rural areas.[72] The situation, clearly, is far from acceptable. As one headteacher remarked:

> Can we really expect teachers to introduce innovation, can there seriously be talk of bringing the school closer to the community and serving its educational needs, when so many establishments find themselves in such poor repair? My staff remain committed to their profession despite all of these problems, but there is a limit to what we can achieve. (Headteacher of comprehensive school, interview with the author. December 1995)

Efforts are underway to introduce innovation into the way that funds are allocated to and managed by the schools, yet while they recognise the need for a new mechanism and, indeed, welcome a good number of the changes that this drive has brought, many of the headteachers and administrators whom I interviewed admitted to a certain nostalgia for the relative stability and security of school funding in the Soviet system, notwithstanding the drawbacks of the 'leftover principle.' The uncertainty of the new era, in which planning the school's budget can be an almost impossible task because of the high level of inflation and the difficulties of supply, along with the requirements for all concerned to acquire complex skills of financial management, renders the new order of school financing a frightening prospect for many.

In the Soviet system, by way of contrast, the amount of initiative that could be employed by individual schools in deciding how to use the funds allocated to them was limited, and those funds, whose sum was calculated through tightly controlled mechanisms, may have been inadequate for the school's needs, yet there was at least some element of certainty underlying the model of finances. Now, as that stability has been replaced by financial uncertainty, and as inflation has caused havoc in the planning of budgets, the schools have found themselves left with far greater responsibility for managing their finances, in the most difficult of circumstances. As one headteacher put it:

> We're not accountants or financial experts, or even business people, but teachers. It is nice to have control over your own money, but we are amateurs in what has increasingly become a very professional game, and a lot of people have found to their cost what 'business' means in Russia today. (Headteacher, December 1995)

The problems of the schools are increased by the fact that the funds allocated by the educational authorities have proved insufficient, at times drastically so, for their needs. As a result, schools have had to develop strategies for generating extra income through a wide range of activities. Attracting such external support is not a new idea, of course: revenue from the sale of produce was a factor during the Soviet period, particularly under Khrushchev, although this was, apparently, a controversial issue.[73] More significantly, many schools received material assistance from local factories or collective and state farms, assistance that was often instrumental in ensuring that the school managed to maintain its buildings and equipment in good repair. In recent years, however, such support has diminished considerably, as enterprises and farms struggle to cope with the transition to the 'market' and decide to cut back on extraneous expenditure. As the Russian reforms were getting underway in the early 1990s, it was hoped by the centre that new approaches to external fund-raising could redress the loss of such support, and could be in turn a major source of additional funding for the schools, that would simultaneously relieve the burden on the budget, bring the schools closer to their community, and even contribute to the overall process of 'marketisation' in the economy.

In the early 1990s, for instance, schools were actively encouraged to offer 'services' to the local community, including the leasing of school premises to small companies, running educational, vocational and recreational courses for the population, even selling 'goods' produced in the school's workshops or, in the case of village schools, from its holdings of livestock and crops. However, doubts soon began to emerge about the extent of the usefulness of such activities, and the consequences that they sometimes held for the schools. As one headteacher commented to me with evident concern:

> Schools are not sausage factories. We are supposed to be educational establishments, serving the needs of the young, the population, the country. We are not here to make a profit. If we divert our energies into fundraising in this way then it is education that will suffer. (Headteachers of comprehensive school, interview with the author, April 1992)

To some extent, the early hopes placed on fund generation have often been disappointed, as the realities of business life in the new Russia have taken their toll. Many establishments which leased premises, for instance, found it to be a loss-making exercise that interfered with the educational functions of the school; indeed, in many regions such activity is now strictly forbidden by the educational authorities.[74] In those schools that still do engage in such business, the lion's share of the income is often taken by the 'owner' of the property. In general, the issue of 'ownership' in education remains a somewhat ill-defined concept, which the Law on Education has only partially addressed (Article 39). A complex discussion on property rights has taken place in recent years, and many issues remain unresolved.[75]

One effect of the revolution in financing, and the onus that has been placed on establishments to engage in a never-ending search for funds, has been to sharpen the divide between schools in working-class and middle-class districts of the towns and cities. While such differences were not so noticeable in the material condition of the schools in the Soviet period, in the new atmosphere, as the gap between income brackets has grown, certain schools find themselves in a comparatively favourable position with regard to potential parental support. This is particularly true of those schools that are 'fortunate' enough to be able to attract sponsors, whether from among parents or from the wider community. Certainly, money generated in this manner can be seen as welcome income, but it does raise questions about educational equality and provision, and about the involvement of the community in education. Further concerns have arisen because of the introduction of fees payable by pupils in certain schools. (Fee-paying education in non-state schools is permitted under the Law on Education, but a growing number of state schools have interpreted the law to mean that they can also generate income in this way.)[76]

As has proved the case in many educational systems, headteachers in Russia have often found that they are ill-prepared to deal with the increasingly diverse administrative burden placed on them, having to learn quickly to adjust to new patterns of decision-making in curricular issues, and to master the complexities of local management of finances. In addition, the social problems found in society at large are, of course, reflected among the staff, pupils and parents, and pose a further challenge to the headteacher, who must take responsibility for addressing such issues as drug and alcohol abuse by teenagers, the consequences of increased criminal activity and its effects on the pupils, and the threat and reality of unemployment among school-leavers and their families. Of course, such problems did exist in the Soviet era, and schools had to find ways of tackling them then, but the scale of the problems now, continued with the degradation of the social security system in Russia, and the comparatively underdeveloped support mechanisms available for the school to call on, all place a strain on the schools and on the headteacher and his or her deputies in particular. This strain has been evident among most of the headteachers with whom I have communicated during my research. Indeed, two headteachers from my sample, both in their late thirties, decided to resign their post and find employment elsewhere, one commenting to me subsequently:

> I came into this job with such high hopes, such enthusiasm. Now, in the era of reforms, we would surely be able to achieve something. I was committed to the school, to the teachers, pupils, parents. But there is a physical and mental limit to what one can force oneself to do. Perhaps they should have employed a businessman, or an accountant, rather than a teacher to deal with the amount of administrative overload I was faced with? (Headteacher of comprehensive school, interview with the author, April 1992)

The urgent need that such cases highlighted for the authorities to provide comprehensive support to headteachers was neglected in the early years of the reforms, and headteachers complained in interviews that they were often left to fend as best as they could. As the reforms have progressed, so the system has begun to respond better to the needs of headteachers: the rôle of the head has been the subject of research, conferences and publications, which have attempted to provide a framework of analysis to study the problems of headteachers and suggest possible solutions;[77] the number and quality of in-service programmes provided for heads has increased substantially; and a journal titled 'School Director' (*Direktor shkoly*) was launched in 1994 and, on the whole, welcomed by headteachers. Headteachers whom I interviewed, however, emphasised that the most important measure required, in their view, concerned the need to revise the pattern of administration within the school. With regard to administrative workload, for instance, apart from the responsibilities covered by the deputy heads, there is usually only a small group of secretaries, and perhaps, now, a financial administrator, a level of administrative support that is inadequate, as the interviewees stated unanimously. Employing additional administrative staff, however, would be impossible for most establishments. A less costly answer to at least some of these problems, however, might lie in addressing the amount of responsibility that the headteacher has to assume for running the school, and the lack of development of community involvement in the school's affairs.

Apart from the internal pedagogical council (*pedsovet*) in each school, which was made up of the teaching staff and which was responsible for the management of the curriculum, each Soviet school also had a parents' committee (*roditel'skii komitet*), which comprised one parent representative from each form, with sub-committees divided by year group. The parents' committee fulfilled a function similar to that of Parent–Teacher Associations in the UK, organising extra-curricular activities, school trips, helping with the redecoration of classrooms and so on. Apart from such work, however, there was very little direct involvement of parents in the actual day-to-day running of the school. The same was true of the involvement of local factories and farms, whose activity was limited to material support.

The pedagogical council and parents' committee have now been joined by the school council (*shkol'nyi sovet*), an idea that had emerged in the late 1980s under the democratisation drive of *perestroika*,[78] and which can trace its roots back to the promotion of greater parental and community involvement in education included in the 1984 school reforms. School councils comprise teachers, parents, members of the local community and pupils,[79] and are intended to act as a forum for discussion of all aspects of the school's life. In principle, this promises to relieve the burden of responsibility that currently hangs over the headteacher, sharing out this responsibility among the members of the council. Indeed, this is included as a recommendation in the School Statute (*Ustav shkoly*) that was introduced by the Ministry of Education in 1995 to serve as a guideline for schools in developing their own statutes.[80] Whether or not the councils will be able to fulfil their promise remains to be seen. The picture across the country appears to be quite diverse, with some schools possessing an active school council that has truly begun to effect change in the way that the establishment is run, while other schools, for one reason or another (e.g. lack of interest from parents, pupils and other potential members, resistance from the headteacher; abandonment of the project after an unsuccessful launch) have found it difficult to organise a council, or otherwise the council has failed to achieve a great deal. As some headteachers argued during interviews, a more coherent framework for such activities is required, in which the council, or its executive, would assume legal responsibility for the running of the school, and would have defined functions *vis-à-vis* financial matters, staff employment, curricular issues and so on, suggestions which have yet to be taken up in the Russian system.

If school councils operate effectively, alongside the benefits of improved school–community links the element of accountability, stressed in the reform agenda, should also be strengthened. According to anecdotal evidence collected for the current study, some schools and teachers are finding it difficult to adjust to this aspect of democratisation, although certain regional and local authorities are, apparently, taking the issue seriously, publishing information for parents with regard to their rights (including the choice of school for their children), and detailing, for example, the outcome of disputes between schools and parents.[81]

5
The Culture of the Russian School and the Teaching Profession

Before we attempt an assessment of the process of implementation of reform in Chapter 6, it would be helpful to consider the nature of the organisation of the Russian school, to examine the extent to which the school culture can be said to be suited to the task of introducing and developing change. The considerable resources that have been employed in the West to study the culture of the school have produced evidence of the important rôle that such factors as the nature of professional relations within the school play in the process of reform, by shaping the nature of the school's response, defining its capacity to engage in change.[1] An ideal type of establishment to have emerged from the debate in the West on the culture of the school and the quest for school improvement is that of the 'learning organisation,' in which, as Dalin and Rolff explain:

> Initiatives for change may come from within the school, as well as from the environment. The school is *open* to improvement [original emphasis], clear about strengths and weaknesses, and has motivation and capacities to cope with improvement processes.[2]

In other words, change has become part of the culture of the school, the evolutionary approach coming to replace the stop–go, reactionary model common in most systems.[3] However, as yet, most schools in most systems across the world are, in fact, a long way from reaching the lofty heights of the 'learning organisation':

> The school is not now a learning organisation. Irregular waves of change, episodic projects, fragmentation of effort, and grinding overload is the lot of most schools.[4]

We should not, therefore, be tempted to judge the Russian school too severely against such paradigms. Nevertheless, it does serve as an example of what can be achieved, if the factors that have been shown to exert a strong influence on change patterns are all afforded the attention they require, and the school approaches change as an evolutionary matter that is integral to the life of the school as a whole. Given such criteria, to what extent can the Soviet school model be said to have been a learning organisation? An examination of aspects of the culture of both the Russian school, and the teaching profession, allows us to understand better the course that reform has taken in the Russian system.

The Soviet tradition of reform

The top-down approach to reform ingrained in the Soviet system reflects a drawback common in many systems, where the potential significance of the teacher's participation in the change process has tended to be overlooked. As Hord notes: 'In school change, teachers tend to be recipients rather than initiators of change.'[5] In the case of the USSR, however, the possibilities for open and active participation seemed to be especially restricted; the application of individual initiative in curricular matters was not encouraged, indeed, it was actively discouraged, and the teacher was supposed to act as a 'teacher–fulfiller' (*uchitel'–ispolnitel'*), who would ensure that the centrally imposed timetable was delivered according to plan. Failure to do so could result in sanctions of various kinds being imposed on that teacher and her or his headteacher by the authorities.

This does not mean that initiative was stifled completely; in addition to such high-profile cases as Sukhomlinkskii, ordinary educationalists who were sufficiently determined were able to introduce an element of individuality and diversity into the curriculum through employing approaches and materials that differed in some way from the official norm. (In Yaroslavl' I interviewed one such 'innovator', a retired primary-class teacher, who told me of the textbook which she had prepared in secret in the 1960s and had retained without showing it to the authorities ever since, but the contents of which she had used in her teaching.) Nevertheless, the lack of attention paid in the Soviet system to the potential input that teachers might make to reform has undoubtedly handicapped Russian teachers in adapting to the new expectation that they participate actively in change, and become, to employ the current Western terminology, 'change agents'. (This drawback applies, in particular, to those teachers who qualified and taught in the Soviet system before the reform era.) This is not to say it would be impossible to adjust; indeed, there is a genuinely positive attitude to change present among a good number of teaching staff, a motivational factor that could help to overcome some of the difficulties teachers face in learning to approach change in the new paradigm of empowerment. Yet enthusiasm, while important, is no substitute for the skills required for successful implementation. As systems across the world have found, the complex nature of change requires staff to become adept at understanding the processes of change as they operate at the classroom level. It was important, therefore, that the educational authorities in Russia appreciate the need for teachers to be given the opportunity to acquire those skills, before embarking on the ambitious programme for change.

The hierarchy of power in the school

Research findings in the West demonstrate the key part played by headteachers in those schools which are seen to be successfully implementing change, and the handicap caused by inadequate leadership in other schools suffering setback or failure in change.[6] Much depends on the headteacher's ability to manage the staff, guide them through the problems of reform, and set the agenda for the broader tasks that the school faces in adjusting to new educational and social conditions. Such patterns hold true in the case of Russian headteachers as well, for they face challenges which are very similar in their nature to those experienced by principals in the USA or headteachers in the UK. Indeed, the conservative tendencies observed among some American headteachers[7] might be seen to be even more firmly ingrained into the culture of the headship in Russia, given the amount of control imposed on heads by the authorities in the Soviet era, an experience which still shapes the attitudes of many headteachers in Russia today.

Now this control has been significantly reduced, of course, as a result of devolution, leaving headteachers both to take advantage of the opportunities that this brings to assume greater control over their school, and to face the greater responsibilities that have come with devolution and the general nature of change in society as a whole. With regard to the latter, we can observe that in the same way that heads have been given insufficient support in coming to terms with the increased administrative load that they now bear, there has also been inadequate provision of training to prepare them for new challenges in the area of curriculum management, problems which have inevitably contributed to delays in implementation and confusion in schools' approach to reform.[8]

Nevertheless, despite the considerable pressures that they have to contend with, Russian headteachers now enjoy substantially increased influence over the running of their own schools. While they may still be constrained by the nature of the system as far as recruitment of staff is concerned, and while they must devote considerable energy and time to addressing the school's material problems, many heads appear to have welcomed their new-found freedom in the sphere of the curriculum. It may well be that the power thus enjoyed by a headteacher will provide the most effective means of moving a school towards the adoption and implementation of change, as the head is able to 'persuade' the staff of the need for such development. This is particularly true of certain 'charismatic' headteachers (e.g. most notably such well-known figures as Frumin and Karakovskii) who have been able to create an ongoing atmosphere of change in their school, helping staff (and students) to develop the skills required to carry through their vision for the school.

Such cases of charismatic heads are rare, of course, yet for all headteachers, whatever their style of leadership, empowerment brings with it much responsibility, for choosing a suitable course of development for the school, and for creating the right conditions for her or his staff to work towards that goal. In some schools, there will be a conservative core of more experienced teachers who may be reluctant to engage in change, at least to the extent proposed by the head; at times, even an energetic and skilful headteacher may find that such teachers can foil attempts to introduce change. The problem is exacerbated in the Russian case by the low level of mobility of teachers, and the difficulty of recruiting younger staff who might be more able to adjust to the demands of reform. In some cases, therefore, the difficulties of persuading what are seen as 'conservative' teachers to follow the head's views on change have been used by some headteachers as a motive for setting up an alternative school, where they will be able to recruit a new team of staff and, they hope, thereby ensure a greater degree of cohesion and ambition for change.

With regard to the teaching staff, the potential for 'bottom-driven' change, i.e. the ability of individual classroom teachers to influence the course of development in their own school, is still somewhat limited. This is not to say that teachers are not heavily involved in change activities; indeed, many of the teachers interviewed during this research appeared to be taking advantage of the new freedoms brought by empowerment to engage in innovation to varying degrees. Further, in some schools visited for this study a more balanced relationship seemed to have been fostered between the 'administration' (i.e. headteacher and senior staff) and the other teachers. Nevertheless, the fact that the head wields such a large influence can mean that a teacher whose views on change do not coincide with their headteacher may find the possibilities to develop their own agenda are limited, and that they need to follow the line of the head, or face potential conflict with him or her. At times, such control may be justified, if the teacher's intentions for change are seen by the headteacher and others to be ill-advised; however, a good number of teachers, especially young staff, commented to me on their sense of frustration at being held back by their headteacher.

This situation can be ascribed in large part to the 'flat' structure of management traditionally found in the Soviet school (to some extent paralleled in Soviet society itself), in which power was concentrated in the hands of a small number of people at the top of the organisation. Beneath the headteacher the levels of responsibility comprised only that of deputy headteacher (*zaveduyushchii uchebnoi chast'yu* or *zavuch*), with two deputies responsible for the curriculum and 'upbringing work' (*vospitatel'naya rabota*) respectively; *metodist*;[9] form tutor (*klassnyi rukovoditel'*) and classroom teacher. In the English system, in contrast, the hierarchical structure of the school is 'tall', with a varied and complex network of posts and responsibilities, from the headteacher through the deputies, to heads of year, heads and deputy heads of departments, form tutors, examinations officers and so on. In English schools today, junior members of staff are expected to assume responsibility for certain issues of school life from an early stage in their career, the level of responsibility growing as the teacher becomes more experienced, with this work reflected in his or her salary and, possibly, teaching load.

While some would contest that a flat structure can be more

conducive to the emergence of a more 'democratic' workplace, in which collective decision-making is facilitated, in practice the organisation of the Soviet school served to deny the ordinary class teachers, and in particular the younger members of staff, the opportunity to have a real say in the running of the school. In recent years new posts have emerged, including heads of department in a growing number of schools, and additional deputy head positions with responsibility, for instance, for innovative work. Nevertheless, the pattern of responsibility remains orientated towards the senior members of staff; ordinary classroom teachers, and in particular the younger staff, can be given comparatively little opportunity to make an input. As one 24-year-old teacher noted:

> There is little incentive for us younger teachers to put our ideas forward. And if we do, there is a risk that they will not be well received by the headteacher or the deputies. It seems that for most teachers, the requirement is just to do one's job and not try to do anything more than this. (Interview with the author, April 1992)

There is a recognition among some Russian educationalists that a greater degree of power-sharing is needed in the Russian school, to distribute responsibilities among the staff and engender a greater sense of collaboration.[10] Indeed, in some schools, particularly those alternative schools which have adopted a more 'democratic' approach to education in general, progress has been made, judging by anecdotal evidence from my research. However, in many cases one suspects that persuading headteachers of the need to relinquish (as some would see it) the level of responsibility that they have only just begun to enjoy might prove a difficult task.

Teacher overload and stress?

Russian teachers have come increasingly in recent years to talk of being overloaded, and of the new stresses that they have begun to encounter in their work.[11] In one 1994 survey of 500 teachers, for instance, some 30 per cent reported that they were experiencing increased stress in their work.[12] Such problems will obviously affect their capacity to introduce change, and therefore represent an area of concern for the reform planners; yet further investigation of these claims allows us to place the extent of these problems in perspective. There is no doubt that the work of Russian schoolteachers has become more difficult, as they have to contend with the pressures that empowerment brings, attempt to implement reform, deal with growing social problems among their pupils, and contend with the material conditions of the teaching profession. Clearly, problems of non-payment of salaries (which are, in any case, miserly), compounded with the relatively low level of job-related material benefits and other factors (to be discussed later) must have a significant detrimental effect on the work of the teaching force, and must be taken into consideration when assessing the system's capacity for change.[13] In this section, however, the focus is on the nature of the teacher's work itself.

If one compares the experience of Russian teachers with that of teachers in England, one can see that the difficulties of the former are very similar to those of the latter; indeed, in some areas the English teachers, perhaps, could have greater grounds for complaint. The problems faced by Russian teachers may not be as bad as they perceive them to be; it is the speed with which such changes have occurred, and the confusion and anxiety that they have caused in a teaching force which is relatively inexperienced in dealing with such problems, that have caused them to express dissatisfaction.

Take, for instance, the matter of teacher overload.[14] Many Russian teachers decide to assume responsibility for additional teaching hours, on top of the standard load (*stavka*) of 18 hours per week, with some taking on two full loads for a 36-hour timetable.[15] The motivation, of course, is financial: extra salary payments are given for each additional hour, an attractive proposition for staff whose material position, always comparatively weak in the Soviet system, has declined further still in recent years. Naturally, the acquisition of extra hours reduces the amount of time available for staff to engage in preparation, professional development, and reflection on their professional activities, and thus affects their capacity to implement reform. Many interviewees also complained of the physical demands placed on them by such a heavy workload. One can sympathise with the teachers' predicament, and if one were a teacher in the French or German systems, perhaps such sympathy would be stronger, yet for an English teacher, such conditions may appear much more familiar.

Of course, an 18-hour timetable (similar to the norm in France or Germany) does allow more scope for out-of-class, non-contact activities, including professional development, and can help to raise the level of teaching quality. In addition, while Russian teachers are often required to teach on Saturday mornings, they are given the privilege of one day per week free as a 'methodology day' (*metodicheskii den'*), which, in theory, is to be spent on developing materials or for INSET-related work, but which in practice is left to the teacher's discretion, and is often seen by teachers as a 'free' day that compensates for having to work on Saturdays. Furthermore, apart from the *klassnye rukovoditeli*, the pastoral duties of Russian teachers are relatively limited; they are required only to be present for the lessons they teach, and for staff meetings, and are free to leave the premises of the school at other times.

One suspects that many teachers in the English system would dearly like to have an 18-hour timetable; instead, the average is considerably higher (sometimes over 30 hours per week), and additional contact time (including extra-curricular work) brings, for the most part, no additional payment. (In the English system, pastoral duties are obligatory, for instance, and do not bring the entitlement to extra income that is enjoyed by the Russian *klassnye rukovoditeli*.) When not teaching, English teachers are expected to remain in the school, and are often liable to be called to 'cover' for absent colleagues. Finally, while the professional demands on Russian teachers have increased with empowerment and curricular reform, taking a double teaching load may not prove as difficult as the 30+ hour timetable of the English teacher. The latter must now, in the 1990s, contend not only with the traditional aspects of the teacher's duties (syllabus design, materials creation, marking of pupils' work, etc.) but also with the requirements of the National Curriculum, record-keeping, etc., alongside any extra-curricular, pastoral and professional development activities, which combine to make an intensive, demanding workload for the average teacher.[16] Russian teachers still do not face such extensive demands in their work. Traditionally there has been less marking for teachers to do (with less written work in general practised in the school), for instance, and this largely remains the case today; the requirements of the new educational standards are far less comprehensive in terms of teacher administration than the English National Curriculum; and to a large degree, while they may well be trying to implement curricular change, many Russian teachers can still rely on the framework provided by Soviet-era curricula and materials in their work. These traditions of the Soviet system have tended to reduce, therefore, the likelihood of stress-related problems among Russian teachers, as far as the specific issue of teaching the curriculum is concerned. While many teachers are committed to their work and to their pupils, the lower level of freedom that they had under the Soviet curriculum with regard to content and methodology, and the consequent sense of at least partial detachment from responsibility for what was taught, has helped Russian teachers to avoid falling victim to the phenomenon of 'burnout' that has been so widely documented among the teaching forces of, for example, the UK and the USA.[17] This may change now, as teachers take advantage of empowerment and some feel an ever-growing sense of commitment to curricular changes that they, perhaps, feel direct ownership of. For the time being, however, the legacy of the old system acts as a buffer against such problems.

With regard to matters of discipline and stress-related problems, too, some comparative perspective is required, although in the absence of in-depth comparative studies I must again revert to anecdotal evidence and impressions gained from observation in Russia. Many of the Russian teachers interviewed during this research remarked on what they see as the rapidly declining standards of discipline among pupils and the lack of interest that many pupils show towards their studies. Furthermore, teachers complain that they are having to contend with the social problems that have worsened in society in recent years, ranging from drug and alcohol abuse, to hooliganism and criminal activities. I do not contest these claims, for it is clear that such problems have increased. Further, it is clear that Russian teachers have struggled to deal with these issues, owing both to the speed and intensity with which such problems have grown, and to the lack of training and advice given to the profession on how to face such new challenges. A great deal of effort is required on the part of the authorities, the education system and the social service network in Russia in order to adapt to the new realities that transition has brought. Yet if we compare objectively the problems of Russian teachers with those with which many of their colleagues in England have to face, then, to a degree, some of the more desperate conclusions made on the Russian situation are tempered somewhat. In the University of Pedagogical Mastery (*Universitet pedagogicheskogo masterstva*) in St Petersburg, an in-service training centre, I was asked to talk to groups of teachers about the English school system. Many professed to being surprised, even shocked, to hear of the discipline problems that English teachers encounter, the stress that pupils and parents can place teachers under, and the potential threat of dismissal, even prosecution, that can occasionally arise in extreme cases of teacher–pupil conflict. Comparative studies are required to investigate such matters in more depth, but I am confident that the discipline problems of the English school, and related issues of drug abuse, juvenile crime, and so on, are still worse than those found in Russia. However, such problems may well become more prevalent and more serious in Russia in the years to come, especially if social conditions continue to deteriorate. If so, there is an urgent need for measures to be introduced to ensure that the Russian school system is ready for that possibility.

Professional communication: the macro-level

Communication between those working in the same field is, of course, an essential prerequisite of a healthy, developing profession. In the case of Russian teachers, however, there are a number of weaknesses in the nature of the communication that exists, at least at the macro-level, problems which stem to a considerable degree from the legacy of the Soviet era. As Johnson notes, the Soviet authorities were able to restrict the ability of teachers to develop a separate professional identity, controlling the degree to which teachers could influence the nature of such issues as teacher education, educational research, and the type of professional associations which teachers could participate in.[18] Soviet teachers could feel a sense of unity with their colleagues across the country by virtue of the fact that they all worked within a highly centralised and controlled system, in which the experience of teachers was remarkably common from one end of the USSR to the other. Despite such close ties, however, there was relatively very little communication between teachers on a national basis; indeed; even at the regional level, communication was not that extensive. For most teachers the circle of professional communication comprised colleagues in their own school and district, along with staff from their town whom they would meet during in-service training. Apart from this, there were few channels for teachers to engage in a dialogue with their counterparts in other regions and republics. The pedagogical press and the Union of Educational Workers (*Profsoyuz rabotnikov narodnogo obrazovaniya i nauki*) did provide a link between the centre and the grassroots, but these were under the control of the authorities, and offered inadequate scope for the discussion of, say, methodology, not to mention problems of discipline or teachers' complaints about their salary. While the work of teachers across the USSR may have contained much that was similar, the lack of effective means of communication meant that the teaching profession was rather fragmented, and teachers' sense of professional identity somewhat fragile.

From the mid-1980s onwards this situation changed somewhat, as the work of the innovators gained recognition and the momentum of change at the grassroots gathered pace. Apart from the increasingly lively and informative debate taking place in *Uchitel'skaya gazeta* and other sources in the mass media, together with the popular publications produced by the leading innovators, a large number of teachers from across the USSR began to travel to attend seminars and workshops in various locations. Further, the *Tvorcheskii soyuz uchitelei SSSR* promised to lend a sense of professional cohesion to the debate on school reform, and provide greater access for educationalists to these processes. The Creative Union did not live up to expectations, and its demise left the field of trade union activity to the traditional Union of Educational Workers. Although the latter does participate in the debate on educational policy, it tends to concentrate on issues concerning the material position of teachers, and does not provide that much support or advice to members, it would seem, on issues directly relating to curricular matters. This might be seen as an obstacle to the professionalisation of the teaching force, but Johnson's criticism of Dneprov's reformers may be too harsh:

> This [a set of strategic policy errors identified by Johnson] was compounded by the failure to use state or ministerial power to help forge new professional associations and a new, democratically-elected teachers' union, instruments that were absolutely necessary to guide decentralization and democratization.[19]

While one can sympathise with such sentiments, it is perhaps too much to expect of a federal ministry to initiate and oversee the development of, presumably not so independent, professional associations. The fact that the teaching profession has been slow to break free from the legacy of the Soviet practices reflects rather a broader pattern of inertia in Russian society as a whole, with the trappings of 'civil society' taking much longer to emerge than some observers had anticipated.[20]

In other areas of communication, however, as the Soviet reforms became the Russian reforms, so the potential for the development of professional communication has seemed to grow further still. The pedagogical press is now much more varied than before, with the long-running newspaper *Uchitel'skaya gazeta* and the journals *Pedagogika* and *Narodnoe obrazovanie* joined by the popular newspaper *Pervoe sentyabrya*, the journal *Mir obrazovaniya* and other publications such as *Direktor shkoly*. In addition, many subjects have a dedicated journal for their discipline (e.g. 'Foreign Languages in School' – *Inostrannye yazyki v shkole* and 'Mathematics in School' – *Matematika v shkole*). For a time a number of periodicals underwent severe financial problems, with delays incurred in publication and the size of issues reduced. It was feared that some might be forced to close down completely, but for the time being, although financial problems are far from over, most appear to be back to their normal schedules and format. In addition to such printed sources, a relatively small but steadily growing proportion of teachers are able to gain access to the RedLine information site on the Internet, run jointly by *Uchitel'skaya gazeta* and the Ministry of Education. A number of professional associations have been set up, catering, for instance, for teachers of particular subjects, thus providing a forum for focused discussion of issues of particular concern and interest,[21] although their membership appears still to be relatively small. There have also been improvements in the amount and quality of INSET provision, opening up additional opportunities for exchange of experience, and the level of support available from district advisers has, in certain towns, been extended.

Despite the greater availability of opportunities for professional dialogue which now exist, however, in interviews conducted by the author in 1995, 36 of 47 teachers questioned stated that they engage in such activity relatively infrequently, a figure which reflects the survey results given in Table 5.1, although most professed, nevertheless, that they would like to be able to devote more time and energy to such pursuits. The problem for many teachers lies not in the lack of availability of sources of professional information and support, but in material limitations on their access to and participation in such discourse: the school may well have cut down its expenditure on professional literature in favour of more essential purchases, while the fees demanded by INSET providers (and the cost of travelling to attend a course) can act as a further disincentive.

Such are the difficulties facing teachers in their attempts to com-

Table 5.1 Professional communication. Teacher questionnaire q. 10. 'How often do you engage in the following forms of professional communication?' (N = 132)

Form	*Never*	*Rarely*	*Monthly*	*Weekly*	*Daily*	*nr*
1 Read pedagogical literature	23.5% (31)	21.2% (28)	12.8% (17)	9.1% (12)	2.3% (3)	31.1% (41)
2 Discussion with colleagues	2.3% (3)	8.3% (11)	23.5% (31)	40.2% (53)	14.4% (19)	11.3% (15)
3 Read educational press	9.8% (13)	14.4% (19)	34.8% (46)	28.0% (37)	5.2% (7)	7.8% (10)
4 Participation in teachers' association	65.2% (86)	15.9% (21)	5.2% (7)	0.9% (1)	—	12.8% (17)
5 Read official documents	35.6% (47)	43.3% (57)	8.3% (11)	5.2% (7)	3.8% (5)	3.8% (5)
6 Attend lectures/ courses	6.8% (9)	47% (62)	21.2% (28)	6.8% (9)	—	18.2% (24)
7 Research work	52.3% (69)	23.5% (31)	6.1% (8)	9.8% (13)	4.5% (6)	3.8% (5)

municate with colleagues not just across the country, but in their own region. Add to these problems the fact that many teachers complain that the strains of daily life leave them often with no great desire to devote their energy to reading pedagogical literature or attending workshops, even if they are committed to their job and wish to engage in such activities. To gain the benefits of professional dialogue, teachers must have the time to do so, a luxury that is not always available. In addition, apparently minor practical problems can prove a major obstacle. In one teachers' centre (*metodicheskii tsentr*) which I visited in St Petersburg, for instance, periodicals were taken and subscriptions made to associations, thus allowing access for all staff in that district, while local teachers themselves deposited their own work in the centre for the benefit of their colleagues. However, in order to use this extensive range of materials teachers had no option but to copy texts laboriously by hand, since photocopying facilities were not available.

A further barrier to professional dialogue is caused by the relatively low level of staff mobility, owing to the difficulties of obtaining housing and a host of other problems that moving entails. Thus, while Tumalev can state that there is a relatively (for Russia) high level of mobility within the profession, with 68 per cent of teachers in his sample of 1587 St Petersburg[22] educationalists having moved job at least once in their career, it is far more likely that teachers will find posts in another school in the same town, rather than move to a job outside their town.[23] While this does hold certain benefits stemming from staff continuity, it also restricts considerably the opportunities for the 'cross-fertilisation' of pedagogical experience gained in other parts of the country.

Teachers' professional identity: a 'geological' survey

The limitations of professional communication at the macro-level are offset by the fact that the teaching force shares a common heritage, which means that teachers from Petrozavodsk and Sakhalin, should they meet, will be able to identify with one another's experience. The levels of commonality and continuity that characterise the Russian teaching profession stand in some contrast to the pattern of development found in the English system. A British teacher educator once remarked to me that observing British teachers is rather like conducting a geological survey – one could tell exactly during which period a particular teacher had been trained, since the effects of that initial experience almost invariably left their mark, influencing that generation of recruits' approach to teaching for the rest of their careers.[24] Given the frequency with which change occurs in teacher education in the UK, the 'geological pattern' of British teachers can be seen to comprise a series of rather thin layers, indicating the manner in which each wave of innovation has given way to the next, with certain concepts re-emerging perhaps decades after their previous period of domination. To some extent this might be seen to weaken the bonds that tie each generation with its predecessor and successor, and to cause a degree of diversity in the attitudes that teachers of different generations will take towards educational matters, including the question of change. The effects of this fragmented development may have both negative and positive effects. On the one hand, one might argue that it reduces the amount of cohesion and continuity in the profession, with constant changes in approaches and policies causing disruption in the pattern of professional identity of the teaching force; on the other hand, one might see this diversity as a positive influence, allowing greater flexibility and increased scope for progress, as teachers are not bound by tradition.

A 'geological survey' of the Soviet, and now Russian, teaching profession would show a very different pattern, with very little variation discernible across the decades, a reflection of the comparatively far greater degree of continuity and far lower amount of change that characterised the Soviet teacher-education system. Indeed, the basic structure of the system changed little from the 1930s to the 1980s and beyond.[25] Thus teachers trained in the 1970s and 1980s would have followed programmes that differed relatively little from those followed by their predecessors in the 1940s, 1950s and 1960s. This degree of homogeneity and continuity in the profession can be said to have a strong influence on the professional outlook of Russian teachers, whose views on teaching will have been influenced not only by their training and subsequent classroom experience as professionals, but also by their memories of their own school years as pupils – quite literally, they grew up in this system, with the childhood experience of teachers in their twenties remarkably similar to that of staff aged over 60. An additional factor contributing to the continuity found in the Russian system, stems from the fact that one discovers, in the central schools of major cities, as well as in small rural communities, that a good number of teachers are actually former pupils of that school themselves, something which, again, must hold significant implications for the transmission of values between generations of teachers.[26]

To some degree, therefore, the long-standing traditions of the Soviet teaching force act as a unifying bond between the generations. The extent of the influence this has on teachers' attitudes and approaches to various aspects of their professional activities requires further research (a topic, perhaps, for comparative studies), and one should be cautious about drawing too many conclusions on the basis of these hypotheses. Yet these factors do have a bearing on the course of reform in the Russian school, affecting the nature of teachers' attitudes to change, and the general perception that teachers hold of the attributes for a 'good teacher,' the purpose of education and the position of the school in contemporary Russia.

Professional communication: the micro-level

The issue of cooperation among staff has been investigated extensively in the West, and highlighted frequently as an area of concern. A common theme is that of isolation,[27] i.e. teachers tend to perform their professional activities as individuals, without a great deal of collaboration with their colleagues. This may stem from personal choice (a desire to act independently, not to invite the criticism of colleagues, even to protect one's professional 'privacy'), or it may result from the culture of the school (a tradition of 'closed doors' to classrooms, with teachers left to themselves), or a variety of other reasons. It may be felt unethical to encroach on the pedagogical territory of others; experienced teachers may feel they do not need to be observed (or may fear that certain weaknesses will show), and so on. Teachers discuss general issues in staff meetings, but direct dialogue through observation is rare, apart from the cases of trainee teachers and newly qualified teachers (NQTs), or those being observed for appraisal. As a result, teachers lose an opportunity to receive feedback on their work, and have to rely on their own initiative to take them through problems. It is an issue that has been addressed in many systems, but not always successfully:

> Although teacher cooperation is increasing in most systems, and the traditional classroom organization is gradually being replaced by a more flexible organization, the norm in most countries . . . is the traditional one-teacher-one classroom organization . . . Teachers are not used to collegial 'cooperation', simply because it has not been necessary. In fact, much cooperation has been very ineffective and has resulted in even more isolation . . . To share professional thinking with other adults is simply not always part of the school culture.[28]

While isolation affects all teachers, it is perhaps NQTs who suffer most, for they are in great need of advice from experienced staff. The sink-or-swim approach supported by some educationalists ignores the damage (in terms of their pedagogical skills) done to young teachers because of a lack of support, and the 'fossilisation' of certain errors which could have been treated effectively if attended to in time. To some extent, the culture of the Russian teaching profession possesses the potential to overcome these problems, for there is a greater tradition of peer evaluation and peer observation in the Russian system, with teachers expected to visit and be visited by other teachers on a frequent basis. As a result, the school culture is much more one of 'open' rather than 'shut' doors, and teachers often seem to be more prepared to listen to advice and criticism (and praise) from their peers than would teachers in an English school. Yet this apparent collegiality does not necessarily imply that Russian staff engage in constructive dialogue and provide active support to their colleagues as a matter of course. Indeed, in the Soviet system peer observation and support were often seen by the authorities as a means of control by which senior staff would 'guide'

NQTs into the 'right' way of behaving, moulding them into the patterns expected of a Soviet teacher, and 'correcting' deviations from the accepted norm. According to interviewees, the task of 'guidance' was performed very effectively by many senior staff and *metodisty*:

> When I first came to work in school I was still naïve enough to think that I would be able to try out some ideas of my own, at least to a limited extent. Any such notion was soon removed by the older staff who were tasked with my 'upbringing' (*vospitanie*) as a teacher, for they quite forcefully showed me the error of my ways, and impressed upon me the necessity (and virtue) of conformity. (Teacher of Physics, age 38, interview with the author, April 1992)

Whereas student teachers and NQTs in England are encouraged to develop their own personality as a teacher, and bring their own strengths as an individual to bear upon their teaching, the approach in Soviet schools was often to reduce this element of individuality, which was sacrificed in order to satisfy the system's desire for commonality. Although a good number were able, despite these restrictions, to allow their personality to shine through nonetheless, this practice clearly restricted the ability of Soviet teachers to develop styles that suited their own particular needs. This tradition of peer monitoring and control is still very much present in many Russian schools, and is a legacy that headteachers and others need to deal with if true progress is to be made in school development; indeed; it can be a source of conflict between older staff, for whom change may be proving a difficult and painful process, and some younger colleagues, who enter the school with substantially different ideas on how to approach the task of teaching.

While the control element may have dominated in the old system, there were senior teachers who did approach the task of mentoring junior colleagues in a constructive manner, seeking to assist them in the development of their skills. In the contemporary reform effort, such positive uses of peer appraisal and professional communication at the micro-level are being exploited successfully in some schools, where younger staff (especially NQTs) are benefiting from the support that such collaboration can offer. The task for the Russian school now is to build on the foundations of collaboration and collegiality that it has inherited, and to develop the positive elements within this tradition. There should be a degree of 'control' in the socialisation of young teachers into the profession, yet to meet the needs of the Russian school, which is supposed to be assuming a more change-orientated culture, such support needs to be given sensitively and flexibly, to allow NQTs to learn from their more experienced colleagues but at the same time to bring their own talents and views to bear on the overall development of the school.

The status of the profession

Despite propaganda to the contrary, the Soviet teaching profession never enjoyed a high level of status in material terms, with teachers' salaries and other benefits (such as housing, access to kindergartens, etc.) set at a lower level than the norm in the industrial sector.[29] Nevertheless, in terms of professional status, Soviet teachers fared somewhat better, as they were afforded a good deal of respect by parents and citizens in general.[30] The teacher's views on the pupils' progress and behaviour were comparatively rarely challenged openly by parents, who were often passive recipients of praise or admonishments delivered by form tutors at parents' evenings. This amount of reverence shown towards teachers stemmed in part from the general culture of Soviet society, in which education, upbringing, the virtues of a good citizen and the acquisition of knowledge were portrayed as noble matters which transcended the perspective of the individual, and were related directly to the development of the State and the progress towards communism.

For many teachers, therefore, belonging to this profession was a matter of pride, notwithstanding the poor material rewards. This perception still continues: in Tumalev's study of St Petersburg teachers, 76 per cent of respondents stated that they valued their profession highly.[31] Indeed, this apparently strong sense of confidence in their profession may have been increased in the case of some teachers, who feel that the greater pedagogical freedom they now enjoy has heightened their status as professionals. The changes in the social structure of the 'new' Russia, however, and the worsening state of the teachers' material position cannot but detract from the greater sense of professional autonomy that empowerment may have brought: in stark contrast to the high level of self-belief shown in the survey just referred to, a mere 2 per cent of teachers stated that they felt their profession was highly valued by both the State and by society at large.[32] It is not uncommon, of course, in international experience for the relatively highly qualified members of the teaching profession to feel that their skills are under-appreciated; in the Russian case, however, the extent of the material problems of teachers – often seen as the most tangible sign of a profession's status – are serious indeed.

The common pay structure (*edinaya tarifnaya setka* or ETS), introduced in an attempt to protect salaries from the rampant inflation suffered by the Russian economy, has proved incapable of meeting the demands placed on it, while the actions of the federal and regional governments have proved ineffectual, or, indeed, have made the problem worse. As Kerr notes, the resetting of the ETS in 1995, in response to the fact that it had risen only 1.4 times over the preceding 15 months while prices had increased on average by 4.2 times, achieved nothing, and even led to a decrease in income in real terms for a good number of teachers.[33] Meanwhile, across the country teachers continued to complain of the problem of non-payment of salaries, perhaps for as much as four months at a time, as the regional administrations, their own budgets severely limited, sought to impose control over their expenditure.[34]

Russian teachers did not have a tradition of taking political action, and for many the strike option was still viewed with unease (as it is by teachers and employees of the social sector in many countries), yet the severity of their financial problems, along with concern for the schools and the pupils, gave rise to a feeling of deep dismay and considerable anger among a growing number of teachers, expressed in an ongoing round of local and national strikes,[35] which grew in scale during the 1990s. Indeed, educationalists have consistently been the most active participants in strike action among employees of all sectors in Russia (although such strikes have, on the whole, been given less media attention in Russia and abroad than that afforded to certain 'key' industrial sectors). In 1991, for instance, some 58 100 teachers engaged in strikes in 1177 sites across the Russian Federation, compared with 15 900 industrial workers striking in 324 sites (by 1992 the figure for teachers on strike had risen to 222 100).[36] In September 1995 a national strike of educational workers was called, with over half a million teachers from 11 000 schools taking part.[37] A further two-day national strike was mounted in December 1995, and actions continued throughout 1996 and 1997,[38] with some teachers going to such desperate lengths as a hunger strike to make their feelings known.[39] At the start of 1997, some 11 289 educational establishments (all levels) were involved in strike action (with some 531 200 educationalists participating).[40] Although the amount of strike action died down somewhat in the autumn of that year, owing to the federal government's ability (willingness?) to divert some 3 trillion rubles to pay off wage arrears of educational workers,[41] strikes in the education sector nevertheless accounted for some 92 per cent of all strikes conducted in the Russian Federation in 1997.[42] Moreover, the relief provided by the government's actions proved short-lived, as wage arrears continued into 1998: by April of that year they totalled some 8.3 billion rubles, with Irkutsk *oblast'* the worst-hit region, at some 798.6 million rubles. As a result, there was strong support from teachers for the All-Russian day of protest organised by the unions on April 9, 1998, with over 1.8 million teachers taking part.[43]

While one could argue that one positive result of such strike action may be the development of a greater sense of professional identity and cohesion among Russia's teachers, the negative factors which also accompany participation in action must surely counteract any such gains, at least to a large degree. With regard to the achievement of the aims of strikes, the weakness of the teaching profession's bargaining power, in comparison with workers such as miners, who can exert economic pressure on the government, has meant that it has only achieved partial victories, which have often been overturned or rendered ineffective by subsequent actions on the part of the central and regional authorities.[44] Given such pressures, it is not surprising that the morale of the teaching force has declined yet further. It is remarkable that so many still retain a commitment to their job, for which they are often not paid for weeks and months, and that some can even be trying to introduce change in the schools. How much longer such resilience can last, however, remains to be seen. Meanwhile, the prospects for successful implementation of reform, to be discussed in the next chapter, must surely be tempered by the problems described in this chapter.

6
Signs of Change?

Assessing the amount (and quality) of change activity

Change of some kind is, undoubtedly, taking place in Russian schools, as the numerous accounts of innovative activity published in educational journals and newspapers testify. One study conducted in the early 1990s concluded that some 90 per cent of Russian schools were engaged in some form of innovative activity,[1] while the Tumalev survey of teachers in St Petersburg noted that 75 per cent of teachers claimed to be introducing innovative ideas in their teaching.[2] To some extent, the presence of such activity may be considered to exert a positive influence in itself, engendering an atmosphere in which change is portrayed as a desirable and common occurrence, a natural, essential part of school life in a system which had discouraged grassroots initiative for so long.

Evaluating such claims of implementation, however, is difficult: many reports of change at the school level, for instance, are supplied by the teachers engaged in the process themselves, rather than independent teams of researchers. When studies are conducted by researchers from specialised institutes and higher education establishments, the emphasis is often on the micro-level of a relatively small number of schools. Larger-scale studies of implementation at city-, region- or nationwide levels have to rely principally on the inadequate statistics available, and on the use of quantitative surveys, a legacy of the Soviet system's neglect of qualitative research and of the financial restrictions on the conduct of research in contemporary Russia. As a result, the system must operate 'blind' to a considerable degree, unable to draw on the type of detailed analysis which it desperately needs in order to make an informed assessment of the progress of change, of positive and negative areas of experience.

For these reasons – and for those highlighted in the Introduction to Part II, with regard to the analysis of implementation in any system – the following review of trends in change activity must, necessarily, serve only as an impression of a process whose outcomes will only be visible some time from now. The issues to be examined are:

- the experience of change at the level of the school (with particular attention paid to the position of alternative and selective schools)
- the teachers' perspective on change
- the pupils' perspective
- the material aspects of reform implementation.

The experience of the schools

Although it is impossible to quantify the type of experience of reform apparent in the schools, it can be seen to fall into one or more of the following categories:

- positive change
- over-experimentation
- 'shallow coping'

In the case of most schools, most teachers, indeed, the overall pattern of approaching the demands of change will be made up of a combination of the three types of experience, with the outcomes of change dictated by the extent to which any one factor is more influential than the others.

Positive change experience

There is a great deal of innovative work being practised in Russia's schools, in some cases allowing Russian educationalists justifiably to claim that such work is in the *avant garde* of current educational thinking in the world. The application of Bibler's 'Dialogue of Cultures' approach and the adoption of the 'developmental education' model by many schools has already been remarked upon in Chapter 3, while frequent mention is made in the Russian pedagogical press of the work of high-profile educationalists such as Adamskii, Tubel'skii and others, who are carrying on the mantle of the 'teacher–innovators.'[3] Tubel'skii, for instance, along with other leading representatives of the reform movement, set up an association of innovative schools and centres (*Assotsiatsiya innovatsionnykh shkol i tsentrov*), which organises workshops and conferences, and seeks to act as a voice for such establishments on a national level.[4] There is also a considerable number of so-called 'experimental sites' (*eksperimental'nye ploshchadki*) around the country, with schools attached, for instance, to a research institute, and used as a 'laboratory' for the development and testing of new approaches.

Apart from such prominent examples, however, there is a great deal of evidence, provided again in the pedagogical journals and newspapers and confirmed by my research and that of others, of innovative activity among 'ordinary' educationalists. In one school (an ordinary comprehensive) in St Petersburg, for instance, I discussed at great length with the deputy headteacher responsible for experimental work the school's plans for innovation in all areas of the curriculum. A 5-year timetable for change had been established with phases defined, the goals of change indicated, the approach to be taken to achieving those goals debated and agreed upon, responsibilities distributed among the staff, and a system for evaluation of progress agreed with the local authorities and the city's in-service training providers. The whole staff felt that it was working together towards change, although sufficient flexibility was retained to allow individual teachers to explore avenues of innovation by themselves. The pupils and parents were kept well informed of the aims of innovation, and appeared to be content with the school's work, offering it their support (there was, apparently, a good deal of interest from parents across the city, who wished to enrol their child at the school).

The extent to which such work is truly 'innovative', in the sense that it is pushing back the frontiers of pedagogical knowledge is not that important. Rather, it is the fact that such schools are creating an atmosphere of change, of progress and development, in which the staff are combining efforts to improve the nature of the education that they provide to their pupils. If it is approached in such a manner, the prospects for schools to achieve positive outcomes of change may be strong. However, much depends on the degree of professionalism and sense of responsibility among the staff. At times, there can be a narrow margin between innovation and over-experimentation.

The dangers of over-experimentation

The experience of the accredition committees of regional educational authorities bears witness to the appearance in recent years

> of enthusiast–teachers (*pedagogi-entuziasty*) wishing to realise at any cost their utopian dreams of the ideal educational establishment.[5]

Thus far, at least, the professional attitudes of the majority of Russia's teachers have prevented wide-scale fragmentation and loss of systemic cohesion. Nevertheless, there have been numerous cases of over-experimentation, of schools and teachers indulging in what may be called pedagogical adventurism. This trend was perhaps strongest in the early years of the reforms, as the old mechanisms of control were relaxed, and schools were urged by the reformers to engage in innovation before new mechanisms of cohesion had been put in place.[6] Some teachers and schools – especially, it seemed, the new alternative schools – took advantage of this opportunity to break away from what some saw as the shackles of the Soviet tradition to try out a wide variety of 'new' ideas, often without paying due attention to the implications which uncoordinated introduction of change might hold.

Such excesses can take various forms. In some schools, teachers decided to introduce what some might term as 'non-traditional' approaches, such as the ideas of Montessori, without sufficient understanding of the nature of such approaches, of the extent to which they would have to adapt their teaching style and produce new materials, of the viability of using such methods with large groups in the setting of a traditional school, and so on. The attempt to change attitudes towards discipline and teacher–pupil relations, for instance, while perhaps well-intentioned, has often fallen victim to the harsh realities of the classroom. In some cases, the decision to embark on such an experiment was made with little or no consultation with the education authorities, the parents or the pupils.

A more common example of over-experimentation has been the tendency of some schools to increase the workload on pupils (and teachers) by introducing additional subjects into the curriculum and/or by making the study of particular subjects more intensive:

> In the overwhelming majority of cases the so-called 'schools of a new type' are nothing more than educational establishments with strengthened, intensive, narrow or specialised preparation of pupils for entrance to higher education of a particular profile.[7]

In some cases it has been possible to 'muddle through' the problem of over-experimentation, with relatively little disruption caused. Such fortunate cases may occur because of the limited scope of the experiment, or a decision to revert to a more standard approach before too many problems arise. In other cases, however, the results of experimentation have been more damaging, as schools have pushed ahead regardless of the risks.

The contribution of alternative and selective schools

The expansion in the numbers of alternative and selective schools in both the state and the non-state sectors continued into the mid-1990s. The number of 'profile' schools, offering in-depth study of certain subjects, rose from 6955 in 1991 to 8200 in 1995, before dropping back to 8097 in 1996, and more sharply to 7580 in 1997. The number of state *gimnazii* and *litsei* showed a constant annual increase (1991–177; 1992–506; 1993–897; 1994–1160; 1995–1282; 1996–1421; 1997–1606 (952 *gimnazii* and 594 *litsei*)). With regard to non-state establishments, the number rose rapidly in the early 1990s, from 85 in 1991, to 300 in 1992, 368 in 1993, 447 in 1994 to 523 in 1995, although the tempo of growth slowed subsequently, reaching figures of 530 and 540 in 1996 and 1997 respectively (although some of this decline in the rate of increase may be attributed to the fact that some establishments included in the 1995 figure may have closed subsequently).[8] With regard to geographical location, 47 non-state schools were operating in Moscow city and region in 1997, and 48 in the north-west of Russia (including St Petersburg), demonstrating the more favourable material conditions present in these cities.[9]

In terms of student numbers, by 1997 some 50 500 pupils were enrolled in non-state schools, in comparison with 32 600 in 1993,[10] which represents some 0.24 per cent of the total of 21 million children of secondary school age (6–17 years) in Russia.[11] Approximately 1.5 million pupils (7 per cent of school-age population in Russia) were studying in 'profile' schools in 1997, and some 1 174 000 pupils were enrolled in *gimnazii* and *litsei* (768 000 and 406 000 respectively, together representing some 5.6 per cent of school-age population). While such schools, and the pupils they teach, are clearly outnumbered by the 'comprehensive' school, their experience of change is significant. Many have, after all, been set up with the ostensible purpose of introducing substantial change into the nature of education; further, it is in the alternative schools that the reform camp, in the early 1990s at least, appeared to lay hopes that they could act as 'beacons of change'. In this section, therefore, the impact that alternative schools have had with regard to reform implementation is examined, as well as the extent to which they can be seen to be contributing to the overall process of change in the school system.

What is an 'alternative' school?

Evaluating the progress of change in alternative schools is made difficult by the extent of the diversity among the establishments which are covered by this rather imprecise description, for the term 'alternative' is often applied to any school which declares itself to be 'different' from the standard state comprehensive. Such establishments may call themselves, for example, 'Montessori' or 'Steiner' schools; other alternative establishments, meanwhile, may seek to offer what would be called by some in England a 'traditional' education, in which the study of academic disciplines is stressed, and the goal of attaining higher education entrance is afforded considerable importance. In some cases schools have, literally, attempted to offer a traditional education, by reintroducing certain subjects which were studied in the pre-revolutionary Tsarist school, such as Latin and Greek. (Some, indeed, even call themselves 'classical gymnasium', *klassicheskaya gimnaziya*.) Some schools are wholly non-state, private establishments which charge fees for all aspects of the services provided to the pupils; others operate on a part fee-paying basis (although the practice of charging fees for certain elements of a pupil's education has become quite widespread, even in those schools which are, ostensibly, 'free').[12] Many alternative schools use selection procedures to choose their pupil intake, although not all do so, and the procedures in those which do vary considerably. In some cases, selection is made on the basis of presumed intellectual and academic ability, in others on the basis of the emotional needs of the pupil, and in others on the basis of the ability of the parents to pay the required fee. In some cases, the school itself may not be completely 'alternative,' but may select pupils into alternative 'classes' alongside the mainstream groups. There may be, for example, a so-called gymnasium class (*gimnazicheskii klass*) which serves as a top 'stream'; in another school which I visited, in Moscow, three parallel primary-level classes were organised, it was claimed, according to 'standard', 'Montessori' and 'Steiner' approaches.

Despite such diversity, however, it is possible to identify certain characteristics in the approach that these establishments have taken to reform implementation, and to assess the potential contribution which they might make to the school system as a whole.

The achievements of some alternative schools

Among those schools which belong, in my judgement, to the category of those which show signs of innovative practice, alternative schools are relatively well-represented in comparison with ordinary comprehensives. To some extent, this might be expected: the decision to break with the traditions of the comprehensive school signifies a degree of commitment to change on the part of the headteacher and her or his deputies. Even in those cases where the motives for creating an alternative school rest more on a desire to follow a trend, rather than on a vision of what such a transformation is supposed to achieve, there is an onus on such schools to engage in some kind of change in order to demonstrate that they deserve this status. While change is occurring in the comprehensive schools, therefore, the impetus for innovation may well be greater in the alternative school, and can be seen, along with a number of other factors, to give the alternative establishments certain advantages over their comprehensive school counterparts, perhaps serving as justification for the hopes that the reformers placed on diversification, as a means of allowing educationalists to free themselves from the restrictions which the legacy of the old system is perceived to impose on the development of the post-Soviet school. Indeed, one could argue that some examples of positive change noted in alternative schools would have been far more difficult to achieve in the standard comprehensive, not just because of any material advantage that the former might enjoy, but also because of the more dynamic change culture which some alternative establishments have been able to develop.[13] While diversification has brought some kind of result in certain schools, however, as far as the system as a whole is concerned such developments will be valuable only if the experience of good practice is effectively transferred to the rest of the school network. Is this taking place?

Passing on experience

Some alternative schools have proved unwilling to share their experience. One headteacher of an alternative school, in answer to my question on the level of interaction between her establishment and other schools in the system, remarked rather dismissively: 'Our methods just would not work in a "mass" school' (conversation with the author, October 1994). To some extent, a degree of pedagogical snobbism can be discerned in such attitudes, a product of the mood of élitism on which some alternative schools were founded. Perhaps it is a little harsh to criticise these attitudes; indeed, in some cases the 'mass' schools themselves may prove unreceptive to advice from the alternative sector. Nevertheless, while some alternative schools may wish to distance themselves somewhat from their comprehensive school counterparts, it has to be remembered that both sectors share a common heritage, with the vast majority of staff in alternative schools having worked in the Soviet system. Moreover, many alternative schools remain wholly or partially funded by the State, and thus have, one could say, some kind of obligation towards the state-maintained sector. Further, although plans for the direction and scope of change may differ, the problems faced by the alternative school and the comprehensive are still very similar, and there is, accordingly, potential for constructive and beneficial dialogue between the two sectors.

A good number of alternative schools do engage actively in such a dialogue, for instance through the provision of INSET workshops for teachers from other schools, at which experience of innovation can be related, and through the publication of articles in the pedagogical press and journals (although it should be noted that many 'ordinary' schools also offer INSET courses and make a considerable contribution to this dialogue). Those schools which have a state or semi-state funding base can be seen to have a greater input than those which are truly independent, as they still have direct access to the system through the teacher-education establishments, *metodischeskie tsentry* (teachers' centres) and the local education authorities. The rôle of alternative schools as beacons of change is being fulfilled, therefore, at least to some degree. However, the extent to which the experience of these schools can be seen to be directly applicable to the system at large can be questioned, for many alternative schools enjoy significant advantages in certain key areas.

With regard to staffing, for example, while many schools are created on the foundation of an existing establishment, and thus 'inherit' the incumbent teachers, the title of alternative school may serve to aid the recruitment (and retention) of staff who are themselves committed to the idea of change (perhaps with the added incentive of a larger salary than that earned in comprehensives). In other cases, usually where the alternative school is a 'new' establishment, the headteacher may be able to select staff who s/he feels will be suited to her or his plans, thus overcoming, as suggested earlier, potential problems of conservatism and resistance to change. As one headteacher of a non-state school noted, the staffing issue had been a key element in the setting-up of her school, which she had decided to create as a 'new' establishment, bringing in an entirely new staff, rather than trying to build on the foundation of an existing school:

> If I had not been able to bring in like-minded staff when I set up our school, the conservatism of the 'old guard' would have killed the idea before it was born. (Headteacher of non-state school, interview with the author, April 1994)

One should also note the advantage that such schools often enjoy in material terms over their traditional counterparts. Some have truly become élite establishments, in that they cater for the offspring of the wealthy and powerful in Russian society (although the richest tend to send their children abroad to study in private schools), and can thus draw on the substantial fees that such parents are prepared to pay. More typical are schools which educate the children of the less affluent, but nevertheless relatively prosperous, 'middle classes' (business people, better-off members of the 'intelligentsia'), and which can charge fees for all or part of the education they provide. (Popular magazines and journals have taken to offering advice to parents on how to choose an appropriate school.)[14] Other schools may be lucky enough to attract the support of 'sponsors', who might be the parents of a child for whom entrance was gained to the school not by academic selection, but by virtue of his or her family's wealth. As a result, the alternative schools are likely to have greater access to up-to-date teaching materials, can afford to pay their teachers more, and can restrict the number of pupils in a class to a much smaller level than is the norm in the 'mass' schools.

Finally, the selection of pupils by ability allows the schools to make greater academic demands, and since such pupils tend to come from the new 'middle class' or the traditional 'intelligentsia' and white-collar backgrounds, these schools are likely to have to contend less with the results of various social problems that pupils from less well-to-do families may encounter. Given the weight of such advantages, therefore, it is not surprising that many alternative schools can be seen to have greater opportunities to embark upon and implement change. One might argue that even when a dialogue is maintained between alternative and comprehensive schools, and experience of positive change passed on, the various advantages which many alternative schools enjoy provide a false impression of what is possible for the system as a whole, as the majority of schools cannot hope to emulate such material conditions.

Experience to pass on?

In may be the case, however, that the alternative school has little to offer its 'mass' school counterpart. While many of the examples of positive change to be found in the system have come from alternative schools, so too have many of the examples of over-experimentation discussed earlier. In a good number of cases, change has been pushed ahead too rapidly, too ambitiously, without the restraining influence of inertia that one might find in an ordinary school. Some schools have failed to provide the pupils with the appropriate level of knowledge of certain core subjects, with pupils as a result failing entrance examinations to higher education establishments. Of course, one cannot condemn teachers for wishing to introduce variation into the curriculum – the curriculum itself is in need of change, after all – yet a school's responsibility is to its pupils and the education system. Ignoring the standards and practices of the system constitutes destructive change, as opposed to the constructive approach of working with others across the system to introduce effective and cohesive measures.

The mechanisms of cohesion and control which the Ministry of Education has introduced, accordingly, might be seen to be of particular importance in dealing with such 'excesses'. They have had a mixed reception, however, in the alternative school network. The Association of Innovative Schools and Centres issued a statement in 1994 demanding that the ministry revise its plans for teacher appraisal, and attacking the moves to bring in a core curriculum, standards and the accreditation of educational establishments. These initiatives, the association claimed, threatened 'the reversal of innovative processes in education'.[15] Such criticism did contribute to the process of consultation on these matters, and some of the points made in this statement were not without foundation (e.g. on the setting of the levels of attainment contained in the proposed standards). Nevertheless, opposition towards such mechanisms on the part of some alternative schools was, it seems, motivated at least partly by a desire to protect themselves from criticism over poor standards and, in some cases, professional incompetence. Those alternative schools which had nothing to fear were more positive in their reaction to the introduction of these initiatives, and, indeed, have welcomed them, recognising the benefits that quality control measures can bring to the image of their establishments, if operated effectively.[16]

As in the system as a whole, however, in most 'alternative' schools it is more common to find not deep change or over-experimentation, but superficial change, as highlighted by studies conducted by Russian researchers[17] and by my own investigations. Many have been tempted into following the trend of adopting prestigious-sounding titles, yet the substance of their approach to the curriculum has, in fact, altered little if at all, with the same teachers using the same materials as before, with little change of note in their use of this material, in their overall delivery of the curriculum, or in their stance on teacher–pupil relations. The incentives for acquiring such a title can be substantial: the schools may be able to receive extra income, and their efforts to ensure that their pupil cohort is biased towards the more able can help them to achieve apparently good results with rather less effort than would be necessary if they had to work with a greater range of ability (although selection does not always guarantee better results). The potential contribution that these schools can make to the wider system is, accordingly, somewhat limited.

The social meaning of alternative schools

Apart from the question of these schools' significance in educational terms, the development of the alternative and non-state sectors clearly has potentially far-reaching social implications. However, while the debate may have moved on from the initial curiosity shown in such schools in the late 1980s and the shallow treatment of these issues in the early 1990s,[18] and while there may be wider recognition of the shortcomings of certain alternative schools,[19] there is still little discussion of the importance of such issues as selection and élitism in education. When these matters are dealt with, the arguments advanced tend to retain a superficial, ill-informed character. In 1996, Minister of Education Tkachenko, for instance, could state that:

> The move away from a unitary, common form of education towards education by choice has become a reality. Today we can offer

> pupils and parents a choice of educational establishment, profile (i.e. specialisation) of studies, of programmes, textbooks, final examinations and the form of receiving education, even in rural areas. Education by choice and the core curriculum have become powerful instruments in the protection of children, of their personality, their individual paths of development . . . This is helped by the reshaping of the structure of the network of educational establishments. The number of non-traditional establishments is rising constantly – lycées, gymnasia, colleges, professional lycées, educational complexes (kindergarten–primary school–gymnasium), etc.[20]

Opponents can argue – with some justification – that choice for one pupil is the denial of opportunity for another. Meanwhile, those who are against alternative or private schools have also made their point at times in a rather undemocratic manner, which has not contributed to the constructive debate that is required. I was told of cases in which municipal authorities have tried, apparently successfully at least in some instances, to prevent private schools from being set up in their town, or even trying to close down existing schools (without sound reasons for doing so) (information supplied by headteacher of state *gimnaziya*, June 1995).

By the mid-1990s, there were some signs of polarisation in the debate on alternative and non-state education, and supporters of non-state establishments were beginning to speak with growing concern of the threat posed to such schools by the attitude of the federal and certain regional authorities, as shown in the proposed amendments to the Law on Education which were introduced for discussion in 1994.[21] It was feared, for instance, that the application of measures such as the accreditation of establishments and the mechanism of competitive bidding for funding may serve not only to bring into question the development of non-state education, but its very survival. In late 1994 a 'Concept for the Development of Non-State Education' was drawn up on the initiative of a *Duma* deputy, L.V. Babukh, which sought to provide a framework for constructive discussion of the issues involved.[22] However, a few months later a bill was introduced entitled 'On non-state education in the Russian Federation' which, while supported to a degree by the proponents of non-state schools with regard to certain of its provisions, also attracted widespread criticism from this same group, displeased with the failure of the bill to address adequately the questions of accreditation and financing in particular.[23]

In the democratic society that Russia, ostensibly, has committed itself to building, there should be room for state and non-state sectors of education to exist alongside and to complement one another. However, while there are pockets of positive development of this kind in various parts of Russia, the scope for holding a rational and wide-ranging debate on this issue on a national scale is restricted by the immaturity of civil society. As will be shown in Part III, both the non-state and state sectors of education have had to contend with considerable pressures in recent years, which have acted as a barrier to the rationalisation of relations within the system, and, indeed, increased the potential for damaging rifts.

'Shallow coping'

Returning to the issue of school reform, it can be suggested that for most schools, whether they consider themselves to be alternative establishments or ordinary comprehensives, the experience of change to date is still restricted to relatively shallow implementation and innovation. This is not to say that they are not trying to implement change – indeed, many may think that they have already achieved it. In the majority of cases, though, real change is some way off. Some schools, some teachers are actively trying to engage in change, yet for a variety of reasons, change is proving to be elusive. Others may have a more negative stance, reluctant to change, perhaps through anxiety about its outcomes, or confusion about how to go about it. The result, a common phenomenon in any system, is what Louis and Miles term 'shallow coping'.[24] Within the issue of coping, however, there are a number of interrelated strands concerning the culture of the system, the system's management of change, and the schools' ability to respond to reform.

Confusion continued into the late 1990s over the definitions of such terms as humanisation, humanitarisation, or even the apparently more straightforward concept of differentiation. In the case of the last-named policy, confusion has arisen because of inconsistency in the application of the term at all levels within the system, including ministerial level. At times, it is used to apply to the differentiation of approach used to teach pupils of varying ability, at others to refer to the placement of pupils in various types of establishment according to various criteria, including ability and inclination towards a particular specialised field of study:

> The majority of schools (up to 60 per cent) are engaged in developing, experimenting with and orientating themselves towards the differentiation of learning by level of ability and by subject (profile). By this is meant the differentiation of the children, but not of the means, methods and materials of teaching.[25]

Until a greater degree of clarity can be achieved, teachers (not to mention pupils, parents and other lay people) will remain confused as to the nature of the changes that the schools are supposed to be engaged in, and such phenomena as shown in the following section will continue to affect the development of the school.

'Lip-service'

Many teachers and many schools are paying lip-service to change, rather than actually engaging in it meaningfully. This may stem from a 'self-defence' motivation, a desire to appear to be changing and thus hide one's difficulties in adapting to change, a tendency which can occur at the level of the individual, but which is also frequently found at the institutional level. This is strengthened by the legacy of the Soviet period, in which all members of society knew when to appear to be conforming, and when and how to make it seem to the authorities that everything was going smoothly, in order to avoid any sanctions for failing to comply with instructions. While the Russian school reforms are much less tightly controlled than in the Soviet era, and schools are, indeed, encouraged to make their own decisions in many matters, old habits die hard. Such false, or incomplete, conformity could, one might think, be of concern to the authorities, for beneath the apparent veneer of compliance might lie a hidden element of opposition to change, expressed through inertia rather than through open refusal to follow the reform agenda. Here, again, the lack or clarity over policy aims can play a part.

By way of example, in 1995 I observed (along with a *metodist* and a number of other teachers) a lesson of physics taught by a deputy headteacher, in which the teaching style was very much taken from the traditional Soviet didactic, teacher-centred approach, with pupils given only limited (and controlled) opportunity to participate in the lesson, no opportunity to discuss with one another, or to conduct experiments themselves. During the lesson the teacher referred briefly in passing to the work of a number of English physicists, giving a small amount of biographical detail. She also showed a photograph from a newspaper article, depicting a car crossing a bridge made of paper, thus demonstrating the principle of physics that she was focusing on in this lesson. The *metodist*, in her analysis of the lesson (given immediately afterwards with all observing staff present) stated that this could be considered a model lesson, and that the younger staff should take particular note of the 'excellent' inclusion of humanisation, in the form of the two references to 'real life' cited earlier. This shows the degree of confusion that exists in the system over the concepts introduced in the reforms, for this lesson did not meet, I feel, the criteria for differentiation and humanisation intended by the reform leaders. While such variation can be tolerated for a certain time, if it is allowed to continue for too long such misconceptions will become embedded in the culture of the teaching profession, and will be difficult to address subsequently.

Adaptation

This example also points to another strand in the coping scenario, namely the adaptation and modification by the teachers and the schools of the ideas contained in the reform agenda. This, again, is a common occurrence in any system, as the profession imposes its own interpretation on changes to make them fit in with their own views. From the point of view of the initiators of reform, this may be seen as a negative phenomenon, for it threatens to distort, even disrupt the passage of their planned innovation. It may be that the further away the initiators are from the level of the classroom, the greater the risk of such adaptation; innovations that originate at the school level will have less far to 'travel,' although the changes introduced by the headteacher may also be adapted versions of the intended changes proposed by the centre or the region.

At the same time, adaptation can have positive effects, for the schools may be acting as a filter for the reform effort, diluting some of the more radical elements that seemed to threaten the integrity of the system. To some extent, the ability of the schools to effect such adaptation in the relative freedom of the decentralised scenario may also have offset the risk of outright opposition to change. Teachers may perceive the aims of the reform (as seen in their diluted state) to coincide more or less with their own views, whereas the introduction of the reforms in unaltered form might have proved less acceptable.

The question of adaptation, however, despite any negative or positive perceptions on the part of those connected with the system, does raise a number of issues which deserve urgent attention from the authorities. Adaptation can be tolerated to a degree, but over-indulgence in adaptation may hold serious consequences for the ability of the system to maintain the *edinoe prostranstvo*, especially while the mechanisms of cohesion are still only just being put in place. It highlights yet again the need for a more detailed debate on the reforms to inform the views and actions of the schools, and the associated requirement for a greater amount of research and research dissemination on practical issues of implementation, to establish a greater level of clarity.

The teaching force's reaction to change

There has been relatively little qualitative research to date on the experience of change of Russian teachers. In this section, therefore, I draw heavily on the findings of my own small-scale research, and draw the reader's attention to a number of significant factors relating to teachers' attitudes which have implications for the system-wide process of reform, and which merit further, more in-depth study.

The prospect of change can be rather daunting for any professional group, and its introduction is bound to cause disruption and dispute, with, almost inevitably, a certain amount of resistance to reform. In the case of teachers, as Fullan notes, the arrival of a new round of innovation and reform is often greeted with mixed feelings by teachers:

> The fact that those who advocate and develop changes get more rewards than costs, and those who are expected to implement them experience many more costs than rewards, goes a long way in explaining why the more things change, the more they stay the same. If the change works, the individual teacher gets little of the credit; if it doesn't, the teacher gets most of the blame.[26]

The situation may be different in the Russian scenario where teachers felt themselves to be more detached from holding responsibility for the curriculum. Nevertheless, the reform agenda does seek to alter fundamentally the pattern of professional experience of the Russian teaching force, and this, coupled with the accompanying factors of social change and the political/ideological implications of the reforms would seem to indicate that some degree of reluctance to change might be encountered, a factor that the educational authorities needed to be aware of. For while reforms can be introduced against a backdrop of reluctance, even opposition to change, as has been the case to some extent in England and Wales after the 1988 Education Reform Act,[27] implementation is likely to be more effective if the teaching force both understands and supports the aims of the change programme, especially if there is a sense that the profession enjoys a degree of ownership of the policies.

I have already referred to evidence provided in various surveys which seems to indicate a good degree of dissatisfaction among Russian teachers with regard to the state of the school system. Despite the factors that I highlighted that may have influenced such negative appraisal of the status quo, there does appear to be a general acceptance of the need for change of some kind. This is an important point, particularly since a positive attitude to change can be discerned not only among the younger teachers, but also in the older age group (i.e. over 40 years old), those for whom change can prove the most daunting. Would this acceptance of change extend to the policies proposed by the Ministry of Education in the Law of 1992? Has a process of 'institutionalisation' of the reform agenda occurred? Has teachers' support for the agenda increased or diminished? Do they feel that the policies of reform reflect their own views on the needs of the school? (See Table 6.1.) Have they succeeded in 'adapting' elements of the agenda to fit in with their own views?

The anecdotal evidence of my research suggests that teachers have given the policy of decentralisation a mixed reception. While some welcomed the new freedoms that these developments brought, others urged a more cautious approach to devolution from an early stage, their concerns receiving a growing amount of support from colleagues from 1994 onwards, as some of the negative outcomes of rapid decentralisation noted earlier became more noticeable. Empowerment, the element of decentralisation of most immediate concern to the teachers themselves, was given a warm reception by a little more than half of the teachers surveyed, as Table 6.2 shows, a figure reflected in the results of my interviews, where 27 of 43 teachers questioned directly on this issue in 1993 reported that they were satisfied or very satisfied with the results of empowerment, with one stating:

> At last we have been given the opportunity to make our own decisions, as experienced professionals. It is like a breath of fresh

Table 6.1 Views on the need for changes. Teacher questionnaire q.1a. 'With regard to the following changes in the school system, indicate the extent to which they were required according to the scale: 4–very necessary, 3–necessary, 2–not that necessary, 1–not at all, 0–do not know' (N = 132)

Change	*4*	*3*	*2*	*1*	*0*	*nr*
Decentralisation	18.3% (24)	38.6% (51)	13.6% (18)	10.6% (14)	8.3% (11)	10.6% (14)
New types of school	16.7% (22)	23.4% (31)	28.8% (38)	15.2% (20)	7.6% (10)	8.3% (11)
Democratisation	35.6% (47)	22.7% (30)	15.9% (21)	6.1% (8)	6.8% (9)	12.9% (17)
Humanisation	25% (33)	31.1% (41)	21.2% (28)	9.8% (13)	5.3% (7)	7.6% (10)
Humanitarisation	19.8% (26)	31.8% (42)	20.4% (27)	14.4% (19)	4.5% (6)	9.1% (12)
Core curriculum	18.3% (24)	34.8% (46)	21.2% (28)	12.9% (17)	6.8% (9)	6% (8)
State educational standards	15.9% (21)	27.4% (36)	23.4% (31)	14.4% (19)	13.6% (18)	5.3% (7)
Private schools	14.4% (19)	28% (37)	28.8% (38)	11.4% (15)	3.8% (5)	13.6% (18)
Appraisal of teachers	12.9% (17)	25% (33)	34.1% (45)	15.9% (21)	6.8% (9)	5.3% (7)
Differentiation of instruction	20.4% (27)	28.8% (38)	22.1% (29)	10.6% (14)	8.3% (11)	9.8% (13)
Common exam system	9.1% (12)	16.7% (22)	21.2% (28)	9.8% (13)	23.4% (31)	19.8% (26)
Selection to 10th form	11.4% (15)	22.1% (29)	24.2% (32)	13.6% (18)	12.9% (17)	15.9% (21)

Table 6.2 Views on empowerment. Teacher questionnaire q. 3a. 'What is your opinion of the granting of greater freedom to teachers in the choice of curricular content and the methods of teaching?' (N = 132)

Very positive	*Positive*	*Negative*	*Very negative*	*Do not know*	*No response*
20.5% (27)	31.2% (41)	12.8% (17)	5.3% (7)	16.7% (22)	13.6% (18)

> air. Maybe we will make mistakes to begin with, but at least they will be our mistakes, and we will be responsible for rectifying them. (Teacher of history, 'comprehensive' school, April 1993)

On the basis of my evidence, however, a considerable number of teachers (16.7 per cent and 13.6 per cent respectively, in the survey) either did not have an opinion or did not respond at all to

Table 6.3 Views on the ownership of reforms. Teacher questionnaire q. 2. 'To what extent does the direction and content of reform reflect the opinions of teachers?' (N = 132)

Large	*Fair*	*Little*	*None*	*Do not know*	*nr*
9.1% (12)	22% (29)	38.6% (51)	5.3% (7)	17.4% (23)	7.6% (10)

this question, displaying a sense of uncertainty with regard to empowerment which was also reflected in the interviews. It seems that many teachers were, at least initially, unaware of the implications that it held, particularly with regard to the increased burden of responsibility on them. As time has passed, a more sober appraisal of the impact of empowerment has come to light, although I would argue that many teachers have yet to feel the full impact of the policy, since they are still 'protected' to a considerable degree by virtue of the fact that they are able to teach according to old curricula. Positive outcomes are possible if empowerment is managed effectively, but when teachers decide, or are asked, to assume full responsibility for curricular design and implementation, problems can occur, and the shortcomings of certain aspects of the teacher-education (i.e. teacher-training) system are highlighted. More thought should have been given by the education authorities to the problems which arise with the introduction of empowerment, for empowering teachers without adequate preparation is akin to handing the keys of a sports car to someone who does not know how to drive – the risk of costly errors is substantial.

Levels of ownership and influence

The results given in Table 6.3, responses to a question in my questionnaire that was intended to establish the extent of ownership felt by teachers, may seem to be rather surprising. As has been shown, the ideas of reform came from the more change-orientated section of the grassroots, and received widespread support in the early stages of the moves towards change in the mid-1980s. While they may not have participated directly in the formation, development and promotion of these ideas, one might still have expected greater recognition of the fact that the path that they have taken stands in considerable contrast to the traditional top-down pattern of Soviet reforms. How can this be explained? To a large extent, opinions are still conditioned by the Soviet experience, in which ordinary teachers (and citizens) felt little if any control over the

Table 6.4 Degrees of influence on the course of reform. Teacher questionnaire q.3. 'What amount of influence do the following exert on the course of reform? Give your answer according to the scale: 5–very large, 4–large, 3–fair, 2–small, 1–none, 0–do not know' (N = 132)

Person/organisation	*5*	*4*	*3*	*2*	*1*	*0*	*nr*
1 Headteacher	8.3% (11)	16.7% (22)	31.9% (42)	19.7% (26)	12.1% (16)	6.8% (9)	4.5% (6)
2 Municipal education authority	12.1% (16)	18.2% (24)	28.8% (38)	20.5% (27)	10.6% (14)	5.3% (7)	4.5% (6)
3 Ministry of Education	17.4% (23)	35.7% (47)	24.2% (32)	10.6% (14)	2.3% (3)	3.8% (5)	6% (8)
4 Russian Academy of Education (RAO)	6% (8)	9.1% (12)	10.6% (14)	24.3% (32)	13.6% (18)	20.5% (27)	15.9% (21)
5 Teacher	3.8% (5)	11.4% (15)	19.7% (26)	43.9% (58)	9.1% (12)	6.8% (9)	5.3% (7)
6 Regional (*oblast'*) Education authority	19.7% (26)	40.2% (53)	15.9% (21)	12.9% (17)	6% (8)	2.3% (3)	3% (4)
7 Municipal / district education authority	6.8% (9)	9.8% (13)	16.7% (22)	37.2% (49)	12.9% (17)	8.3% (11)	8.3% (11)

decisions being made about their country's policies, and were resigned to the rôle of merely reacting to, and being seen to fulfil the directives delivered from above. Although these ideas came from the grassroots, the fact that they are now being promoted by the centre has somewhat distanced teachers from them. At the same time, there seems to be a continued sense of 'obedience' among teachers towards policy implementation, of feeling oneself obliged to state that one is implementing a policy, even if one is uncertain of the goals of, and the need for, such measures.

Of course, there is an element of 'obedience' in any system; further, the fact that legislation has been passed is a compelling reason, one might argue, to comply with the policies. Yet in the Russian scenario, the presence of 'obedience' is accompanied by a certain apathy with regard to the powers of the ordinary citizen to change the course of development in Russia, mixed with a degree of mistrust, of passive opposition to the authorities. The limits of the individual are seen in Table 6.4, which shows teachers' perceptions of the relative amount of influence exerted by various figures and organisations within the system.

Many of the teachers whom I interviewed felt that they had little influence over issues outside of their own immediate environment, with other bodies exerting far more influence over the direction of reform. It is interesting to note, however, with regard to the question of devolution that regional and municipal authorities are seen as having a greater say than the central Ministry of Education. This may reflect changes in the pattern of system-wide relations under devolution, yet may also be due to the fact that the vast majority of teachers have little direct contact with the centre in Moscow, and may not be *au fait* with the current debates taking place in the Ministry of Education. In contrast, the work of the district and regional authorities may be more visible to the classroom teacher, who will have contact either directly or indirectly (e.g. through their headteacher, inspectors, etc.) with these levels.

Pupils' attitudes to the reforms

There is relatively little material available on the specific question of pupils' attitudes to the policies of the reform agenda. Among English-language sources, Westbrook's study, while limited to only a small sample of pupils studying in independent schools in St Petersburg, does provide an interesting analysis of student views on the process of change in the early period of the reforms in 1992.[28] Most Russian studies of pupils' attitudes to school that I have seen, however, tend to focus not on pupils' views of the need for and impact of particular features of the reforms, such as humanisation, but have concentrated instead on wider issues relating to education, such as career intentions,[29] or on problems of socialisation.[30]

Evidence can, nevertheless, be gleaned from the Russian studies with regard to the process of change in general terms. In the Sobkin and Pisarskii survey of 1991, for example, of a sample of 1063 pupils of the 10th form (15–16 years old) in Moscow, some 47.7 per cent stated that they were 'pleased' with their school, while 34.9 per cent were 'indifferent' and 15.7 per cent said that the school 'did not suit them at all', an interesting reflection on the pupils' perception of the need for change, given that the survey was conducted a year before the Law on Education was introduced.[31] The authors of a 1993 survey of 1131 pupils of the 9th to 11th forms from various Russian cities, however, give a more critical appraisal of the school, stating that:

> For half of the pupils the school remains a prison-like place, an obligation. Only for one in three or one in four senior-grade pupils does the school represent a place where they can hope to receive a good education, and the knowledge they will need in life. Only one in six pupils likes her or his school.[32]

This evidence, the authors claim, demonstrates both the pressing need for school reform, and the fact that reform had not yet begun to have an effect in the schools. While there is an element of truth in both claims, they also contain a degree of naïvety. First, in any system, a question to pupils on whether or not they like their school will often receive a rather negative answer – even if the pupil concerned *is* content. Further, as I have argued earlier, in the Russia of the early 1990s it was common for everyone to criticise everything; pupils may well have been carried along on the tide of national discontent. Finally, to expect real change to have occurred in the school so soon after the launch of the reforms represents wishful thinking. This is not to say that such evidence should be ignored, for there are good grounds for pupils to be dissatisfied with the nature of their schooling, as will have become apparent from what I have stated in the rest of this work. Such quantitative studies needed to be supplemented, however, with comprehensive qualitative research.

From the anecdotal evidence of the 38 interviews which I conducted with pupils (27 of whom were pupils of the 9th to 11th forms, i.e. 14–17 years old), it appeared that the impression which pupils had of change varied considerably. One pupil whom I interviewed, who attended an alternative school which clearly differed substantially from the traditional Soviet model, in its organisation of the curriculum and its approach to teacher–pupil relations, remarked on the fact that he felt 'comfortable' in this new establishment, and was able to communicate with the staff, while in the ordinary schools that he had attended he had never been able to adjust. Other pupils from the same school, however, noted that the staff's attempts to introduce elements of the Montessori and Steiner approaches to teaching had not been well received by all pupils, who were used to a very different pattern of learning. Indeed, in those schools that have tried to move to a more pupil-centred approach, even on a modest scale, it has often been difficult for pupils to adjust, having grown accustomed to a teacher-centred approach.

In other schools where change had not been so radical in nature, pupils commented on the element of discussion and group-work that had begun to appear, although the use of such approaches are still only slowly emerging in many schools, with teachers cautious about making the transition to a pupil-centred style, and sometimes noting that the pupils themselves seem to prefer the teacher-directed lessons to the group-work sessions. (This apparent reluctance on the part of the pupils, however, may stem from the teacher's inappropriate use of group-work, rather than a negative reaction to the concept of such activity itself.) Some pupils did refer to the greater sense of freedom they felt in being able to express their views more openly to teachers, and even to challenge staff, although it seems that teachers and pupils are only slowly getting used to communicating with each other in a more relaxed manner in which the teacher does not seek to dominate. A number of pupils complained that some staff still tended to treat them in a condescending manner, even trying to humiliate pupils on occasion. Others, stated that they could identify little real change in their school over the ten years that they had been there, apart from the fact that pupils no longer wore uniform.[33]

In other words, a mixed reaction (with views that might just as well have come, one feels, from pupils in England). While certain changes had registered with the pupils, for the majority school seemed to be, as one 15 year old noted: 'just school.' Some were bored with studies, some were engaged in ongoing conflicts with staff or other pupils, others were working hard to pass their examinations, others still were preoccupied with boyfriend–girlfriend relationships. The wider issues of school reform and its implications for them personally were given little thought, at least in the interviews conducted for the present study. In most cases, it seemed, they accepted school as it was, and saw little opportunity to influence it. Of course, given the small and unrepresentative sample of pupils interviewed broad conclusions cannot be drawn, although the anecdotal evidence provided by the comments of pupils and teachers would suggest that Russian pupils, as is probably the case in the vast majority of schools across the world, are somewhat detached from the process of change taking place in their school. This state of affairs may hold serious implications for the overall course of reform, and, again, deserves more detailed analysis by researchers.

Pupils' participation in change

The tendency in most education systems has been to ignore the pupils as a potential participant in change, even to fail to acknowledge their interest in the results of innovation that will, after all, affect their education.[34] In this sense, the Soviet system has as poor a track record as most. There was, of course, an element of responsibility for one's studies (and, indeed, the progress of other pupils) attached to membership of the Pioneer and Komsomol organisations, and there was also a tradition (which had some positive traits) of using more able children as peer teachers to assist pupils in need of extra learning support. This all fell short of allowing pupils a real say in the way that the school was run, however, apart from token input into such matters as the organisation of extra-curricular activities. Would pupil participation increase with the introduction of the Russian reform effort?

This was the intention of the reformers, who promoted the vision of making the school the property of its local community, with the pupils active participants in the school's transformation (Article 13 of the Law on Education). The school councils were supposed to include pupil representatives, and pupils were supposed to be able to influence decisions concerning a wide range of matters. Some innovative schools, such as Tubel'skii's 'School of Self-Definition' (*shkola samoopredeleniya*) in Moscow, have been able to introduce complex systems of pupil–teacher 'governments' and other initiatives, which give pupils the chance to acquire experience of 'real' responsibility, along with the chance to develop their skills of communication and negotiation. For the majority of schools, however, it seems that neither the school nor the pupils were ready for such a rapid transition to this form of power-sharing, even on a relatively limited basis, and that much more effective preparatory work would be required to develop pupils' experience of holding real responsibilities, an element of upbringing only partially addressed in the Soviet system. As a result, there was, at least for a time, a downplaying of the importance of pupil involvement in school councils, with more emphasis given to teacher and parent participation (although subsequently there seemed to be renewed interest on the part of the Ministry of Education in pupil involvement).[35]

In some schools that I visited pupils do appear to be involved in the process of reform, at least as relatively passive partners, informed by the staff of the aims of innovations, and asked to give feedback on their perceptions of the outcomes of change. This in itself represents a considerable advance over what used to be, and what still is in the case of most schools, not just in Russia but in any system. For the most part, pupils continue to play their traditional rôle as recipients of knowledge, and are not expected or encouraged to take a more active part in the discussion or implementation of change. One should note, however, that the attitudes of youth in Russia today are undergoing rapid transformation, and the outlook of young people today is quite different, in many respects, from that of pupils of this age ten, even five years ago. It may well be that in a few years' time, pupils will be more assertive in making their views known on issues of education and other matters relevant to the school. The teachers will need to be ready to adjust to this change in the pattern of pupil–teacher relations, and try to ensure that pupils are given the opportunity to express their concerns in a constructive manner, and not feel that they are being stifled. Tomorrow's generation of Russian pupils is unlikely to be as willing to display respect to teachers as automatically as has been the case to now.

Obstacles to change

Apart from the difficulties encountered in developing an effective culture of change, however, Russian schools also have to contend with practical problems on a huge scale. Indeed, in the light of such difficulties as those outlined later, one might think that change would be almost impossible to attempt. It is one thing to declare a radical transformation of the curriculum; it is another to provide teachers with the materials they need to introduce such change. The need for new resources was most keenly felt by the teachers of social science disciplines such as history, in which there is a clear need to introduce revised materials in order to replace the Soviet-era textbooks, and the new subject of civic studies (*grazhdanovedenie*), for which entirely new materials needed to be devised. Unfortunately, while a number of the new history textbooks produced by Russian authors in the early 1990s received positive reviews by Western analysts,[36] the financial constraints on the education system have held back the development and production of such resources, and what seems to be an annual battle over the funding of textbook publication now takes place, with the schools left as the victim as promises are made and broken by the central government.[37] In 1997, for instance, as the start of the school year approached, only some 82.5 billion rubles from a planned target of 400 billion had been allocated for textbook production, and schools faced the prospect of having to work with only 20–30 per cent of the textbooks from the so-called 'federal set' (i.e. funded from the federal budget) that they should have received.[38] The situation was described by one deputy minister of education as 'catastrophic', and he warned that it could lead to the 'derailing of the entire reform process'.[39]

Even when textbooks are produced, there is no guarantee that they will reach the classrooms, at least through the route of federal financing. One headteacher from a city located some 300 miles from Moscow told me of a visit she had made to the bookshop of a major publishing house in the capital, where she had been surprised to see large numbers of copies of textbooks which she had been informed could not be delivered to her school since they had not been published. When she asked a company representative to clarify the situation, it transpired that the publisher had, indeed, published the books, and had put some on sale at high prices to the public, but was meanwhile hoarding large numbers of the book in anticipation that the high inflation rate would guarantee a greater profit margin when it was decided to distribute the books to the schools.

Various initiatives have been undertaken to try to bypass the problems in government funding of textbooks, notably by the Soros Foundation and other foreign-sponsored projects. The Soros group's 'New Books for Russian Schools' programme began in 1995 on the basis of an earlier initiative by the Foundation in which teams of authors across the country worked to write a range of new materials. The Foundation is now overseeing the distribution of a million copies of 25 textbooks.[40] Further Western involvement has included a project run by the International Movement Toward Educational Change (IMTEC) organisation, and a joint Canadian–Russian project to produce a textbook on civics education.[41] Such schemes represent a welcome additional source of materials for the Russian system, extending the opportunities for teachers to engage in change, even providing an element of choice in the resources on offer. Nevertheless, while some schools (often those in the major centres) have been fortunate enough to obtain such new materials, many others have had to struggle on with their existing resources.

Some teachers have attempted as far as possible to develop their own materials, for instance using newspaper cuttings for teaching history, yet there is a limit to which such self-made materials can meet the needs of the curriculum. Most teachers are not able to spare the considerable amount of time that it takes to produce large quantities of high-quality material; further, it is very difficult to provide additional copies of those resources they are able to make, for photocopying facilities are still a rarity in Russian schools. Indeed, many schools are restricted in the amount of technical facilities and teaching aids that they are able to afford (including computer equipment, video recorders, overhead projectors), thus further restricting the scope for curricular change.

Even if teachers do have the time and materials necessary to produce additional resources, or even if they are lucky enough to have acquired new textbooks and materials, the culture of the Soviet school may still act to restrict their capacity to take advantage of such opportunities. In the Soviet era, with single textbook titles produced *en masse* and used for the teaching of that subject across the school system, the quality of instruction in a particular subject could depend to a considerable extent on the quality of the textbooks written for that subject. Some subjects (along with the teachers who taught them and the pupils who studied them) were fortunate, as those 'experts' chosen to write the textbooks produced materials of a good standard; in other subjects, the quality of the resources could be less satisfactory. The central authorities, however, committed the system to enduring such drawbacks by not allowing schools any choice in the materials they could acquire, and by retaining, in many cases, the same textbook for a considerable length of time.

Teachers had little option but to follow slavishly the approach laid down in such materials, whether they felt it to be suitable or not. The restrictions placed on the expression of individual points of view, and the control exercised by the authorities over the teacher's delivery of the curriculum, led to a very passive stance among teachers with regard to materials design, and the management of the learning process in general. Indeed, for many, it could be argued that the textbook came to be seen as the curriculum itself, with both handed to the teaching staff from above. Despite the greater freedoms that empowerment and curricular change have brought, many teachers retain the mind-set which was present in the Soviet system, and are ill-prepared for the opportunities now afforded to develop new materials, or even to adapt existing resources: the textbook is still held to be the curriculum, in many cases, rather than one element in a range of potential resources which teachers could use in their delivery of the curriculum. Given such problems, then, with both the supply and use of resources, the education authorities should be under no illusion with regard to the potential for rapid implementation of curricular reform in the schools.

Staffing problems

If curricular reform is difficult with insufficient materials, then it is even more so if there is a shortage of teaching staff. The Soviet system traditionally suffered from the difficulty of attracting young people to choose teaching as a career, principally because of the comparatively poor material rewards that teaching brought. (While a graduate job in the industrial sector may well have had a good salary and additional benefits such as the prospect of housing provided by the enterprise, teachers' salaries were lower and there were few extra material rewards to speak of.) In the 'new' Russia, as opportunities for employment in the commercial sector have opened up and teachers' income has fallen progressively further behind the average earned in industry (dropping from between 65 per cent to 75 per cent of the industrial average during the *perestroika* era to less than 55 per cent in September 1995),[42] one might expect that this problem would intensify. Indeed, one deputy minister of education, Mariya Nikolaevna Lazutova, warned in 1995 that by the year 2000 there would be a 50 per cent shortfall of teaching staff across the country, if current rates of decline continue.[43] Figures on the scale of the crisis vary considerably. According to former minister Tkachenko, by the start of the 1994–95 school year there was a shortage of some 81 600 teachers, with 32 000 of these representing vacancies in village schools.[44] Another source, referring to the start of the 1995–96 school year, cited figures of an overall shortage of 74 500 teachers, with 13 100 of these required in primary classes, and some 43 600 needed to fill vacancies as teachers of mathematics, science and humanities subjects.[45] Contacts in schools in Yaroslavl' and Moscow told me that the worst-hit subjects tend to be computer studies, foreign languages and Russian language and literature, with teachers of these disciplines the most in demand by companies.

A more positive view, which somewhat contradicts this evidence, was provided by the collegium of the Ministry of Education in May 1996 (strangely, given that this body includes the very ministers who had issued such dire warnings about this problem). At the collegium it was stated that trends were actually showing favourable signs, with the number of vacancies nationwide (i.e. all schools, not just those in rural areas) having fallen from 31 900 in 1991 to 29 800 in 1996. Further, it was claimed, the number of teachers working in the system had actually risen by 488 000 over the preceding ten years.[46] These somewhat contradictory trends are difficult to account for – explanations offered by educational administrators to me tended to be at variance with one another – but it is likely that the increase in the overall number reflects, to some extent, the fact that a growing number of teachers of pensionable age are staying on, or returning to, the schools, and perhaps shows an encouraging improvement in the retention rate of teachers in general. Meanwhile, a 1998 source cited a figure for the shortage of teachers of 'approximately 2 per cent' of the teaching force of some 1.7 million, i.e. 34 000, or an increase on the 1996 figures given by the Ministry of Education collegium.[47] Whatever the true extent of the problem, it is clearly a large thorn in the side of the schools' reform effort.

Some, however, manage to maintain a more optimistic perspective: a senior education official suggested to me in 1995 that the decrease in the birth-rate in Russia meant that the resultant overcapacity in the primary-level classes would allow the authorities to free staff to work in the senior school. Further, he claimed that the teachers among the immigrants and refugees from former Soviet republics who had moved to Russia would also be able to help to relieve the problem. Finally, he noted that the number of applicants per place in pedagogical institutes and universities had risen, albeit only slightly, from 2.2 in 1993 to 2.3 in 1994.[48]

Perhaps these developments can help to alleviate the problem, yet these arguments are not convincing. True, there will be less demand for spaces in kindergartens and primary classes in the years to come, but to ask a primary-level teacher to move into a secondary-level classroom is not at all a simple proposition. This would require a huge retraining effort, which would still not guarantee a successful transition. Further, the reliance on such unpredictable and uncontrollable phenomena as migration trends is not a sound basis for a staffing policy. With regard to the claim that an increase had taken place in applications to teacher-education establishments, it is obvious (or should be) to all in the Russian system that the important figure is not that of entrants but of those who actually go on to teach in school. Many students enter pedagogical institutes and universities with the goal of obtaining higher education, with little if any thought about the profession for which they are, ostensibly, being trained, a fact that is reflected in the figure of 40 per cent for graduates who do not go on to work in school.[49] The problem of recruitment will not go away so easily.

One result of the problem of shortages and the difficulty of attracting younger staff to work in school has been an increase in the number of retired teachers remaining or returning to the classroom. In 1995–96, for instance, pensioners made up 9.3 per cent of the total teaching force, in comparison with 7.9 per cent in 1992–1993;[50] by 1997, the figure had risen to roughly 10 per cent, and was said to be set to rise at the rate of 1 per cent annually.[51] As far as the reforms are concerned, it is likely that these older staff will not be as motivated (or able) to introduce change as their younger colleagues. In the case of the majority of these older teachers, their purpose in coming back to the schools is not, primarily, to engage in change but to supplement their meagre pension. At the same time, however, they will be able to bring their experience to bear, and are at least providing the possibility for the children to continue their studies (it was reported that at the start of the 1996–97 school year some schools remained closed because of the severity of their staffing problem).

Teachers' material problems, the trials of daily life, the perception of increased discipline problems, and the demands of reform implementation combine to weigh down the teacher, whose morale may well be sapped by such difficulties.[52] It is not surprising that a large number of teachers leave the profession each year; in 1994 the figure just for staff with higher education qualifications who had left for jobs in commerce and industry was some 34 600.[53] Those who decide to stay, willingly or unwillingly, may find that they suffer from stress-related problems. All of this reflects, of course, on teachers' capacity to work towards reform. As one teacher of chemistry in her mid-thirties noted:

> I love teaching, love working with children, and would like to be able to develop new syllabuses, new materials, new approaches. But I am so exhausted and frustrated by all of the problems around me that I simply have no energy for creative work. (Teacher, comprehensive school, interview with the author, April 1993)

The pupils: It is not that easy to be young in the New Russia

As Russia's social problems have increased, so too have rates of illness among children, with the poor environmental situation in many large industrial centres adding to such difficulties. According to figures provided by the Ministry of Education, in 1994 some 80 per cent of school pupils were afflicted by some kind of health problem, ranging from the relatively minor through to heart conditions.[54] Another source cites figures of only 14 per cent of children who are considered 'healthy', with 35 per cent categorised as being 'chronically ill'.[55] While the chief concern is clearly with the need to improve this situation for the sake of the children, such a state of affairs can only act as a detrimental factor on these pupils' ability to perform well in their school work.

Apart from physical ailments, a significant and rising proportion of children are also affected by a range of psychological problems – to a far greater extent, so Russian experts affirm, than would normally be expected in a stable society.[56] This is not surprising, given the extent of the social upheaval going on around these children, the difficulties imposed on families by economic hardship, the prevalence of crime in certain areas. Even in 1992, when some 2.4 per cent of children under the age of 14 and some 3.7 per cent of those between 14 and 18 sought or were referred for psychiatric treatment, research estimated the true figure of those requiring treatment to be some 10 times higher than this.[57] In one school in Yaroslavl', the resident educational psychologist claimed that in some classes up to 50 per cent of children displayed signs of various neuro-psychological conditions, but only a handful would be able to receive the attention they required, owing to a lack of funding for such treatment.

The amount of 'anti-social' behaviour among children has also increased, with growing numbers (some 600 000 in 1994) of young people involved in substance abuse of one kind or another,[58] such activity often leading, of course, to other problems. Criminal activity among the young has also grown, with theft seen as an answer by some children to their material problems, and violence towards other children and adults (including teachers) a disturbingly more common phenomenon.[59] Children are easy prey for the criminal community (including the so-called 'Mafia'), as victims for, say, drug-pushers, or as recruits for the criminals to use in their activities. Meanwhile, a good number of children in recent years have spent at least some of the time that they should be in school engaged in various forms of 'commercial' activity on the streets, perhaps in order to supplement their family's income or just for their own gain, often earning more in a few hours than their teacher would make in a month.

The problems endured by many young people in Russia can hardly be seen to be conducive to the promotion of democratisation and marketisation. There is a real danger that the country may be storing up so many problems that in some years' time there will be a veritable social explosion, as the young, a good number of whom feel increasingly marginalised and rejected by a society too wrapped up in its own problems,[60] reach the limit of their tolerance. With regard to the question of reform implementation in the schools, of course, there are also serious implications, for social problems of this order cannot fail to be reflected in the classroom. For some time in the early 1990s, at least, there was worried talk among teachers and others in the education system of the fall in interest that young people were showing towards schooling and the need to obtain education; the lessons of the street, where easy money could be made, seemed to be proving more enticing than the lessons of the classroom.[61]

In some ways the trials of transition affect the young perhaps most of all, for it is they who have to come to terms with the disruption in the transmission of social norms and values that transition has brought, and it is they who will have to bear the brunt of reshaping Russian society. Indeed, evidence provided by Russian colleagues suggests that the attitude of young people towards education has now recovered from the dip of the early 1990s, with greater numbers now applying for places at higher education establishments, for instance, as the young recognise that long-term employment stability is more likely to be guaranteed by qualifications.

A number of initiatives have been introduced in an attempt to provide a measure of protection for the young against the problems they face. The federal government has operated a programme entitled 'Children of Russia' (*Deti Rossii*), for instance, which was launched in accordance with Presidential Decree No. 543 of June 1, 1992, and which included a number of sub-programmes, such as 'Disabled Children', 'Orphan Children', 'Family Planning', Children of Chernobyl', 'Children of the North' and 'The Development of the Child Food Industry'.[62] Other measures have included an effort to support the continued provision of summer camps for children, to counter the trend in recent years of the contraction of the camp network (owing to the demise of the Pioneer organisation and the increased costs of running such establishments), thus denying children the opportunity traditionally afforded under the Soviet system of spending an extended period in a relatively ecologically clean environment. The Ministry of Education has sought to take a more active rôle in supporting such camps, and reported that in 1995 some 5.2 million children were accommodated in summer camps, thus reversing, albeit partially, the decline.[63]

In the schools themselves, teachers with the new specialisation of 'social pedagogue' (*sotsial'nyi pedagog*) have begun to take up posts, with the task of offering support for children (and staff) in matters concerning the personal development of pupils, thus offsetting the trend in recent times of the relative neglect of the upbringing element in Russian education. There has also been an attempt to improve the work of the educational psychology service,[64] and schools have seen an influx of educational psychologists (in some schools that I visited there were four or five resident, full-time psychologists, a figure that will seem incredible to most teachers in the UK, who are used to having to share the services of a small number of psychologists among a large number of schools). However, doubts were cast on the level of professional competence of such psychologists by the head of a centre for the 'rehabilitation' of children in Moscow, whom I interviewed in 1995. He noted that most of these staff had gained the title of psychologist after passing a 9-month training course, and could therefore by no means be seen as fully qualified. Indeed, he cited examples of incompetence among such psychologists, suggesting that the work they perform is mainly of a superficial nature (i.e. compiling statistical data on pupils from questionnaires), and that problems therefore remain untreated. This may well be true, yet one can sympathise with the authorities, who are at least trying to deal with this issue with limited resources. If they were to wait until sufficient money could be found to train psychologists adequately, then there would be even less support offered to schools in dealing with these matters.

The need for support

From the evidence provided in the preceding sections it will be clear that the task of reform faces considerable challenges, yet offers too the prospect of achieving meaningful results if the conditions are sufficiently conducive. Tackling the obstacles effectively will require the efforts not just of the education system but of society as a whole. Whether or not Russia is ready to respond to that need will be discussed in Part III; one might say that to a large extent the matter is beyond the control of the schools themselves, for they cannot hope to solve their material difficulties by themselves. Nevertheless, it is important that as much as possible is done within the system to ensure that the schools are able to approach change in as efficient a manner as they can, by providing them with a range of support measures which can both promote good practice, and serve to foster cohesion. The measures introduced to support the reforms are discussed in the next chapter.

7
Mechanisms of Cohesion and Support

The need for a comprehensive set of measures which would both ensure cohesion across the system and, it was hoped, stimulate the process of change, was recognised from the beginning of the reforms. The measures comprise:

- a core curriculum and state educational standards
- a system of inspection and advisory support
- an accreditation process for evaluating the work of schools
- a licensing programme to confer the right of a school to operate as an educational establishment
- a staff appraisal scheme.

It has taken time, naturally, to develop these mechanisms and put them into practice, with the intervening period between the decision to introduce change, and its actual appearance, giving rise to certain problems of direction and coordination. Once in place, would these measures prove to be effective in providing the schools with the framework they require?

The core curriculum and educational standards

The core curriculum (*bazisnyi uchebnyi plan*) was presented at an early stage in the reforms, published in June 1993.[1] With it the reformers hoped to move the system away from the rigidity of the old curriculum, while at the same time retaining a sufficient degree of commonality across the network.

It is divided into the so-called 'invariable' and 'variable' elements (*invariantnaya* and *variativnaya chasti*), which lay down respectively a framework for studies which are considered to be essential for all pupils, and the parameters of choice which allow schools to respond to the needs and interests of individual pupils. These two elements are presented through a combination of three types of programme:

- compulsory studies which form the basis of general secondary education
- compulsory studies in which pupils choose the nature of the programme to be followed
- optional studies.

The number of hours which can be allocated to each of the three types of programme in each form are established in the centrally designed curriculum, as Table 7.1 shows.

The responsibility for the management of the curriculum is divided, again, into three elements:

- the federal component
- ethnic-regional component
- school component.

The federal component includes those parts of the curriculum which are deemed to relate to universal cultural issues or to matters of national (state) importance, and covers Russian language, mathematics, information technology, physics and astronomy and chemistry.

The ethnic-regional component is intended to meet the particular needs of the various ethnic groups in the Russian Federation, and covers such matters as ethnic languages and literatures, and regional history and geography.

The school component, which covers both compulsory choice-based studies and optional studies, is intended to allow each individual establishment to draw on its own specific strengths to enrich the curriculum offered to pupils, within the overall framework established in the federal and ethnic-regional components.

The core curriculum was to be accompanied by sets of state educational standards (*gosudarstvennye obrazovatel'nye standarty*), which would give a detailed (yet, it was intended, non-prescriptive) guide to schools and parents of the levels of attainment that should be expected of pupils in each subject.

The initial reaction

Before the curriculum was introduced across the system, a trial period was used to give the centre, the regions and the schools an opportunity to discover its strengths and weaknesses, and suggest modifications. Further, in 1994, the Ministry of Education decided

Table 7.1 Core curriculum of the Russian school system

Area of knowledge	*Number of hours per week by form*[2]													
	I	*II*	*III*	*I*	*II*	*III*	*IV*	*V*	*VI*	*VII*	*VIII*	*IX*	*X*	*XI*
Russian language as state language	*4*	*4*	*4*	*3*	*3*	*3*	*3*	*3*	*3*	*3*	*3*	*3*	–	–
Languages and literature	4	4	4	4	4	4	4	8	8	6	5	5	4	4
Art	2	2	2	2	2	2	2	2	2	2	2	–	–	–
Social sciences								2	2	2	3	4	4	4
Natural sciences	–	1	2	2	2	2	2	2	3	6	8	8	4	4
Mathematics	5	5	5	4	4	4	4	5	5	5	4	5	3	3
Information technology	–	–	–	–	–	–	–	–	–	2	–	–	–	–
Physical education	2	2	2	2	2	2	2	2	2	2	2	2	3	3
Technology	2	2	2	2	2	2	2	2	2	2	3	3	2	2
TOTAL	19	20	21	19	19	19	19	26	27	28	30	30	20	20
Compulsory subjects, subjects chosen by pupils	5	4	3	1	3	5	5	3	3	4	2	3	12	12
Compulsory studyload of pupil	24	24	24	20	22	24	24	29	30	32	32	33	32	32
Optional, individual and group studies	2	3	3	2	3	3	3	3	3	3	3	3	6	6
TOTAL	26	27	27	22	25	27	27	32	33	35	35	36	38	38

Source: 'Bazisnyi uchebnyi plan: uspekhi i problemy', *Uchitel'skaya gazeta*, no. 31, September 30, 1996, p. 3

to hold a competition to develop the federal component of the curriculum. Five teams put forward proposals, with the winning proposal (developed by the Institute of General Education of the Russian Academy of Education) selected by a panel of experts in 1995. This proposal was then to be published for wider discussion among the country's educationalists, and further refined, before it could be adopted by the ministry for general application.[3] The curriculum and standards debate can thus be seen to be open, with time allowed for reactions from practitioners to be heeded, and a sense of dialogue cultivated.

This factor was appreciated by virtually all the teachers I interviewed, although reactions to the introduction of the core curriculum and the standards themselves have often been cautious. For some, they represented the imposition of renewed control over the work of the teacher:

> The core curriculum and educational standards are, in practice, returning the school to a system of strict regulations, in which the teacher is once again denied any initiative.[4]

Among some of my interviewees (principally older staff, i.e. above 45 years), the heritage of the Soviet school and its centrally defined curriculum appeared still to represent a certain degree of security, as the following comment suggests:

> When we had the old curricula, many of us used to grumble that Moscow did not give us any leeway in deciding what to teach and how to teach it. But I don't think we really anticipated just how difficult it would be to adapt to deciding such matters on our own. Some of us now secretly long to return to a more passive role. (Teacher of Geography, age 48, interview with the author, December 1995)

Some teachers, then, predicted that the standards would not provide a sufficiently detailed guide to the levels to be achieved by pupils, others saw them as overly prescriptive, even restrictive. For some, the standards were seen to measure only superficial indicators of a child's achievement, and did not value broader issues of 'formal intellect'.[5] It was also feared by some that the standards would be used to judge the work of teachers, thus failing to move away from the result-driven assessment of teaching that dominated in the Soviet system. So, alongside the promise that the curriculum and standards seemed to hold, there was also a good deal of anxious anticipation on the part of teachers, eager to see whether this would really signify a new approach to the organisation of the learning process, or merely a revised version of the old pattern, themes echoed in the extensive debate that has taken place in the pedagogical press over these issues.[6]

Patterns of implementation

There appears to be considerable variation in patterns of implementation across the country, with some regions already possessing several years of experience of working with their own ethnic-regional component (Moscow had already developed its component by 1991, St Petersburg brought in its component in 1993, Samara in 1993–94), while certain other regions were still considered by 1996 not to have devised a true regional component.[7] The relative state of advance at the regional level obviously affects the ability of the cities and the schools themselves to move forward in implementation (although many schools have pushed forward, nevertheless, often by 'borrowing' examples of practice from schools in neighbouring regions).

In some cases, it is reported that certain regions have ignored the 'rules' laid down by the Ministry of Education to some extent, by demanding that the schools increase the allocation of curriculum space to the ethnic-regional component, at the expense of the school component. In other cases, it is the schools themselves which have distorted the process, by introducing subjects that, as Tkachenko complained, are not to be considered as strengthening the nature of the general educational process, but are rather very 'narrow' specialisations that are based either on some 'fashionable' ideas or on the preparation of candidates for entrance to a particular higher education establishment.[8] In order to address such issues, and ensure that the adoption of the curriculum and standards move towards 'institutionalisation', an effective mechanism of inspection would be essential.

School inspection

The challenge for the Russian system would be to move away from the Soviet practice of control and sanction towards a more supportive and positive approach to school inspection, which would provide teachers with the expert advice they require, yet which would also serve to encourage system-wide cohesion and identify cases where such cohesion was likely to be compromised.

According to the Law on Education, all schools have to pass through a round of 'attestation' (*attestatsiya uchrezhdeniya*) once every five years (Articles 15, 28, 30–33 of the Law on Education). This has placed great strain on the inspection system, which has to inspect a large number of establishments with an inadequate number of inspectors, using criteria for inspection which should differ considerably from those previously employed. It is not surprising, therefore, that the results to date have been mixed. One problem, for example, stems from the fact that the inspectors are themselves only beginning to adapt to the changes that are taking place in the school system. The urgent need to provide training for inspectors to prepare them for the task of conducting school evaluation is often not met, owing to a shortage of resources (and, sometimes, a shortage of qualified staff to train the inspectors), thus adding to the problems of implementation of this system.

A fragmented pattern has also been observed as a result of the Ministry of Education's decision to allow regional and municipal authorities to develop their own procedures, which has led to inspectors in some areas using criteria and techniques which differ considerably from those used in others. In some cases, lesson observation is emphasised as a key factor in the inspection, while in others it is not even included.[9]

The introduction of alternative schools, including non-state establishments, has given rise to a need for a mechanism of accreditation and licensing. State schools are granted a licence automatically (although there may be grounds for removing this licence in extreme cases), but non-state schools have to pass through the accreditation process before they are given a licence. Without it they cannot operate as educational establishments.[10]

In those regions or cities where it is operating effectively the system can be said to be fulfilling a function of 'quality control', identifying, for example, cases where curricular guidelines are not being adhered to. Some non-state schools, for instance, have been found not to have provided pupils with the level of educational provision demanded by the Law on Education and the core curriculum, and have, as a result, been refused a licence. Often, however, the accreditation procedure suffers from similar problems to those encountered in the conduct of general attestation, with regard to the retraining of committee members to prepare them for the task, levels of diversity in the criteria used for evaluation, and so on. In some instances, municipal authorities were reported to have allowed private schools to open before they had obtained a licence,[11] while in some cases (a small minority, it would appear), bribes were used to acquire licences (information supplied by teacher in Moscow school, April 1994). This situation suggests that much refinement and revision is still needed before this can become a truly effective measure.

Staff appraisal

In the Soviet system comparatively little was done to stimulate and reward professional development over and beyond the 'norm' defined by the central authorities. Exceptional achievement (interpreted in a variety of ways) might be recognised by the award of coveted titles such as *Zasluzhennyi uchitel' RSFSR* (Honoured teacher of the RSFSR) or *Narodnyi uchitel' SSSR* (People's teacher of the USSR), yet these titles were not seen so much as incentives, but rather as a symbol of respect for a teacher's past work. This arrangement suited the nature of Soviet education well, of course, for the authorities did not want to encourage change which might lead to the initiative passing to the classroom teachers, but to control the rate of development of the schools themselves. Thus, while teacher appraisal was introduced into the Soviet school in the mid-1970s, its function was apparently perceived by many teachers and administrators to be one of supporting the overall culture of control over teachers' activities.[12] In the new Russian school, as one might expect, a different approach would be required.

Staff appraisal is seen as a multi-purpose mechanism, that allows the authorities to introduce greater clarity and order into the organisation of teachers' salaries, while also serving to promote, recognise and reward professional development. The end result, it was hoped, would be the adoption by the teaching profession of a positive attitude to change, encouraged by the tangible personal benefits that their efforts might bring. With regard to salaries, for instance, the teaching profession (in common with other professions) has moved onto a system of scales (*razryady*), which determine the teacher's salary status. The scale runs from the 1st to 14th *razryady*, with teachers automatically entering the scale at point 7 upon joining the profession. This scale is in turn linked to the common salary network (*edinaya tarifnaya setka*), introduced in 1993, which is supposed to guarantee stability and commonality in salary allocations across the country. Teachers progress through the scale from the 7th to the 11th point according to number of years served or position held.

The final three points on the scale, however, are reserved for 'categories' (12th point = 2nd category; 13th = 1st category; 14th = higher category), which are awarded to staff who are deemed to have reached a particular level of professional achievement. Advancement through the lower scales (7th to 11th) is more or less automatic, but the attainment of a category requires considerably more effort on the part of the teacher. It is with these categories that the system of teacher appraisal is principally concerned. While it will often be the older, more experienced teachers who apply for a category, the option is also open to younger staff, in order to stimulate change at all levels in the profession. Each category is assessed by an expert commission, which has a different composition according to the level being appraised. For the 2nd category the commission is drawn from the senior staff of the teacher's own school; for the 1st, a district-level commission is appointed, with, for example, *metodisty* as members; while for the higher category the 'chief appraisal commission' is called in, with representatives from the municipal, or even regional authority.[13] As with the other mechanisms of cohesion and control covered thus far in this chapter, the teacher-appraisal scheme is a complex and ambitious measure. How would it be received by those it was intended both to assess and to assist?

Not surprisingly, many teachers were apprehensive about the implications that appraisal held. In the Soviet system, teacher appraisal was conducted in a situation of far greater stability, in which one was rewarded for *not* being innovative, but instead for abiding by the rules and teaching as one was meant to. Now, teachers are being asked to introduce wide-ranging change into the curriculum, to adapt their teaching methods, to devise new materials, to adopt a different attitude to teacher–pupil relations – in short, to effect a transformation in their professional lives. With the onset of appraisal, it seemed that they were to be assessed against these new criteria, an unsettling prospect.

It was not a surprise to see that in my interviews with teachers and in my questionnaire survey, responses can be divided according to age groups, with younger staff displaying more support for the concept of appraisal than their older colleagues. In the questionnaire survey, for instance, the majority of staff below the age of 35 stated that appraisal was 'very necessary' or 'necessary' (28.7 per cent and 33.4 per cent), with only 9.6 per cent seeing it as 'completely unnecessary', while the corresponding figures for those over the age of 35 were 6.8 per cent, 22.3 per cent and 38.6 per cent respectively. These results support the impression gained in interviews with teaching staff. Such a situation is quite natural. The task of adapting one's approach to fit in with the new ideas of the reform agenda is more difficult for the more experienced staff, who have been used to working according to another pattern for many years. While in the old system they may have expected to receive due recognition of their seniority, now they find that they are being assessed in skills that may be very new to them, and in which younger staff may hold an advantage, since they may be able to adjust to the new demands more quickly.

The teams of inspectors assigned to conduct appraisal need to show a considerable amount of subtlety and understanding when working with older members of staff, in order not to damage the sense of professional esteem of the latter group. Simultaneously, they must ensure that the work of all teachers, including those not in senior positions, and in particular the younger staff, is encouraged and recognised appropriately. It is difficult enough to recruit and retain young teachers to work in the schools at present; once they have entered the profession, everything possible should be done to persuade them to remain in teaching.

As might be expected with the introduction on a nationwide basis of a complex scheme which marks a significant innovation in the life of the school, there have been a number of 'teething problems' associated with appraisal. The test for the system lies in its ability to react to these problems, and also in the extent to which such problems are seen as minor drawbacks or major flaws in the concepts being employed.

Once the scheme is fully in operation, of course, the appraisal load will settle down and be evenly distributed, yet in these early stages the demand for appraisal has exceeded the capacity of the system to provide it. This problem is exacerbated by the complexity of the appraisal procedure; the Russian system has gone from having almost no formal appraisal scheme to introducing one that is extremely thorough; indeed, it is more thorough, I would suggest, than that found in the English and Welsh system. As Table 7.2 shows, the procedure is time-consuming, both for the appraisee and

Table 7.2 Outline of teacher-appraisal procedure (by category)

Typical forms of assessment	*Higher*	*First*	*Second*
Analysis of documentation	2 hours	1 hour	–
Observation of professional activity	6 hours	4 hours	–
Analysis of communicative culture	2 hours	2 hours	2 hours
Analysis of the educational outcomes of tests, continuous assessment, etc.	4 hours	2 hours	2 hours
Discussion	1 hour	1 hour	1 hour
TOTAL	15 hours	10 hours	5 hours

Source: *Attestatsiya pedagogicheskikh i rukovodyashchikh rabotnikov gosudarstvennykh, munitsipal'nykh uchrezhdenii i organizatsii obrazovaniya Rossiiskoi Federatsii: Sbornik dokumentov Ministerstva obrazovaniya Rossiiskoi Federatsii–vypusk 2* (Moscow: Ministerstvo obrazovaniya Rossiiskoi Federatsii, 1994), p. 23

the commission, with the former obliged to submit examples of his or her teaching materials, descriptions of innovations introduced in methodology, and other forms of evidence, which must then be scrutinised by the commission. The complexity of the procedure and the demands it makes on a system with limited resources have contributed to further problems, which suggests that streamlining will be required if the scheme is to prove effective yet manageable.

A frequent complaint from teachers has been that the members of the appraisal commission did not appear to be sufficiently well-qualified to conduct the process, thus putting the appraisee at a disadvantage and disrupting the pattern of appraisal across the system.[14] To some extent this is unavoidable; the appraisers' experience is similar to that of those being appraised, for all have had to come to terms with the nature of reform in the system, and few have been able to effect a rapid and effective transition to meet the requirements of the change agenda in education. Yet this begs the question – why was it decided to rush into implementation before those charged with introducing the procedure were ready?

The problem has, of course, been recognised by many regions, which have emphasised the pressing need to provide training for appraisers, but financial limitations act as a severe restriction on the amount of provision that can be offered. Meanwhile, the inexperience of commission members has compounded problems concerning the interpretation of the criteria that are to be used in the appraisal.

The guidelines for the conduct of appraisals and the criteria to be employed in assessment are both complex and thorough, yet contain an element of vagueness with regard to the interpretation of certain aspects of the culture of teaching (especially with regard to such 'novel' concepts as the need for humanisation). This mixture of complicated procedure and ambiguity make the task of conducting appraisal difficult, of course, with the problem compounded by the relative inexperience of the assessors, as noted earlier. As a result, there can be a good deal of variation in the approach adopted by commissions, and the standards they apply when assessing appraisees. A commission whose members have a good understanding of the principles underlying the reform agenda will be likely to give a significantly different type of appraisal than one whose members remain somewhat unsure of the meaning of such concepts as 'humanitarisation' or 'differentiation.' Some appraisals, therefore, are conducted in accordance with the policies of the post-Soviet reform era, others are based more on an approach that targets teaching qualities that were stressed under the Soviet system.[15]

That the old system's values are being used as criteria is not bad in itself, of course, for it has yet to be shown that the new policies are necessarily better than those they are designed to replace. Indeed, the inertia that such cases illustrate serves to bridge the gap, to some extent, between old and new. Rather, the major problem that such divergence creates is that of disharmony and a lack of consistency in the conduct of appraisal. While one candidate may be required to produce a comprehensive account of the significance of introducing differentiation in the teaching of a class, including a review of the research background of this topic and the implications that the innovation holds for methodological and resources issues, a counterpart elsewhere may be required to provide a much less detailed account, or may advance a much weaker argument, yet both may be awarded the same category, just one example of what appears to be a common occurrence of variation in appraisal procedures.[16]

Questions have also been raised with regard both to problems of subjectivity and the danger of personal relations interfering with the process, and with regard to the lack of knowledge that the commission may have about the candidate. In the case of the second category appraisal, for instance, which is conducted internally in the school, there is potential for the personal relationship between the appraisee and the members of the commission to influence the outcome of the appraisal (a problem that has been noted in the system employed in England and Wales, too, where in-house appraisal is used). This risk is somewhat diminished in the first category appraisal, which includes district-level representatives, yet the scope for transferring the second category to this arrangement is probably out of the question, given the resource implications that this would hold. The higher category appraisal, however, has been criticised for the comparative lack of familiarity of the commission with the appraisee, who is judged on the basis of the materials viewed and interviews held in the course of one day, a situation that does not, some teachers argue, allow them to show their true abilities to the appraisal team.

Finally, the results of appraisal have drawn attention to a number of issues concerning finances and the salaries of teachers. In some schools, for instance, it was felt that the best way of approaching appraisal was to award categories to as many staff as possible, as this would have the effect of demonstrating the school's potential for innovation and high-quality educational provision. Unfortunately, in many cases this move proved to be a mistake, for the award of a category brings an automatic salary increase, with which these schools and their local authority were then burdened.

At the same time, it was pointed out by many teachers that the actual advantage in salary terms held by a teacher with a higher category over a colleague with no category is not that great, thus removing the potential financial incentive that teachers might have looked for when deciding whether to make the effort to prepare for appraisal.[17] This matter, however, as with all questions concerning salaries, remains out of the hands of the educational authorities to a large extent.

Despite the problems, however, in those cases where the conditions have been right, teacher appraisal has achieved impressive results. A *metodist* involved in first category appraisal recounted, for instance, that:

> Appraisal has allowed us to take a more positive view of the need for change, change at the personal level, within one's own classroom. Despite the early uncertainty, most teachers whom we have appraised have stated that they felt the experience to be rewarding, and that it is a fair way to assess the work of the profession. (*Metodist*, St Petersburg, interview with the author, December 1995)

This view was endorsed by a teacher of biology who had recently gained the first category:

> The preparation for appraisal was exhausting, but all the effort has paid off, and I feel that I am a better teacher for it. It has made me focus on a variety of factors, and increase my theoretical understanding of the teaching process, as well as develop a better understanding of the needs of my pupils. (Teacher, *gimnaziya*, interview with the author, December 1995)

On a broader scale, in those areas where appraisal has proceeded effectively and has been well received by teachers, there has been a noticeable increase in the demand for in-service training and support from advisory services, and in applications from teachers wishing to enroll on postgraduate courses on aspects of educational studies.[18] Appraisal can thus be seen to be promoting ongoing professional development, and acting as a stimulus for innovation as staff see the value, both professional and material (despite the problems mentioned earlier) of furthering their theoretical and practical knowledge of their classroom skills. The scheme is contributing, as a result, to the establishment of a culture of change 'agentry' that is so essential to the long-term prospects of development in the school system as a whole.[19] The future progress of the appraisal scheme will depend on the resources that are allocated to it.

Revision of the examinations system?

The traditional pattern of examinations and assessment in the Soviet/Russian school system was based on oral assessment, with relatively little emphasis given to written assessment procedures. While the continuous nature of assessment in the school did have advantages (e.g. in reducing the amount of pressure on pupils seen in, for example, the English system's traditional preference for assessment to be based on end-of-school examination results), the fact that teachers, in the Soviet system, assessed their own pupils for the most part, and that no recordings were made of the oral examinations, clearly had implications for the level of objectivity and commonality that it was possible to achieve.

The urgent need to reform this model was quickly recognised in certain other post-communist countries, such as Poland, which had operated an assessment system very similar to that seen in the Soviet

Union. The Polish system, for instance, began work on the development of a new examinations system soon after the fall of the communist regime (personal communication with officials of the Polish Ministry of Education, 1994). In Russia, however, relatively little attention was paid to the need to reform the assessment system in the early 1990s. There were isolated attempts in certain regions to introduce written examinations, to be assessed by a centralised group of examiners, yet such localised approaches could not offer to solve the problem of system-wide cohesion as a whole. Meanwhile, at the level of the Ministry of Education some concern was expressed regarding the need to tackle the question of assessment, but no concrete proposals were forthcoming for some time.[20]

By the late 1990s, however, the Russian system had also started to devote more attention to these matters, and a set of measures was introduced with the apparent aim of moving to a national 'centralised' system of examinations, in which commonality of procedures and content would be stressed, and in which written assessment would be given a greater emphasis.[21] By 1998 schools were already beginning to operate according to the revised assessment procedures,[22] and although, as might be expected, certain problems were encountered and a degree of resistance and uncertainty was being expressed by teachers,[23] the innovation appeared to get off to a mostly positive start. Of course, the introduction of a truly nationwide examination system, to a level of complexity seen in Western countries, will prove be a costly venture, placing an additional strain on the already stretched resources of the system, and will also demand yet another adjustment to be made in the professional culture of the teaching force (and, indeed, in the way that students, parents and employers view the meaning of qualifications). Such developments do promise, though, to lend additional support to the overall goal of ensuring commonality and cohesion across the system, while also bringing Russian educational policy into line with international practice. A national examinations system which includes objective assessment of candidates would improve the degree of comparability among school-leavers, thus providing a more accurate picture of educational attainment across the country, and would also allow for a more flexible system of entrance to further and higher education, moving away from the current targeted approach of having to pass entrance examinations to individual establishments.

Research in education and the dissemination of experience

Educational research is still recovering from the legacy of the Soviet era, in which the conservative Academy of Pedagogical Sciences held a virtual monopoly over the conduct and dissemination of research. The APN was succeeded by the Russian Academy of Education (*Rossiiskaya Akademiya Obrazovaniya* or RAO), which includes in its ranks the most prominent figures of the reform movement, and which, far from discouraging innovative activity, actively supports it through its own network of research institutes, which it inherited from the APN, and whose number has swelled in the post-Soviet period.[24] They include, for instance: the Institute for Pedagogical Innovations, formerly VNIK–Shkola; the Moscow Institute for the Development of Educational Systems (MIROS); the Moscow Academy for the Development of Education (MARO); the Institute of Theoretical Pedagogy and International Research in Education, and many others, based predominantly in Moscow.

These institutes, and researchers from higher education establishments across the country, have turned increasingly in recent years to the development of classroom-based research with a greater accent on practical application than was previously the case, thus taking advantage of the new possibilities afforded after the abandonment of ideological constraints on such activity. Further, as innovative practice has progressed in a good number of schools across the country, teachers themselves have become actively engaged in the conduct of research.[25] This work needs to be coordinated and systematised, in order that support may be provided to researchers, communication fostered within the academic community, dissemination facilitated and excessive overlap avoided, yet such organisational capacity remains beyond the scope of the Russian system for the time being, as resources for research suffer from the same constraints as education in general. Research funding, for instance, is severely limited, and opportunities for publication and dissemination of research findings, while they exist, have also contracted as a result of the crisis in educational publishing.

There are positive signs, however, from the teacher-education establishments, which appear to be placing far greater emphasis on educational research than was ever the case in the past.[26] In the Soviet system, the pedagogical faculties of the pedagogical institutes were severely restricted in the nature of work that could be conducted, given the requirements to follow a Marxist-Leninist interpretation of education and the desire of the APN to maintain a stranglehold on research in this field. Now, in contrast, many pedagogical institutes and pedagogical universities are attempting to develop their research profile in education. Novgorod State University, for instance, formed on the basis of a pedagogical institute and a number of technical institutes, has a faculty of continuing pedagogical education which engages in a range of educational research aimed at supporting the school system of the region. A good number of pedagogical VUZy maintain close links with local schools, perhaps even with access to an 'experimental site' in one particular school where innovative work can be closely monitored. Further, many teacher-education courses now appear to be moving from a 5-year model leading to the *diplom* (the qualification obtained on completion of higher education) to a '4 + 2' model of a Bachelor's level degree (*bakalavreat*) after four years, and an optional 2-year course leading to a Master's degree (*magistratura*), which includes a far greater element of research work. It is hoped that practising teachers will be encouraged to take advantage of opportunities to register on Master's courses, either full- or part-time.

These are encouraging developments for the system, for they offer to build up the research base of the system at the grassroots level, and thus create a larger pool of investigation and data which the school system can draw on to inform its approach to reform and other matters. Much remains to be done, of course. The pedagogical faculties are only slowly adapting to the changed circumstances and the potential for research that they open up, while the pedagogical universities themselves often remain to be convinced that educational research is an area that they should treat as a priority. Meanwhile, the scholars are still in desperate need of the support of the academic community, to provide a more substantial framework within which to proceed with the reforms.

8
Teacher Education: Questions of Quality and Quantity

If teachers are to understand and support the aims of change, then they must be equipped with the knowledge and skills necessary to effect implementation; furthermore, it would seem to be logical to conduct this process of training and re-training well in advance of the actual launch of such changes in the classroom.[1] In many countries, however, teacher education is often not seen as a priority, with due consequences for the development of the school, the career experience of teachers, and the progress of reform and innovation.[2] The Soviet Union was no exception, with the teacher-education (teacher-training) system suffering from a lack of investment and recognition of its importance.[3] This legacy has meant that in the post-Soviet period the teacher-education network, instead of leading the way for change, struggled in the early 1990s to keep pace with developments in the schools, with due implications for the prospects of system-wide reform across the school network.

A 'new' model of teacher?

According to the rhetoric of the reform agenda, the Russian school needs a 'new' type of teacher, a *pedagog*, who is capable of reacting to the educational needs of his or her pupils and drawing on a range of pedagogical skills, to replace the traditional *uchitel'-ispolnitel'* or teacher-fulfiller, who saw his or her task as the transmission of knowledge according to the curriculum. Achieving such a transformation in the professional culture of the teaching force, whether through remedial or constructive measures, however, is far from simple. Indeed, an attempt to do so may cause more damage than good, if the process is not managed properly. The task is perhaps easier in the case of new entrants to the profession, if initial training patterns have been suitably amended. The rate at which such new entrants will replace older staff, and thus bring in new approaches which they have had from the start of their careers, will be limited, and this process may well be slowed down further by the fact, referred to earlier, that only half of those trained go on to teach, and many subsequently leave the profession. Instead, as was noted earlier, a process of 'ageing' is occurring, with considerable numbers of teachers of post-retirement age continuing to work in the schools. It is very difficult for a teacher who has worked according to one pattern for many years suddenly to change his or her approach, or even educational philosophy, and adopt the guise of a new model of teacher. The authorities would need to work with these senior staff and assist them in adjusting to the changes.

Reform of the system, however, was seen as desirable by many teachers, judging by the results of surveys conducted in recent years. In one survey conducted in 1989, for instance, 83.6 per cent of respondents stated that they were not content with the quality of the initial teacher education they had received,[4] while a 1992 study of teachers in Moscow found that 85 per cent of respondents complained that course content had not been brought up to date, and thus did not reflect the needs of teachers faced with the prospect of introducing radical change into the system.[5] In the following sections an evaluation is made of the response made by the system since the early 1990s, beginning with a review of in-service training (INSET) provision.

In-service training: coping with demand?

Soviet teachers were entitled to receive comprehensive in-service training only once every five years, the training lasting one school term, with this provision offered by the local INSET centre, at an Institute for the Advanced Training of Teachers (*Institut Usovershenstvovaniya Uchitelei* – IUU) or at an Institute for the Raising of Qualifications (*Institut Povysheniya Kvalifikatsii* – IPK). Teachers complained that the system was too inflexible, that the interval of five years between retraining was far too long, that there were few or no incentives for teachers to attend such courses.[6] Instead, they argued, they required a range of short-duration courses that would target specific issues of direct relevance to the teachers' classroom experience.

As the momentum for change grew in the late 1980s, changes did begin to occur in the nature of INSET provision, with such innovators as V. Shatalov of Donetsk running training sessions which were attended by teachers from across the USSR, while growing numbers of INSET institutes themselves began to offer a greater variety of programmes. The system as a whole, however, was slow to react, and demand far outstripped the supply of training sought by the teaching force.

Changes have occurred both in the structure of the INSET sector, and in the nature and content of the courses provided. Many IUUs and IPKs, for instance, have embarked upon a process of apparently substantial reorganisation, some changing their titles to, say, University of Pedagogical Mastery (*Universitet pedagogicheskogo masterstva* – UPM), in an attempt to reflect the changes and the new functions that they now claim to perform, such as combining their in-service activities with the development of a profile in educational research.[7]

The extent to which such changes represent real transformation rather than superficial adaptation varies, of course. In the UPM in St Petersburg an impressive range of courses of various length is offered to teachers, who professed to being very pleased, on the whole, with the quality of the service provided. In other cities, staff complained that their IUU had not changed at all. Nevertheless, as positive experience continues to accumulate in other cities and regions, those IUUs that have proved more reluctant or less able to change will find that the demands of their 'clients' will force change upon them anyway. The INSET sector now contains, after all, an element of competition, with independent providers having entered the market, along with innovative schools offering to pass on experience.[8]

The problem now is not so much one of the type of courses provided, for there appears to be a wide choice available, at least in the major cities, but one of access to these courses. The fees charged by the alternative providers in particular place their courses beyond the reach of many teachers. The introduction of a voucher scheme in Samara, under which the educational authorities give schools vouchers for a certain value, and which the schools can then use to purchase courses from providers of their choice, goes some way to responding to this problem,[9] yet there is still a limit to the resources available, even if their distribution is made more efficient. Many teachers, consequently, continue to have little meaningful access to the kind of INSET provision that they so desperately need, a fact that has important implications for the reform process, for provision can only be effective when it is received by sufficient numbers of teachers. As might be expected, the problem is most acutely felt by teachers in rural areas, whose schools are likely to be less well-off in financial terms than many town schools, and for whom travelling to courses, even in the nearest centre, can be fraught with difficulties.

To some extent the problem of access is compensated by the increased activities of *metodisty*, acting in an advisory capacity, and teachers' centres (*metodicheskie tsentry*). Where the system is working efficiently and has sufficient funds, there will often be a *metodist* for each curricular subject or area, for instance, who will travel around the schools in their district to provide support for staff in developing curricular approaches, monitoring the induction of NQTs, and helping staff to prepare for appraisals. On a broader scale, teams of *metodisty* may also be involved in the development of school-wide plans of action, in collaboration with the headteacher and senior staff of the school.

Initial teacher education: the problems of the old system

The problems of initial training revolve around two interrelated issues – quality and quantity, the former concerning the content of the training provided to the future teachers, and its relevance to the realities of the modern Russian classroom, the latter referring to the difficulty of recruitment and retention of teachers. The roots of these problems lie in the drawbacks of the Soviet system.

In the later years of the Soviet system, the vast majority of secondary-level teachers (90 per cent) were trained on 4- or 5-year courses in a pedagogical institute (*pedagogicheskii institut*, or *pedinstitut*), which had higher education status, with the remainder coming from universities, whose courses included a compulsory element of teacher training. From 1985, students wishing to teach at primary level were able to follow a higher education course in a pedagogical institute, although the principal route for primary-level teachers remained a 3-year course in a pedagogical college (*pedagogicheskoe uchilishche*, or *peduchilishche*), where they received a secondary-specialised education qualification (i.e. *not* higher education). From the late 1970s onwards, an element of teacher training was also available in certain secondary schools, which organised a 'pedagogical class' (*pedagogicheskii klass* or *pedklass*) for pupils in the senior grades. Some of these pupils would go on to study in a *pedinstitut* or a *peduchilishche*.

The teaching force comprised a mixture, therefore, of teachers who had received higher education and those who had not; despite a steady increase in the numbers of the former group over the years, the proportion of those who did not have higher education was still large enough by the mid-1990s to be spoken of with concern by figures in the educational establishment. (Some 74 per cent of teachers have a higher education degree, while 22 per cent graduated from a *peduchilishche* with a secondary-specialised education qualification, and 1 per cent received only general secondary education.)[10]

If the Soviet education system was funded under the 'leftover principle' (*ostatochnyi printsip*), then teacher education was usually allocated what remained of the leftovers. Teacher-education establishments lacked the material base and support from industry that many technical institutes enjoyed, and lacked too the prestige of the university sector. Despite attempts to remedy the situation during the *perestroika* years (for example through experiments with financial self-management, and a scheme of 'selling' graduates to commercial organisations) the network was still gripped by financial difficulties as the post-Soviet era began, a situation which would become worse as the transition to the 'market economy' progressed.[11]

The teacher-education curriculum, in common with the curriculum of all educational establishments in the USSR, was centrally controlled, thus ensuring a high degree of commonality across the country, and restricting severely the amount of individual initiative that could be practised by lecturers in adapting courses to meet the needs of their current cohort of students, or indeed the needs of their city or region. Some attempts to break away from this pattern were made in the late 1980s, but the result in practice was that little change took place; pedagogical institutes received the right to manage only 15 per cent of the curriculum independently, and then only after gaining permission from the central authorities.

A review of the curriculum itself gives an indication of the lack of emphasis placed on the 'pedagogical-psychological cycle' (i.e. that part of the course devoted to teacher education), which over the years consistently lost more and more of its share of the timetable to the so-called 'specialised subjects' (i.e. the disciplines that students were ostensibly being trained to teach in the schools) and the compulsory 'social science' subjects (such as 'Scientific Communism', 'Marxist-Leninist Philosophy' and the 'History of the CPSU'). The specialised subjects came to comprise between 60 per cent and 70 per cent of the overall timetable, while pedagogy was given fewer hours than the social-science cycle, and fewer even than the total hours for the subsidiary subjects (such as military training for male students or medical training as military reserve nurses for female students).[12] The view taken by the authorities was that, since the school curriculum and the methods to be used for its delivery were predetermined, there was not such a great need for Soviet teachers to develop their skills as all-round educationalists. The pedagogical cycle itself was biased towards theory, and contained relatively little practical knowledge or opportunity to develop ideas through practical experience of such matters as classroom management. As a result, there was considerable dissatisfaction among headteachers with the level of preparedness of graduates for coping with the practical demands of teaching upon completing their training.[13] In this regard, the training provided by the *peduchilishche* was often of greater use to its students, who were able to receive a better grounding in practical issues concerning teaching, a reflection of the fact that a higher proportion of the staff of these establishments had come from school-teaching backgrounds, in contrast to the *pedinstitut* staff, many of whom had only experience of working in higher education.

Apart from the questions of quality there was the eternal problem for Soviet and Russian education of teacher shortages and the unpopularity of the teaching profession among the young. The fact that the problem continued to be such a thorn in the side of the system, with its legacy extending into the Russian period, can be explained to a large extent by the unwillingness of the authorities to accept the true causes of the issue. Rather than attempt to deal with such matters, the Soviet system sought both to blame the student body for its lack of commitment, and to engage in cosmetic change that was bound to achieve little, while leaving the roots of the problem unaddressed. As with so much else in Soviet society, the problem revolved around a dichotomy between the declared aims of the state and the personal decisions of the individual, and the subsequent inability of the system to adjust to such realities.

The Soviet teacher-education system was designed to operate in the conditions of a centrally planned economy, in which specialised-secondary and higher educational establishments were, for the most part, tasked with the preparation of graduates to work in specific professions. Consequently, the authorities in Moscow decided how many teachers they needed, and directed the pedagogical institutes and colleges to oblige. To ensure control over the direction of newly qualified teachers a system of 'distribution' (*raspredelenie*) operated, under which NQTs were assigned to a school, often in a rural area, for three years. In practice, graduates often managed to find a way to avoid this obligation, for example through marriage. The reality was that many entrants, from the very start of their studies, had little or no intention of going on to teach in school. Instead, they were more likely to see this route merely as a means of gaining higher education *per se*, with the *pedinstitut* acting as a surrogate university for many Soviet students.[14] Indeed, the choice of *pedinstitut* was often made on the basis of the availability of suitable higher education establishments in their town or region – in many cases the *pedinstitut* would be the only institution to offer programmes that the student wished to follow.[15]

Despite the introduction, during the late Soviet period, of such initiatives as preferential entrance procedures for teacher-training applicants from rural areas (in an attempt to address the acute problem of attracting and retaining village teachers), and the ongoing practice of running 'pedagogical classes' in the senior grades of secondary schools, in the hope of winning young people over to the teaching profession early, the crisis of recruitment remains unresolved.

To a large extent the unattractiveness of teaching can be explained by the material weakness of the profession. For the most part, however, the linkage between salaries and conditions and the question of recruitment and retention was not admitted by the authorities, an oversight that is still present in the Russian system, and which continues to deny the schools the ability to attract greater numbers of motivated, talented staff.

However, while the education system could not have been expected to tackle the issue of low salaries by itself, the introduction of certain internal changes could have had an effect on the system's ability to counter the problem of teacher shortages. The system was also restricted by its inflexibility. No short-duration teacher-training courses were offered at the postgraduate level, to cater for those who may have thought about a teaching career only after having completed their general higher education, or indeed who wished to transfer from another profession, while within the system itself, *peduchilishche* graduates who wished to gain higher education in a pedagogical institute would have to repeat much of the material from their earlier course, since the system was not designed to meet the needs of such students. In the post-Soviet era, with the distribution system abandoned and a wider choice of careers, often better paid than teaching, available to those seeking employment, the task of persuading young people to enter teaching would be harder than ever. The Soviet tradition of organising higher education according to the type of profession which establishments were preparing graduates for would, it seemed, need to be replaced by a more flexible approach of general university-style education, with the prerogative in the choice of professions now shifting to the student, who would decide upon graduation, rather than on leaving school, which career to opt for. Would the new Russian system be able to tackle these issues effectively?

Responding to change? The initial teacher-education network

The trend in the early years of the reforms at least was to *strengthen* existing patterns of organisation, rather than embark upon real change in the structure of the network. In the teacher-education system, as in Russian society as a whole, and indeed in the school system itself, there has been a wave of renaming of pedagogical establishments over recent years. Table 8.1 shows, in the left-hand column, the titles of teacher-education establishments found in the Soviet system (titles which were still retained by some establishments in the late 1990s); in the right-hand column, a list of 'new' titles is given, with pedagogical institutes having been 'transformed' into pedagogical universities in many cases, for instance. The procedure of renaming involves a process of assessment by a team appointed by the Ministry of Education, which is supposed to conduct a rigorous appraisal of the establishment's current and potential capacity to meet the required criteria, although in practice, according to Russian contacts, the application of these criteria can vary considerably.

As at the school level, of course, it is one thing to change an establishment's name, quite another to bring about real change in the running of that establishment. Some pedagogical universities and colleges display a high level of resolve to bring about real change,

Table 8.1 The Russian initial teacher-education network

Existing system (Soviet model)	*'New' establishments*
A. Higher education	
Pedagogical institute (*Pedagogicheskii institut*)	International pedagogical university (*Mezhdunarodnyi pedagogicheskii universitet*)
University	Regional pedagogical university (*Regional'nyi pedagogicheskii universitet*)
	Pedagogical university (*Pedagogicheskii universitet*)
B. Secondary-specialised education	
Pedagogical college (*Pedagogicheskoe uchilishche*)	Pedagogical college (*Pedagogicheskii kolledzh*)
C. Secondary education	
Pedagogical class in X and XI grades in certain secondary schools (*Pedagogicheskii klass*)	Pedagogical lycée (*Pedagogicheskii litsei*)
	Pedagogical gymnasium (*Pedagogicheskaya gimnaziya*)

having instituted development plans and, importantly, addressing the key issue of staff training. The regional pedagogical university initiative, too, appears to have been pursued in a constructive manner that promises to render such establishments a valuable tool for the regions as they develop their own economic and social potential. In other cases, establishments appear content to pay lip-service to the slogans of reform. The results of these efforts should begin to emerge in the next few years. It is significant, however, that a number of such new universities seem to be playing down the importance of the word 'pedagogical' in their title, seeking instead to expand the general university element of their mission, with due implications for teacher supply, should the pedagogical universities decide to reduce their teacher-training activities further.

Over recent years a considerable amount of attention has been paid to increasing the coherence of the system by addressing the need to establish continuity in provision.[16] Pedagogical institutes and universities are actively developing collaborative programmes with pedagogical colleges, lycées, and gymnasia, to facilitate, among other goals, the transfer of 'credit' for education received at one level to a higher level within the system, building on earlier experience of experiments which brought together various establishments.[17] While such initiatives promise to increase the effectiveness of the system, it is important that attention is paid not just to the redefining of vertical links between establishments at various levels, but also of horizontal communication across the network. A degree of commonality in the teacher-education system in the country as a whole can help to offset the danger of fragmentation that has been mentioned frequently in this study. Indeed, the central authorities have made an attempt to control this situation with the introduction of a set of standards for teacher education, which are designed to establish a framework for the development of the system, along the same lines as the standards used at school level, while still allowing the network to retain and exploit the freedom it has received to introduce new approaches and courses. Ultimately, however, it will be the responsibility of individual rectors to ensure that fragmentation does not occur.

The regional pedagogical university initiative is part of a broader effort to adapt the content of teacher education to the educational, cultural and economic requirements of its local region. With regard to teacher supply, this should facilitate a more flexible and quicker response to local need, with regional authorities better placed to assess that need than the centre in Moscow. However, along with such benefits the drive towards decentralisation has exacerbated the teacher-education network's perennial problem of financing.

The 'regionalisation' of the financing of education has meant that a good deal of the responsibility for funding teacher education has been passed to the regions, an issue taken very seriously by the Ministry of Education, which opposed the measure, warning that this could lead to the collapse of the entire educational network in Russia.[18] In an attempt to counter such moves, the Ministry of Education has suggested the possibility for teacher-education establishments to come under the joint auspices of federal and regional authorities, and thus establish a clearer framework of responsibilities for financing from both levels.[19] Meanwhile, establishments have been encouraged to look for other means of supplementing their income. Some are reorientating a proportion of their courses towards the commercial sector and/or offering courses to the public, others have sold off or rented out buildings. Another source of revenue comes from the introduction of a 'contract' system (*kontraktnaya sistema*) for students, as a successor to the 'agreement' scheme (*dogovornaya sistema*) that was brought in during the last years of the Soviet era, and under which students were supposed to sign an agreement with a sponsoring organisation at the start of their studies. The intention was that the organisation (commercial or educational) would then pay for a proportion of the student's course, with the student subsequently obliged to work for his or her sponsor for a specified period on graduation (thus replacing the unpopular distribution system). Even if such a scheme is effective, however, it is not clear how it will benefit the schools, which will still be unable to sponsor students (unless they themselves receive a funding allocation from the cash-strapped education authorities).

While such measures may bring some relief for the financial position of teacher-education establishments, they will not provide a complete solution. The system needs a large amount of investment simply in order to survive, not to mention the implementation of wide-scale changes in the curriculum and the pressing need for retraining lecturers. There is one possible way out, but it is one that many establishments have not, to date, found appealing.

The idea of mergers, under which pedagogical institutes would join with other higher education establishments in that city or town to form a general university, was aired in the early 1990s, but has proved to be a matter which many teacher-education establishments have preferred to ignore, despite the fact that mergers would mean that pedagogical institutes and universities would gain access to the facilities of better-equipped former technical institutes, and staff resources could be shared, with benefits for teaching and research. A large university of this kind would also be in a stronger position to attract funding from state and commercial sources.

The concept of mergers, however, while attractive to some, is not so welcome to administrators in the institutes concerned, particularly in the smaller establishments, who feel that their institutes would be 'swallowed' up and their posts threatened, a possibility that the administrators are not keen to contemplate. Opposition is particularly strong from institutes which have renamed themselves as pedagogical universities – they would see their 'gains' turned into losses by such a move. Some pedagogical institutes, though, have decided to throw caution to the winds and merge with others. The institute in Novgorod, for instance, merged with a large technical institute in 1994.[20] Teacher-education courses are now offered in a separate faculty within the larger university, and early results are encouraging, according to staff accounts. Given the ongoing problems of funding, other teacher-education establishments may have no choice other than to follow a similar path.

Course organisation

This need seems now to have been recognised, as the nature of course provision is set to undergo fundamental revision. Under the proposed modifications, the old 5-year course model is to be retained, while two further patterns of training are to be phased in: a 4-year course leading to the qualification of bachelor (*bakalavr*), with a further two years of study to gain the degree of master (*magistr*); and a 1-year training course at post-graduate level. These ideas have been under development for some time, and a number of establishments have begun to implement them more fully.[21] The Herzen Pedagogical University in Saint Petersburg, for instance, now offers a so-called 2 + 2 option for the *bakalavr* degree, with students taking a 2-year foundation course before choosing a 'major' subject for the remainder of the course.

The introduction of short courses means, at last, that the selection of a career in teaching will be possible at the postgraduate level, when students are able to make a more reasoned choice. This offers greater flexibility in career development for the individual, while the authorities will be able to respond more rapidly to changing staffing needs. It is likely, too, that the retention rate of NQTs in the schools will be higher. There is considerable disquiet, however, among many teacher-education lecturers who feel that a 1-year course is insufficient to provide a high-quality foundation for novice teachers. To highlight the problem, they refer to the recently introduced 9-month courses being operated to train school psychologists, a measure that has proved effective at producing an abundance of staff, but not at ensuring their quality. One lecturer told me that, far from reducing the training period, it should be *increased* to six years, the minimum period needed, in her opinion, to prepare a teacher.

Such attitudes reflect the influence of old thinking in Russian education, where the idea of 'quantity' of education (i.e. the length of course and number of timetable hours) was often equated with the perception of 'quality'. Of course, any system in the world would be delighted to have as much time as it wanted to prepare teachers, and 1-year courses do represent a compromise over quality. However, a reduction in the length of studies does not have to lead to a reduction in quality. Further, the use of short-duration courses in many systems across the world reflects the need for economic viability in course provision. While such considerations did not feature prominently in the Soviet era, in the New Russia solutions must be sought to overcome the severe financial constraints on the education system. There is even a case for arguing that the Russian system will at some point in the future have to look at the possibility of running a licensed teacher scheme (i.e. with school-based, on-the-job training), to reduce the training process yet further, although this is a suggestion that, presumably, will be anathema to many Russian lecturers, still coming to terms with the changed environment around them.

Curricular matters

Students in the pedagogical institute could face up to 36 hours of study per week, in an academic year that extended over 9 months, a workload which gave little scope for the students to engage in reflective study. While certain institutes have attempted to reduce the number of hours in the timetable in recent years, using their new freedom to decide curricular issues themselves, in practice many students find that hours are added again by individual departments, leaving the timetable problem unsolved. It seems that the problem of overloading, which obviously reduces the effectiveness of the course of studies, is often not recognised by very many lecturers, still used to the principle of 'quantity' rather than 'quality' with regard to studies. Indeed, one lecturer mentioned to me that she thought there was room for more lectures per week in the timetable.

The position of the 'social science' disciplines in the curriculum was eroded during the process of 'deideologisation' of the early 1990s, although there is still a significant social science element in the curriculum, with courses on, for example, 'Politologiia' (political science) having taken the place of Marxist-Leninist theory. Indeed, often the same lecturers that taught on the old courses are now found teaching the new 'deideologised' programmes, sometimes without having changed their approach or course content a great deal. Students now, however, are much more likely to question openly the nature of the material presented to them, thus compensating for the effects of the inevitable inertia that will continue for some time in the curriculum.

The specialised subjects (e.g. physics, chemistry, history, English) have given up little, if any, ground. Their strength comes from the pedagogical institutes' functions as universities in all but name; indeed, if the idea of mergers gains popularity, the pedagogical institutes' experience in teaching specialised subjects will provide a sound foundation for the new universities.

There are fears among the staff of the pedagogical faculties of teacher-education establishments that mergers of pedagogical institutes and universities with other institutions may lead to a decline in the importance of teacher-training. To an extent this fear has been realised in the cases of those pedagogical universities, as mentioned earlier, which have begun to place greater emphasis on their function as 'universities' and reduce the importance of the word 'pedagogical' in their title. However, the experience of Novgorod University, in which the former pedagogical institute merged with a technical institute, shows that teacher-training and educational research can actually *benefit* from such reorganisation. A separate Faculty of Education now functions successfully, continuing to provide teacher-education courses, engaging in a greater amount of research activity than before, and enjoying the overall support of the wider university body. Perhaps not all cases of merger will produce such positive results, but this example does serve to demonstrate what is possible.

In the area of pedagogical training, efforts have been made to render the nature of courses more suitable to the needs of the contemporary school, in line with the direction of reform. In those establishments that have managed to introduce real change, greater emphasis is now placed on group-work, discussion, simulation exercises and other activities designed to develop the trainee's all-round abilities as a teacher,[22] while much more support is being offered in some cases to the needs of teachers in understanding child psychology and learning how to communicate with their pupils.[23]

More effort is also being made to forge links with schools, with members of pedagogical faculties cooperating with teachers on experimental work, for example, thus allowing the schools to draw on the human and material resources of the institute, and the lecturers to draw on practical experience to feed into their teacher-training programmes.

The lack of a strong tradition in educational research in the teacher-education network has held up its development of a stronger profile, although more establishments are now taking advantage of the new possibilities now available to engage in such work. This base will be supported by the expansion of provision for students to acquire experience of research in their initial training at the *bakalavr* and *magistr* levels, with greater emphasis now being placed in courses on the development of research skills through various activities, thus preparing these future teachers well for their continued professional development as they progress in their career.[24] With regard to opportunities available to practising teachers, further adjustments are still required to the organisation of postgraduate study to increase access for studying on Master's courses. This will allow teachers to enrol on a programme either on secondment or as a part-time student, and will help to strengthen the methodological basis of innovative work being conducted in the schools.

Prospects for teacher education

The failure of the central authorities to place the level of emphasis on teacher education that was required from the very beginning of the reform process has undoubtedly held back both the development of the teacher-training network, and, consequently, the passage of change in the schools. The network has had to react itself to the changing conditions in the schools and in the economy, a task that some establishments have managed to do quite effectively, but which has proved difficult for the majority. By 1991 the teacher-education network had already fallen behind the school; despite progress in certain cases in catching up, even overtaking, the schools and adopting the rightful position of teacher education in the vanguard of change, most establishments are still struggling to keep pace with the schools. Meanwhile, the financial problems referred to above continued to worsen in the late 1990s: in 1998 it was reported that the funding for higher education sector teacher-training establishments was to be cut by a further 26.2 per cent, placing even greater strain on the system.[25]

Such developments can only hinder the system's attempts to tackle the most urgent priority of supplying teachers to the classroom. It may be true that some students are turning to teaching as a refuge from the spectre of unemployment in the industrial sector, and some places may be filled by immigrants and retrained primary-level staff moving to the secondary classrooms, yet such trends are based on negative, not positive grounds. To build a strong foundation for the school system teachers should be recruited at least partly because a positive image of the rewards of teaching are held. For this to happen, considerable investment in (and commitment to) the education system will need to be guaranteed by the authorities.

9
A Progress Report for the Russian School

In Part II a long catalogue of problems and obstacles has been identified, with which the school must contend if it is to develop, and if it is to implement the reforms. As a conclusion to this examination, however, one should note that the presence of such difficulties does not necessarily mean that one should be pessimistic with regard to the system's potential to overcome them, and to adapt to the new conditions and demands it faces. In fact, as I suggest in this chapter, there may be grounds for thinking that *internally*, i.e. within the school system, the change process may have begun to enter a significant new phase of 'settling down', or 'internalisation', of the reforms. This does not imply that the reforms will now move towards successful implementation as a matter of course, but that, perhaps, the dust of the initial period of flux may have now settled sufficiently for the system to be able to take stock of where it is, and what needs to be done next, within a clearer framework of development.

Towards the settling down of the reforms?

To begin with, one can make the apparently unremarkable observation that the reforms are still alive. Given the predominance of failure in the worldwide experience of educational change, the study of school reform can be a depressing task; in the case of the Russian reforms, however, while the scale of the obstacles to be overcome is awe-inspiring, there is definitely no cause to talk of overall failure, of the abandonment of change. Yet according to the experience of change across the world, the Russian reforms should not, perhaps, have managed to survive for so long. After all, a combination of factors – the crippling lack of finances, the coincidence of reform with societal transformation, the very size of the reform agenda – appeared to be heavily weighed against its survival.

Perhaps one of the keys to the reforms' continuing, albeit slow, momentum, lies in their ambitious nature, the huge scale of the task that they have set the schools. Perhaps such all-embracing processes are more effective in the long term than the piecemeal reforms with a narrow focus that have tended until recently to be the norm in many systems. Perhaps it is the fact that the upheaval in society has allowed the schools to consider breaking with certain traditions that would be much harder to discard, or even amend, in a more stable environment. Or perhaps the secret of the reforms to date lies in having the appearance of radical change, while, in fact, little is changing, or the nature of change has been modified to allow for the retention of aspects of existing practices and beliefs under new guise. In our analysis of these processes our task should be to try to differentiate between the superficial signs of change and the deeper currents which can give us clues as to the long-term implications of the developments we see today.

Time for reflection

The extent of continuity in education policy in the post-Soviet period has already been noted, with both Tkachenko and Kinelev generally following the same policy agenda as that laid down by Dneprov's team in the 1992 Law on Education. To a degree, such continuity has been possible because of the broad (and vague) nature of the philosophical foundation which lies at the root of the reforms, and which has contributed to what we might call a state of *false consensus* in educational policy, as perceived both within the field of education and in the political and public arenas, a matter which I will explore in Part III. However, the avoidance of pendulum policy shifts can be seen to have allowed the system time to reflect on what has been achieved to date, on what its needs and capabilities are, and to analyse the processes of change, both positive and negative, to have emerged in the system since the introduction of the reforms. Not all schools or all regions have been able to take advantage of this opportunity, of course, and a good number remain somewhat unsure of the aims of the reform programme, and of the approach they need to adopt in order to react to the calls for implementation. The problem of clarity, of establishing an acceptable degree of consensus on the aims of the reforms, and on how to implement them, is still a major issue, which must be tackled by the school system and by society at large, before there can be talk of the continuation and institutionalisation of reform.

It is extremely difficult, especially given the absence of comprehensive qualitative research evidence, to pinpoint tangible signs of 'settling down', but an impression does seem to have emerged by the mid- to late 1990s (at least, among many of the educationalists with whom I had contact) that in some schools and regions the opportunity to reflect on the issue of change has been used profitably, leading to the appearance of a more reasoned, informed approach which might serve as an example for other parts of the system. As one headteacher commented to me:

> For the first few years of the reforms it was difficult to 'gain one's feet', because we were being asked to respond very quickly to proposals for change which sought to effect fundamental change in many aspects of our work. More recently, however, I have noticed that my fellow headteachers and the local administrators have begun to appear more confident when they talk about the reforms, and there is a greater sense of professionalism, of knowing where we are going. (Headteacher, *gimnaziya*, interview with the author, December 1996)

With regard to signs of positive change in the system as a whole, while such developments represent a degree of success for the institutions and administrations concerned, to some extent their presence is also due, I would argue, to the influence that the forces of inertia have exerted on the process of reform. Although the effects of inertia may cause consternation to those responsible for promoting and overseeing the reforms, and despite the numerous negative consequences which stem from inertia, it can also be seen to have acted as an unplanned system of checks and balances on the system, serving to restrain tendencies towards over-experimentation in certain schools, and contributing to the emergence of a period of reflection in the system. Schools and regions have, therefore, been able to adopt a more moderate pace of reform than envisaged by the reform camp when it launched the Law on Education in 1992, allowing them to avoid certain potential pitfalls. If the centre had placed more emphasis on the need to reorganise the teacher-education system, for instance, and had been able to supply the schools with teachers who had been instilled with the spirit of reforms as envisaged by the original, 'revolutionary' style approach to change promoted by the reformers in the early days, there could well have been considerable conflict between such young 'innovators' and the older staff, whose natural conservatism would have contrasted more sharply with the new ideas of the reforms. Instead, the constraints imposed by inertia have helped to ensure a greater degree of continuity, a slower, more evolutionary approach to change.

'Could do better'

As is the tradition with school reports, while one can congratulate the pupil on the impressive progress that s/he has made in certain areas, one is, nevertheless, compelled to comment on certain aspects of the pupil's activities which could clearly be improved upon. The school system has the capacity to tackle a wide range of the problems identified in Parts I and II internally, through, for instance, the reorganisation of certain aspects of the initial and in-service training provision, and the development of a more profound discussion of the meaning of the reform policies as they relate to classroom practice. Change is also required in the culture of the school, if effective use is to be made of the creative potential of the teaching force, especially the more junior members of staff.

These are matters which can be addressed by the system itself, even without having to rely on a sizeable increase in funding. In the end, however, the system's ability to find an answer to the crucial question of financial and human resources – or the lack of them – is limited. Instead, in order to ensure its survival as a viable societal institution, the school must rely on the support of society at large – as will be shown in Part III, this support is by no means guaranteed.

Part III

Russia's School and Its Society

10
The Vulnerability of the School

An examination of the plight of relatively fragile social institutions such as the school system can tell us much about the nature of the new Russia, about the strengths and weaknesses of civil society, the long-term prospects for the development of democratic practices and a strong, market-based economy. The school reforms described in Parts I and II are taking place, after all, in a period of tremendous societal flux. The decline of what was already at best an inefficiently functioning Soviet social welfare system continued apace in the post-Soviet period, with the notional provision of democratic 'rights' viewed by many in the Russian population as insufficient compensation for the erosion of the kind of substantive entitlements to which they had been accustomed.[1] Moreover, the experience of the schools highlights the growing social divisions which became increasingly apparent in Russia in the 1990s, and demonstrates, too, the limited degree to which Russian citizens felt themselves able, or willing, to assume responsibility not just for safeguarding their interests as individuals, but for developing a greater conscience that could be used as the basis for collective support of the schools.

As a result, the schools were left with inadequate protection from the fall-out which accompanied the country's political and economic crises, with what I would argue are alarming visible and potential consequences. In this chapter the underlying patterns of the school's relationship with society will be examined, and a review provided of the early outcomes of society's neglect, along with their implications for Russia's future.

An inadequate debate

The root of the problem in the school–society relationship centres on what I consider the inadequate nature of the debate on education, which, by the late 1990s, was still some way from being an 'open' or comprehensive debate (see Figure 10.1), i.e. with active and informed participation in the discussion of education policy, and in which such matters as the rights enjoyed by the individual are well-defined and given firm legal status. Of course, one might argue convincingly that such open debates are comparatively rare even in long-established democracies, with discussion of education, when it does take place in the public arena, often reduced to simplistic rhetoric over the 'rights' and 'wrongs' of a particular political party's stance on schooling, rather than a detailed dialogue. This is, regrettably, the case, yet the extent of the neglect of education in contemporary Russia, to the point of ignorance of the gravity, or even existence, of certain developments, not to mention their possible long-term implications, does mark Russia out from the norm seen in many other countries (even, I would suggest, many other post-communist countries).

It is true that the framework of the Russian debate has undergone substantial transformation in recent years. As was shown in Part I, the Soviet state did not hold a monopoly over educational philosophy. Instead, there existed a situation of 'restricted' debate, in which Soviet citizens, as in so many other aspects of their lives, learned to give the appearance of following the official line, while, in fact, pursuing a more personal agenda. A restricted societal debate was, therefore, an integral part of the Soviet system, even if this fact was not acknowledged by the State, or recognised by the population; the task, with the advent of the reform era, would be to develop this debate further, to render it suitable for the needs of a democracy. This debate did appear to develop from the mid-1980s, as a modest public discussion took place on the perceived problems of the Soviet school. With the presence of alternative schools, variety in textbook choice (when textbooks can be obtained),

Restricted debate	⇒	**Shallow debate**	⇒	**Open debate**
(majority of Soviet period)		(late 1980s to present)		?

Figure 10.1 The debate on education: from Soviet to Russian school systems

and the guarantee that anyone was able to put forward their own views on educational issues without fear of retribution, this might be seen as evidence of the development of a more 'open' form of debate in the post-Soviet period. Nevertheless, despite such evidence, I would contest that the scenario of the 1990s is better described as a 'shallow' debate, for a number of reasons that concern both the internal state of the system, and, significantly, the school's relationship with its society.

I have demonstrated in Parts I and II that a good deal of confusion surrounded the reform agenda. In the case of some schools, this contributed to the problem of over-experimentation, while in others, a strategy of coping was employed, as schools and teachers paid lip-service to the task of implementation. A considerable amount of adaptation of the reform aims was observed, therefore, with a wide spectrum of variation in the approaches taken to change, and the interpretations placed on the policies of reform. As is the case with inertia, while there were undoubtedly a number of short-term benefits to be gained from a lack of clarity of aims, the long-term implications give cause for concern. In the short-term, the lack of clarity may be seen to have served a useful purpose, by helping to keep the system together, and retaining what was, in general, the positive attitude to the principle of change that has been noted in the teaching profession. The factors that allowed such positive outcomes to occur can be explained in part by comparing the distance between the declared aims of the reforms (seen from the ministry's perspective) and the actual capacity of the system, and the perceived aims and perceived capacity of an individual school or teacher.

The aims laid before the Russian school in the Law on Education of 1992 were so ambitious, and the system so ill-prepared to make this transition, that had the reform aims been taken up in an 'undiluted' form by the schools I suggest that there would have been severe disruption, great confusion and considerable discontent among teachers, pupils and parents. Instead, through the adaptation of the reform ideas, and the imposition of existing values on the concepts included in the reform agenda, many teachers were able to accept them as notions that did not threaten fundamentally to alter the values which teachers had held throughout their careers. The adoption of this diluted version of the agenda allowed schools to suppose that their capacity to implement these changes was adequate to the task (a factor which was strengthened by the tendency, often noted in school systems, for schools to overestimate their capacity to tackle change).

This may have led to some positive outcomes in the short-term, watering down some of the more radical (and potentially damaging) aspects of the reforms, enabling some in the system to make a more reasoned judgement on the relative merits of the policies and developing a more practical approach to dealing with the demands of change. Yet the extent of the variety of interpretation of the reform aims which exists in the system, and the degree to which confusion and the lack of clarity still remain, are issues which, if left unaddressed, will serve in the long-term both to act as a brake on the reforms and to hinder the development of the system as a whole. Similarly, the eclectic nature of the reform programme put forward by the centre, combined with the vagueness of some of its policies, undoubtedly contributed to reducing the potential for opposition to and alienation from the change process, establishing a degree of consensus on reform in the educational community. The limitations of the debate on change, however, means that this was what we can term a 'false' consensus, whose ability to keep the system together was likely to prove only temporary. Perhaps such shortcomings would be solved in the transition to a more 'open' form of debate?

The transition to an open debate will require the involvement of society and societal institutions (including the political parties), in order to ensure that the discussion of education and the identification of educational values takes place in this wider arena, rather than being confined to the educational sphere alone. The end result of this process, if it proceeds smoothly, should be the provision of a more solid foundation for the future development of the school system, which will have a more precise understanding of the nature of the tasks set before it by society, while the latter, in turn, will possess a clearer idea of what it needs from the schools, and what its own responsibilities are to the school system.

These, however, are long-term goals. In the short-term, the development of an open debate is likely to be a difficult affair, for the level of commitment shown by Russian society towards the school system, and thus its potential to contribute to this debate, remains extremely limited. As a result, patterns of open pluralism are set to appear in a fragmented fashion, and, as Russian society continues to pass through its difficult transformation, the function of checks and balances that operates, albeit imperfectly, in the UK, for instance, will be severely impaired in the Russian case. Accordingly, some elements of the open debate which may later become positive features of the system, may now exert a negative, damaging influence, owing to the weakness of other, less developed elements. This might lead to the development of a greater degree of conflict in the Russian educational debate, as the interests of particular groups and classes, still poorly defined in Russia, begin to emerge in a more explicit fashion.

Taking responsibility for education?

An explanation for the continued shallowness of the debate on education emerges from the following review of the treatment of the issue of education by various sections of Russian society.

Throughout the 1990s, the major Russian political parties professed to have some kind of platform on education, although it was rather difficult to discern the exact nature of their policies, owing to the lack of attention paid to educational issues by the parties themselves. Some degree of variation can be noted, with parties attempting to transpose their overall stance onto the sphere of education. Vladimir Zhirinovskii, leader of the Liberal Democratic Party of Russia (LDPR), for instance, questioned the need for support for national schools for Russia's ethnic minorities, a view which followed his party's position on the need to preserve Russian 'national interests',[2] while Egor Gaidar's Democratic Choice of Russia published a series of brochures entitled 'On the Road to the New School' (*Na putyakh k novoi shkole*), in which the notion of competition in education and the introduction of vouchers were promoted, in line with that party's policies on the development of the market economy.

For the most part, however, the debate on education in political circles suffered from the same drawbacks as the general debate on education within the school system and in society, namely a lack of interest from potential participants, and an inadequate development of the philosophical framework for the debate. As a result, apathy and neglect remained beneath a superficial veneer of glib, general statements on the need for a strong education system, which differed little in their content from party to party, and which did not imply a real commitment from the parties to pursue such aims with any real vigour. Instead, the focus was on the more immediate concerns of the politics of the day, and the struggle to gain influence and power.

The *Duma* has a cross-party committee on education which oversees developments in the area,[3] and parliamentary hearings on education are held regularly. Yet while such hearings do attract the participation and interest of all parties, and quite detailed debates can take place, these proceedings are still very overshadowed by much of the rest of the parliament's business. At the regional and municipal levels, a similar pattern can be seen. While some regional heads of administration may devote a good deal of attention to education, the general approach seems to be one of neglect, as governors, mayors and others struggle with the economic problems of their region or city. Before the 1995 *Duma* elections, the chairman of the educationalists' trade union, V. Yakovlev, recommended that his members vote for the Women of Russia party, since this was the only party, in his view, which had anything like a credible policy on education,[4] although even this party's agenda was rather vague and underdeveloped. The prospects for any major improvement in the situation in the near future seem slim, as the political instability continues. The problem for the schools, however, lies not only in the neglect shown by the politicians, but also in the degree of apathy shown in society at large.

The mass media do provide a limited amount of coverage of educational issues: the major television channels broadcast a range of programmes for schools, and there is a regular programme devoted to the discussion of educational topics ('45' on Channel 1), while the major national newspapers maintain educational correspondents. However, the mass media are, of course, driven by major news stories, and there has been no shortage of crises, political and economic scandals, international disputes or crime stories to fill their pages in recent years. Any discussion of educational matters is, therefore, restricted, as it faces an unequal challenge in gaining the editor's attention in comparison with headline-grabbing stories.

Some business people, some companies are taking advantage of an opportunity to 'get rich quick', and appear to have little time, incentive or inclination to spare concern for the interests of the school system. For the most part, however, the world of commerce and industry is engrossed in what it, perhaps justifiably, sees as the more immediate problems of mere survival in the harsh economic climate of the 'new' Russia. The most visible consequence for education is the drastic reduction of support given by enterprises to their local PTU, leading to closure of a good number of colleges, or at least to a considerable restriction on the education they can offer.[5]

As with individual citizens, any support that firms are still able, or willing, to lend to education seems to be very much on an individual, ad hoc basis, with little attempt made to present a concerted front at regional or national level to address the issue of general and vocational education, and the relevance of such matters for the needs of commerce and industry.

The Ministry of Education has consistently held to the line that the state school must remain secular, arguing – understandably – that in a country with as diverse an ethnic mix as Russia, and with the amount of instability and potential for inter-ethnic tension that is present, any attempt to allow the Orthodox Church or any other religion to have a strong influence in the running of the schools would entail serious risks. (Religious study and worship is permitted in non-state schools, however, and the inclusion of lessons on world religions is encouraged in the state sector.) For its part, the Orthodox Church appears to accept, and support, the ministry's policy.[6]

Gauging the attitudes of the population towards education is difficult, although the results of research studies and opinion-poll surveys appear to indicate that the general public, in common with the elements of civil society referred to earlier, also does not pay very much attention to this question, in comparison with that which it gives to other issues of more immediate concern. When the public is asked to respond to a question which focuses exclusively on education, for example on whether school-level education should be free of charge or on a partial or mainly fee-paying basis, some idea of the nature of opinions can be ascertained, and variation identified in the types of attitude which are held by the members of different social groups.[7] However, when respondents are asked to state which problems they see as most acute in Russia's transformation, the issue of education tends to figure low in respondents' lists;[8] indeed, education may even be missing altogether from the list of categories presented by the survey organisers.[9]

Naturally, an interest is likely to be seen principally among those parents whose children are currently attending school, thus establishing direct personal involvement. Active involvement in school affairs is more likely to be noted among white-collar, middle-class parents, with some parents now supporting their children's school in material terms, for instance through acting as a financial sponsor. The extent of parental involvement across the school system, however, despite an increased emphasis on the need to encourage such links, is still relatively small. Furthermore, any participation which does occur is almost invariably restricted to the school which those parents' children attend, with few if any attempts made by parents to organise themselves on a wider basis, for example by forming a lobbying group to voice the concerns of parents at the national or regional levels.

Voices from the education system?

If society at large is unable to provide the school with the support it needs, can those within the education system itself do anything to safeguard their interests, and make their views known?

The successor to the old Soviet educationalists' trade union, the *Profsoyuz rabotnikov narodnogo obrazovaniya i nauki* is still, to all intents and purposes, the only union representing teachers' interests across the Russian Federation. It is accused by some of being conservative, even of taking an anti-democratic stance,[10] although its supporters would say that it does, for all its drawbacks, at least offer some kind of platform for teachers to express their views to the national government, as well as regional, municipal and district administrations. While it does take a position on the course of reform in the schools, its chief preoccupation has been and remains that of trying to protect its members' material position, a difficult task, given the huge and seemingly intractable problems of the non-payment of salaries, the inadequacies of the common salary structure, and the material hardships that teachers endure as a result.[11]

The union has adopted an increasingly active stance, through issuing appeals to senior politicians to lend their support to education, by encouraging groups of teachers to travel to Moscow to lobby the *Duma* and the Kremlin, and, of course, through the union's involvement in the wave of strikes which have been mounted by teachers across the country. For all its efforts, however, the union's voice remains weak in comparison with other professional groups. The miners, for instance, frequently threaten to strike, and often do so, confident in the strength of the economic leverage that such action brings to bear on the government. Meanwhile, in recent times a growing amount of concern has centred on the material plight of armed forces personnel, many of whom have come to suffer the same problems of long delays in salary payments that other groups have become accustomed to. The prospect of unrest among the armed forces, however, is afforded closer interest by the government than that which it pays to the activities of striking teachers.

In the Soviet era an organisation named the 'Pedagogical Society' (*Pedagogicheskoe obshchestvo*), which had at the end of the 1970s a membership of 1 300 000 drawn from various walks of life, provided a link of sorts between school and society, although the scope for meaningful debate and activity was, of course, limited, at least until the *perestroika* years.[12] The society still exists today, although its membership has decreased by almost two-thirds, and its influence is minor.

There have been attempts to establish movements which could adopt a more active stance, to act as a lobbying body, for instance, or even try to gain their own representatives in the *Duma* and other bodies at the regional or municipal levels. B.S. Gershunskii, a prominent figure in the Russian Academy of Education, attempted to found an educational 'party', named 'Education and the Future' (*Obrazovanie i budushchee*),[13] although this quickly faded from the scene, having failed to arouse any great interest or support. Another movement, with the similar title of 'Education is the Future of Russia' (*Obrazovanie – Budushchee Rossii*), otherwise known under the acronym DOBRO ('good'), was formed in 1993 on the initiative of a group of senior figures in the educational community, including Larisa Babukh, a deputy in the state *Duma*.[14] DOBRO, however, suffered from a lack of clarity in its formulation of the movement's aims, and displayed a good deal of naïvety (or, perhaps, bravado) in its hopes that it could act as a uniting front for all of the country's educationalists. Despite claims that it would be able to achieve a degree of success in the *Duma* elections of December 1995, either in placing candidates in the parliament itself, or in gaining influence among the major parties, little of any substance was achieved, and the organisation suffered a subsequent decline.[15]

In the lead-up to the presidential elections of June 1996, yet another attempt was made to form an organisation to represent the interests of the education system, this time in the form of the so-called 'Russian Pedagogical Parliament' (*Rossiiskii Pedagogicheskii Parlament*). The pedagogical press had, by this time, become rather sceptical towards the activities of such organisations, and the organisation received rather a dismissive appraisal. It was pointed out, for instance, that the 'Parliament' seemed set to repeat the mistakes of its ill-fated predecessors, by failing to set out a clear agenda, through the naïvety of its expectations, and the failure to attract sufficient support from politicians of the 'real' parties.[16] This is not to say that the idea of trying to present a more cohesive and influential front for the teaching force, through lobbying and other activities, is not a potentially beneficial idea. However, unless a more realistic approach is adopted, such movements seem doomed to achieve only minimal gains, if anything at all, in the harsh political arena which exists in Russia.

Faced with the problem of trying to gain recognition for the cause of education among the political parties, some senior educationalists seem to have come to the conclusion that in order to achieve this goal, they would need to adopt the mind-set of their intended audience. In a parliamentary hearing on education, one group of well-known educationalists and educational psychologists, including V. Slobodchikov of the Centre for Pedagogical Innovations (formerly VNIK) and Yu. Gromyko, President of the Moscow Academy for the Development of Education (MARO), together with Larisa Babukh (of DOBRO) made a presentation which must have had a disturbing (and rather confusing) effect on those Russian educationalists following such events. The group, whose members have, for the past few years at least, been promoting the goals of the reform programme (democratisation, the need to develop a child's personality and character (*lichnost'*) etc.) produced a 'doctrine' which, while incoherent and containing a good deal of internal contradiction, nevertheless sets forth a vision of Russia under threat from malicious and damaging outside influences, and refers to the need to use education to protect Russian interests, the importance of promoting Russian language and culture both within Russia and abroad, the need to instil feelings of patriotism and pride in the achievements of Russia and the USSR among the young, and so on. In isolation, perhaps these sentiments appear innocuous enough, but in the tone of this article they represent a rather unwelcome turn towards the promotion of chauvinism and racist attitudes, betraying the presence of a feeling of national superiority and damaged pride, mixed with a sense of inferiority towards the West, as the following extract illustrates:

> It is impossible to explain to a young person in whose name he should sacrifice his life, when huge numbers of people are looking after only their own selfish interests. The formation of patriotic attitudes has to be conducted today against the tide of the official point of view, the widely-distributed propaganda of the mass

> media, and the nature of formal upbringing work in the school. There are, nevertheless, still wonderful teachers who, at their own risk, continue to promote the need to serve the Motherland. It is due to their self-sacrifice that we still exist today as a nation and as a great power.[17]

Perhaps the apparent commitment to the more liberal ideas of the reform agenda, which those who signed this document had professed to hold, was not so genuine after all? Or perhaps the simplistic and philosophically unsound nationalistic ramblings of this document represent an attempt to pander to the conservative forces in Russian politics? Whatever the motive, it is not the stance that the Russian school system expects or deserves from its more influential representatives.

The school left to its own devices?

From this brief résumé of the nature of society's stance (or lack of one) on education, and from the evidence provided in Parts I and II, it is clear that the safety-net functions are only partially being performed by Russian society. With regard to the function of monitoring developments in the schools, some positive and negative consequences can be observed in the lack of interest which society has paid to developments in the school system. While no school system can lead a separate existence from that of its society, the Russian system, in recent years, has enjoyed, or endured, a degree of autonomy from society, a situation which has placed a great deal of responsibility on the schools, the administrators and the policy-makers. In some cases, certain schools, or even regions, have adopted a rather irresponsible attitude which has ignored the need to keep in mind the interests of systemic cohesion. On the whole, however, the inertia of the old system, and the professionalism of the teaching force, have prevented widespread fragmentation.

In the absence of any clear mandate from society, or interest in the way in which the educational establishment is looking after the schools, one might conclude that it is fortunate that a path towards a 'democratic' system was chosen, almost independently, one might say, by the reform camp led by Dneprov, notwithstanding the lack of clarity which surrounded their plans. Nevertheless, the absence of effective societal scrutiny allowed certain internal contradictions, some potentially damaging, to be included in the reform programme, the effect of which would soon become apparent. The emergence of these problems – which one of my interviewees, not without justification, described as 'attempts on the life of the school' – would prove a severe test for society's safety net.

Selection, rejection and the 43rd Article affair

In its preamble, the Law on Education of 1992 stated that: 'The right of receiving education is one of the fundamental and inalienable constitutional rights of citizens of the Russian Federation,'[18] a concept which is apparently reinforced by Article 5 ('State Guarantees for the Rights of Citizens of the Russian Federation in the Field of Education'). However, certain contradictions in the legislation, and in the authorities' interpretation of it, were to emerge as the school system adjusted to the new 'freedoms' which emerged after 1991. The Law guaranteed state support for free education only up to grade 9 (15 years old), as opposed to the previous limit of grade 11 (17 years old) (Article 5), thus breaking the commitment to universal secondary education of which the Soviet system had, justifiably, boasted. Further, the possibility of moving away from a comprehensive school arrangement, in which the school had to cater for all children in its 'catchment area,' to one in which at least part of the school's pupil cohort passed through a selection procedure, was endorsed in Article 16 of the 1992 Law on Education, and quickly proved popular with a large number of establishments.[19] Indeed, by 1995 it was reported that out of a sample of 77 Moscow schools whose statutes were reviewed by the municipal inspectors, 44 had introduced, or envisaged introducing, competitive selection of pupils.[20] However, if selection of some pupils (as a rule, naturally, the more able or those with wealthier parents) was taking place, this inevitably meant that some children were being rejected by those schools, for the intention was not to increase class sizes (indeed, for most alternative schools the aim has been quite the opposite), but was more likely to be based on a desire to achieve higher academic standards, and to effect appropriate curricular changes towards this goal. It seemed that the presence of average and below-average ability pupils was no longer required in some schools, and the phenomenon of the *otsev* (the expulsion of pupils from the schools) gathered pace. In most cases, the selection process took place after completion of basic secondary education in the 9th grade (age 15), and before entrance to the senior grades (10th and 11th grades, ages 15–17), although the practice soon began to be applied to entrance to other grades, even to the 1st grade itself (age 6).

The problem for those pupils who found that they were unable to gain access to the school, but who wished nonetheless to continue their education, was that the possibilities for doing so were also quickly contracting. As was shown earlier, the PTUs were experiencing considerable difficulties, while evening schools, too, were hit by severe shortages in financing, and could often no longer provide the level of service they had previously given to those who left the secondary school at 15, completing their secondary education in the evenings at these establishments.[21] As Frolova noted in late 1993, while the Law on Education declared the right of every child to receive education:

> The reality of the fate of a thousand ninth-graders in one town [Novosibirsk] is that they are not to be 'honoured' with a place in the tenth form. Technical colleges [PTUs] are closing one after another. The number of technical colleges (*tekhnikumy*) was already pretty small anyway. Evening schools find themselves in an ever worsening situation, since they have been labelled as having 'no prospects'.[22]

Frolova describes the indifference of a number of the teachers towards the plight of pupils who were excluded after the introduction of selection. Male pupils, in particular, suffered in this case at least, with the school visited by Frolova admitting just two boys alongside twenty girls into the tenth form. The decision to remove pupils was made on the basis of a vote cast by the teaching staff; in one case, teachers elected to remove a boy who 'liked dancing too much, and studies not enough'. As Frolova comments astutely:

> Those voting were sixty-year-old teachers for whom complete silence and the absence of any pranks or messing around was essential for the maintenance of comfort in the classroom . . . But who has won, in the end, with these kids having been thrown out of school? Mar'ya Petrovna, in whose lessons there is now complete silence? And who, after lessons, is afraid to walk outside on her own, or go into the lift, into the entrance lobby of her flat, or leave her flat unguarded?[23]

The trend of selection can be said to be at least partly responsible for a process of 'feminisation' of the pupil cohort of the senior grades in the schools, with female pupils making up almost 70 per cent of the total number of pupils who remained in school after the age of 15 by 1998.[24]

The attitudes shown towards pupils in Frolova's account of schools in Novosibirsk may represent the worst-case scenario of neglect and rejection. In some schools, where a more humane and sensible approach was adopted, and where it was realised that any short-term gains for an individual teacher or school would be offset by the problems they entailed for the pupils and for society at large, a degree of protection was granted to pupils. Indeed, it should be pointed out that not all schools decided to adopt a selective stance, and of those that did, the selection procedure has not always been applied as harshly as in the case referred to in Frolova's article. Nevertheless, the Novosibirsk school was far from an isolated example, and the experience of those pupils would be familiar to many thousands of rejected children across the country.

The reasons given by pupils themselves to explain why they have left the schools make interesting (and disturbing) reading. According to one study, some 45 per cent name teacher–pupil conflict as the principal cause of their departure, 38 per cent state simply that they were thrown out, 24 per cent cite a poor academic record, while only 23 per cent confirm that they left because they had found employment.[25] While these figures give only one side of the story (i.e. the child's), beneath the figures which refer to the high level of conflict and the simple dismissal from the school, one suspects that the part played by certain teachers in exploiting, exaggerating, perhaps in some cases even provoking conflict with these pupils may have contributed significantly to those pupils' removal from the school. Expulsion is practised in schools in England, of course, but it is seen as a last resort, only to be used in the case of a pupil for whom all other attempts to deal with the problems have been seen to fail. Even then, the pupil must be afforded appropriate care and educational provision until the age of 16, either in another school or in a special unit. While there is bound to be, of course, an equivalent group of pupils in the Russian system, the size of the *otsev* suggests that schools are being more than zealous in their application of criteria for expulsion on grounds of discipline problems.

With regard to academic performance, while, again, the reason cited by the pupils may not reflect the reason for removal as seen by the school, 24 per cent does represent a disturbingly high proportion, reflecting the desire of some schools to engage in the deselection of pupils whom it feels do not meet the academic standards required in the establishments' revised 'profile.' It may not necessarily be the case, anyway, that it is only the 'low-ability' pupils who are affected by the *otsev*. In a study conducted by the Russian Academy of Education in collaboration with educationalists in the city of Murmansk, it was claimed that the intellectual level of those pupils removed from the schools actually corresponded very closely with that of pupils who remained to study in the 5th to 9th grades. The latter group, however, conformed more to the school's requirement for academically motivated pupils who would be less likely to challenge authority.[26]

The problems of youth did not stem only from the problem of rejection, of course. The material hardships which an increasing number of families suffer from have led a considerable number of children to neglect their schooling in order to engage in money-making activities on the streets, either to supplement their family's income, or because they find more interest and pleasure in such work than sitting in a classroom.[27] Meanwhile, there is a growing problem of 'social orphans,' children who, for one reason or another, have been forced to fend for themselves, enjoying little or no support from family or social-service structures. The end result is that a growing number of children of, ostensibly, school age are to be found instead outside the school's walls,[28] with a disturbing proportion of these children falling into a cycle of crime and destitution. While the *otsev* may not be the principal cause of such problems, the practice of selection and rejection clearly contributed to their development.

The 43rd Article: background

Although the move to reduce the upper age-limit for the provision of guaranteed free education from 17 to 15 years old had been introduced in Article 5 of the Law on Education (see earlier), it was the appearance of the 43rd Article in the Russian constitution of 1993[29] which came to be seen as the watershed in what many came to regard as a retrograde step in the development of post-Soviet Russian education. The importance of this affair lies in the message which it sent to the schools, parents, pupils and society on the degree of protection that the State saw fit to extend to the young, and also in the manner in which it was played out, leading eventually to a rather inconclusive dénouement.

To reiterate, the article stated that henceforth, the upper age-limit for free education would be brought down to the end of basic secondary education, a drop of two years from the existing level, which was supposed to have guaranteed free complete secondary or preliminary vocational education. It was unclear what the implications were for higher and secondary-specialised education, which had also, traditionally, been provided free of charge, yet the effect on the school system, and on its pupils, appeared to be serious indeed, putting a rubber stamp on the practice of selection and rejection, and opening the way for schools to charge fees, should they wish, for any education provided beyond the age of 15, while also endorsing the principle of the *otsev* in general.

The 43rd Article affair served to emphasise the relative weakness of the Ministry of Education within the government. In the ensuing months following the publication of the constitution, Tkachenko did take a stance of opposition to the article, as the following comment shows:

> I am a supporter of universal, free and accessible education. The comprehensive [*massovaya*] school is just that. One cannot use it for commercial purposes. On the whole, the school and the market are concepts that do not go together that well.[30]

However, his ability to influence colleagues in other ministries, or indeed the political élite in general, appeared to be limited, and he was subjected to a growing amount of criticism in the pedagogical press:

> Honestly and openly the minister admits that he saw it [the 43rd Article] in its final form and that no-one had asked him for his agreement to such an article. In this case . . . everything becomes clear: both the weakness of the ministry's position within the government, and the fact that it [the ministry] itself openly pronounces its modesty, its unwillingness to debate, to argue.[31]

Meanwhile, Tkachenko's ministerial team did not put forward a common front on the affair, but presented instead a fragmented and somewhat contradictory line. Deputy Minister of Education Aleksandr Asmolov, for instance, seemed to accept the article's continued presence in the constitution:

> Never before have we faced the question of a sudden turn away from compulsory universal education, which all were supposed to follow without regard for their wishes or abilities, to a completely new system of education which leads to a general education ending in the 9th grade. And we say: 'What a difficult problem, what a tragedy we have on our hands, 200,000 children will be left without an education!' But aren't we reacting according to the principle that, having come up against something new, we must treat it as a cause of stress, as something dangerous?[32]

Others, such as V. Shadrikov (Deputy Chair of the State Committee on Higher Education)[33] and V. Bolotov from the Ministry of Education, came out strongly against the article, the latter commenting that:

> In the hierarchy of priorities it [the State] is not maintaining education as the number one priority. As a result the country is, we can say, entering a risk zone. And the 43rd article . . . is one more step backwards.[34]

This lack of a united response to the problem weakened the ministry's potential to exert pressure on other government departments still further, and added to the confusion surrounding the issue in the perceptions of the wider educational community.

As might be expected, coverage in the mass media was not extensive (although it did increase steadily as the numbers of children affected by the rejectionist tendency grew). Nevertheless, the matter does not seem to have aroused a great deal of interest among the general public, apart from those who were directly concerned because their child was affected, this state of affairs highlighting once more the inadequacies of the monitoring and safety-net functions referred to earlier. With regard to the teaching force itself, a mixed reaction was observed. The pedagogical press and journals did, on the whole, conduct a vigorous campaign against the article throughout the first half of 1994,[35] receiving the support of a good number of educationalists. Some, according to my investigations, reacted negatively to the article and to the practice of rejection out of a continued sense of commitment to the values promoted by the Soviet school, but most did so out of a desire to protect the interests of their pupils and the school system itself. Alongside such opposition, however, at least some educationalists supported the notion of giving preferential treatment to the more able pupils, regardless of the consequences for those not so fortunate, with the following comment serving as one example of the kind of argument put forward:

> If a pupil has no ability, no desire to study, if he has serious problems with his school work, then the teacher has to spend more time and energy on him. Such a pupil needs to study in a particular type of environment, he needs better (different) resources and equipment, effective teachers, whose salary, of course, should be higher. I consider, therefore, that such pupils should have to pay. This 'additional' money could be used towards the education of talented kids, and their overall development . . . After all, the State should ensure that it educates an élite for itself.[36]

The most worrying aspect of the reaction of the teaching force and the rest of society, however, was the extent of apathy towards, and ignorance of, the affair. Among teachers whom I interviewed during this period, for instance, the level of awareness of the 43rd Article and its implications was disturbingly low. While some teachers were knowledgeable about the matter, and expressed concern over it, others stated that they had not even heard of the article. Indeed, some told me that I must be mistaken, for such an article would not have been allowed to appear in the constitution; others noted that it did not have any significance anyway, because what is decided at the level of the government and the parliament in Russia has no bearing on what happens in the country. Perhaps such views are not without some justification, yet concentrating on one's own micro-environment to this extent, and thus ignoring (even denying) what happens at the centre, must be seen as a dangerous phenomenon. Whatever view teachers take on such issues as the 43rd Article, it is surely important that they do have an opinion on events which concern them directly as professionals.

Eventually, notwithstanding the apathy of a certain proportion of the teaching force and of much of the population, the combined efforts of *Uchitel'skaya gazeta*, the more active representatives of the Ministry of Education and others achieved apparent success when President Yeltsin issued a decree which effectively annulled the offending article.[37] The news was welcomed enthusiastically by those who had campaigned against the article,[38] and by the Ministry of Education, with Tkachenko commenting that it was: 'simply impossible to overstate the meaning of this Decree'.[39] First Deputy Minister of Education Bolotov could also report in 1994 that the practice of selection into the 1st grade had been curtailed: 'in full across the Russian Federation'.[40]

However, despite the evident sense of relief present among some in the system, the fact that a presidential decree had been made on the matter did not necessarily mean that the practice of rejection was curtailed. By the summer of 1994, it was reported that over the previous two years some 1 700 000 children of school age had not attended school,[41] while disturbing accounts were made that an ever-increasing number of children below the age of 14 were being excluded from their schools,[42] with some cases reported of children as young as nine falling prey to the trend.[43] Trying to reverse the momentum created over the previous years would prove difficult indeed; it was reported in Novosibirsk at the end of 1994 that the same problems still existed, with schools continuing to neglect the interests of some pupils in the supposed interests of the more able, or better behaved.[44] The practice continues, surreptitiously, to this day, adding to the ever-growing number of children who find themselves, for one reason or another, outside the school walls (in early 1998 the number stood at some 2 800 000, according to information supplied by an official of the Ministry of General and Professional Education in Moscow). In the 1994–95 academic year alone, it was reported that some 90 000 children and teenagers in Moscow left their schools, while selection to the 1st grade appeared to be still in force in some schools where, according to one critic, there was: 'a desire to educate only *Wunderkinder*'.[45]

At the same time, there were signs that the safety net of society was beginning to be more effective, with the public prosecution service trying to address the problems of delinquency among children, identifying schools acting illegally in rejecting pupils, and bringing sanctions to bear against these establishments.[46] Further, an increasing amount of concern was expressed with regard to the immediate social consequences of the *otsev* and the reduction of educational provision. The link between rejection and the subsequent involvement of the juveniles in criminal activity was stressed, for instance,[47] and the need to provide social protection for such children highlighted.[48]

The Ministry of Education, in collaboration with other federal and local agencies, tried to implement a constructive response to the problem of finding some kind of employment or training opportunities for such 'outcasts' from the schools. Many of these children were still too young to be employed legally, while those who were old enough still struggled to find security; the problem of unemployment began to make deeper inroads into the adult population, leaving little opportunity for school-leavers to find jobs, while the possibilities of gaining some kind of qualification in the PTUs or evening schools had contracted considerably. Efforts aimed at alleviating the problem of youth unemployment had to struggle against a tide of broader social problems, therefore, and inevitably encountered serious obstacles,[49] although Tkachenko claimed in 1996 that the Ministry of Education and the Federal Employment Service had succeeded in placing more than 340 000 teenagers in employment in the summer of 1995 alone, and that during the same period some 800 000 places had been created across the country, thus signalling a positive upturn in this matter.[50] With the spectre of much greater unemployment hanging over the working population, however, such optimism may have been premature.

Meanwhile, greater attention was also being paid – belatedly, one should note – to the question of vocational education. The Ministry of Education established a Department for Vocational Education in 1994, to coordinate efforts aimed at revising (and revitalising) the existing system. A federal law 'On Preliminary Vocational Education and Vocational Training' was prepared for presentation to the *Duma*.[51] Nevertheless, at the Collegium of the Ministry of Education held on 17 May 1996, ministers and officials pointed to optimistic signs of an upturn in the fortunes of vocational education, noting that, despite the weakened ties with enterprises, the number of entrants to the PTU network had actually risen, thanks to the introduction of a contract system between the educational authorities, employment service and the enterprises, and the provision of training for workers made redundant following the closure of factories. Further, 38 State Standards for Preliminary Vocational Education had been introduced, and a rationalisation of courses encouraged with the reduction in the number of professions and specialisations catered for by the network from 1250 to 275, signifying a transition away from narrowly focused courses towards more general programmes which will give students training in a wider range of disciplines.[52] Some are also calling for greater emphasis to be placed on the provision of vocational education in the secondary schools, with the establishment, for example, of vocational classes (*klassy real'nogo uchilishcha*).[53] Such ideas and initiatives promised to address to some degree the problems referred to earlier, although their success would depend on the level of commitment (and investment) provided by central, regional and local authorities, and indeed by the world of commerce and industry, which was asked to offer financial support for such schemes.

The privatisation (destatisation) of the schools?

The origins of the *razgosudarstvlenie* (destatisation) debate were described in Part I. The impulse at that time came mainly, it seemed, from a desire to attack the perceived legacy of the Soviet era, and reduce significantly, even remove, what was portrayed as the malign and all-pervading influence of the State in the sphere of education. By the mid-1990s, however, the *razgosudarstvlenie* banner had come to be adopted by some elements in the Russian government as part of their overall strategy for economic reform. Accordingly, the State Committee for Property (*Goskomimushchestvo*), which was overseeing the privatisation drive in Russian industry, decided that the principle of privatisation could be applied to the education system as well. As had been the case with the 43rd Article, which had followed the rejectionist trend set at the grassroots level, so the privatisation idea offered to place an official seal of approval on developments already gathering pace in the system itself, with a growing number of PTUs and kindergartens being sold off to commercial organisations, while some schools had already started to sell off parts of their property. The momentum was now quickening, and with the draft law supported by the powerful *Goskomimushchestvo* and the influential senior government figure of Anatolii Chubais,[54] the Ministry of Education seemed to face a difficult struggle in trying to oppose the move. Although Tkachenko did manage to have the phrase 'privatisation' amended to *razgosudarstvlenie* in the draft legislation, a bill entitled 'On Destatisation and Demonopolisation in the Sphere of Education' was duly introduced in the autumn of 1994.[55] The bill itself was prepared by Larisa Babukh, one of the leaders of DOBRO, and others who demanded greater governmental support for the development of the non-state educational sector.[56]

The aims of the law, as explained by its authors, were to extend the principle of choice in education, allowing parents to select a school through the use of a voucher scheme, and thus render the school system more suitable to the perceived needs of post-Soviet

Russian society. It was intended that 'ownership' of educational establishments could pass to social organisations and charities, including foreign groups, although political parties and religious organisations were not to be permitted to take up ownership. The process of handover would be overseen by commissions in the regions, in coordination with *Goskomimushchestvo*.

Perhaps it was because the educational community had become more aware of what was going on at the centre after the 43rd Article affair, or perhaps an attack on the principle of state education was seen as more serious than the extension of the idea of selection, but the reaction of educationalists towards the publication of this bill was much more audible and determined than had been the case with the 43rd Article. The draft of the bill was leaked to and published by *Uchitel'skaya gazeta* before it was due to be released, and a vigorous campaign was mounted by the pedagogical press, certain politicians and ordinary educationalists, with a heated debate taking place on the matter in *Uchitel'skaia gazeta*, for instance.[57] On this occasion, the opposition of senior political figures was a significant factor in the campaign, with Grigorii Yavlinskii, leader of the liberal YABLOKO faction, a vocal critic:

> While it supports the notion of creating a strong system of non-state education in Russia, the faction [YABLOKO] expresses its deep concern over the hurried preparation of this presidential decree, which has the aim of *forcing through* the privatisation of educational establishments . . . We consider that it would be extremely unwise to experiment [in this way] with such a delicate and exceptionally important sphere as education . . . We declare once again: whatever the financial difficulties the State may have, the comprehensive school must be properly and fully financed. Economising on the school means depriving the country of its future.[58]

With the backing of such heavyweight allies, a counter-attack was launched with a bill 'On the Maintenance of the Status of State and Municipal Educational Establishments and a Moratorium on their Privatisation,' which was passed by the state *Duma* at the third reading.[59] Again, however, as with the question of selection, the matter was not finally resolved. It was reported in the spring of 1995 that, despite a promise by Yeltsin not to privatise the school system, made at the ceremony for the 'Teacher of the Year', only a week later he overturned the bill opposing the privatisation scheme, and preparations seemed to be underway for another attempt by *Goskomimushchestvo* to push their law through.[60] Further, the issue of vouchers was floated again early in 1995, separately from any talk of 'privatisation.'[61] The matter of *razgosudarstvlenie*, therefore, has continued to simmer beneath the surface of the debate on education.

The implications: social conflict over education?

A good deal of attention has been paid both in academic works and in the mass media in Russia, and abroad, to the nature of social stratification of post-Soviet Russian society,[62] with an obvious focus being the growing social divide in Russia, symbolised by the emergence of the so-called New Russians, the *nouveaux riches* of the business and political world who found themselves in a position to take advantage of the opportunities for material gain which the end of the Soviet Union provided, and those members of the population who find themselves living below the officially set poverty line.[63] Within such investigations, however, the question of the rôle being played by education in this matter has received less emphasis,[64] although it is evident that the degree to which the Russian population is given, or denied, access to educational opportunities will have an impact on the future nature of social stratification in Russia (the social meaning of alternative schools has already been discussed in Chapter 6).

This topic was not a major focus of the research on which this book is based, and I do not want to become embroiled in a lengthy discussion of the relative applicability of, say, cultural reproduction or labelling theories to the Russian case.[65] There is a need for a detailed analysis of the relationship between education, stratification and social change in Russia, which, I would suggest, could examine the Russian situation through adapting the sophisticated, if highly contested, theories developed in the West. The following comments, in contrast, serve only to highlight, rather than analyse, the processes which may be at work in redefining the social dynamics of education in Russia.

First, then, do such developments as the 43rd Article and the privatisation of the education system provide evidence of an increasing amount of social conflict in the sphere of educational policy and practice? Some would argue that they clearly do: the *razgosudarstvlenie* episode was portrayed by Lyubov' Rozhkova, then chair of the *Duma* committee on science, education and culture, for instance, as: 'an attempt by certain social forces to carry out the privatisation of the sphere of education'.[66] It is difficult to try to discern the extent to which the kind of social forces which Rozhkova alludes to are actively seeking to alter the nature of educational provision and access, or the extent to which such phenomena as the *otsev* are the net result of individual, unwitting, uncoordinated actions on the part of individual schools and educational authorities at various levels (and should form the basis of an interesting research study).

In the post-Soviet era, the possibilities to express attitudes on education more openly have grown, and in some issues one can identify divisions of opinion according to social group. In surveys of attitudes towards the issue of whether or not fees should be paid for education, for instance, there is, as one might expect, a correlation between social status and income and respondents' views on whether or not fees should be paid. In one survey, the lower and middle-income brackets, 78.1 per cent and 75.7 per cent respectively, felt that schooling should be mainly free, compared with 65.7 per cent of those in the higher income bracket, while the figures for those who felt that there should be a mixture of free and fee-paying schooling were 18.4 per cent, 22.8 per cent and 32.6 per cent respectively.[67] These answers reflect the fact that it has been the better-off parents who have, of course, taken the lead in sending their children to alternative schools, including non-state, fee-paying establishments, or even, in the case of some of the wealthiest families, sent their children abroad to study.

If one wishes to look for evidence of conflict in the sphere of education, it would accordingly be possible to refer to the growing imbalance in the nature of educational opportunities afforded to various social groups, owing to the deterioration in free state provision and the increasing amount of fee-paying which takes place in the state and non-state networks. Indeed, a case could be made with regard to the element of tension between the self-styled 'intelligentsia' and white-collar workers, now joined by the new middle class of entrepreneurs and others who have benefited materially during the transition, and the working class. I have referred in Part I to the handicap that some claim the more able pupils endured under *uravnilovka*; to some extent, the trends of élitism, selection and rejection in the post-Soviet era may be seen as a backlash against this perceived legacy, as the middle class attempts to redress the imbalance that it feels it suffered during the Soviet years.

Perhaps the privatisation attempt was an example of overt conflict, or perhaps it stemmed more from a short-sighted desire to save the government money, or perhaps it was primarily an onslaught on the legacy of the past, or a combination of all these factors. In the case of the 43rd Article, and indeed all developments in the school–society relationship of the past few years, it is difficult to identify with confidence any particular trend, as potential divisions and clashes of interest are obscured beneath a variety of layers of confusion, lack of clarity, ill-informed discussion and apparent consensus. If the 43rd Article and *razgosudarstvlenie* do represent the expression of more clearly defined interests of certain more influential groups in society, however, then this is cause for concern, for such processes are taking place against the backdrop of a predominantly shallow debate, in which the interests of the less influential are protected by what I have shown to be only a moderately effective safety net.

The long-term impact that such developments might have is impossible to predict, of course, although it would not seem too outrageous to suggest that Russia's prospects for truly establishing a strong democratic tradition may not be that strong if this process is not inclusive, but rather one in which a significant proportion of young people feel that they have been rejected by their society. Further, the goal of achieving sustained economic recovery and growth is likely to be elusive, if insufficient investment is allocated to education, and if young people find that the possibility to gain the skills and knowledge required to work in a modern market is to be limited.

Epilogue

On the one hand, conducting research on contemporary Russia and then trying to write up one's findings before they become dated is a risky affair, given the apparent pace and unpredictability of change in that country. On the other hand, *plus ça change*. . . .

In July 1997 the Russian Prime Minister, Viktor Chernomyrdin, announced the setting-up of a commission which was, by November of that year, to present to the federal government a plan for the 'next stage in the reform of the education system' (*ocherednoi etap reformirovaniya sistemy obrazovaniya*), of which the principal aims were:

- to maintain the momentum established by the Law of Education of 1992 and its subsequent amendments, and work towards its implementation (including a goal of achieving a transition to 12-year, as opposed to 11-year, schooling)
- to secure the right of every citizen to have access to educational provision
- to bring the content of education, and the legal and economic bases of the system, into line with the needs of individual citizens, the expectations of society, the interests of the State and the internal demands for development within the education system itself.[1]

A characteristically vague set of statements, at once grandiose and ambitious yet somewhat empty, which received a mixed reaction. Most teachers to whom I spoke in the autumn of 1997 paid scant attention to the development, holding out little hope that it would lead to any substantial changes in their everyday concerns at the 'chalk face,' a mood which was reflected in the (albeit modest) response to an invitation made by *Uchitel'skaya gazeta*, for teachers to indicate the extent to which they felt a 'new round' of reform to be necessary.[2]

In the upper echelons of the educational establishment, however, the call received a more active response, with a number of groups forming to draw up their own 'concepts' to submit to the commission. The composition of the groups reflected the divided opinions apparent within the ministry's current and former personnel: one included the incumbent minister, Kinelev and the former minister, Dneprov,[3] for instance, with another comprising Aleksandr Tikhonov, who would replace Kinelev as minister in the spring of 1998, and his future first deputy minister, Aleksandr Asmolov.[4] These and other proposals were discussed in some detail in the pedagogical press, but in the end, it appeared that the sceptics had been justified after all. After nine months of deliberation, a concept had still not emerged, and the commission's chair, Russian vice-premier Oleg Sysuev, had decided that while work on the formation of the final concept for reform should continue, the first priority was to focus on tackling the socio-economic problems associated with the education system, and the drawing-up of a so-called 'doctrine' for the development of education.[5] Precise details of what was to be included in the latter – described as a document of 'strategic importance' by Tikhonov[6] – remained unclear by mid-1998.

Whether or not the goal of addressing effectively the social and economic concerns of the schools could be met was also open to doubt, however, although potential solutions were proposed at the end of 1997 and into 1998. At the Collegium of the Ministry of General and Professional Education in April 1998, for instance, Tikhonov noted the intention to move, at first in a pilot scheme, towards a *per capita* financing model, in which 'money follows the pupil', i.e. schools are funded through an educational vouchers method according to the number of pupils on their register, a development which had been predicted since the early 1990s.[7] Tikhonov noted that, once again, this had been taking place at the grassroots level anyway, with schools proceeding on this basis even in the absence of the necessary legal frameworks, thus forcing the ministry into taking some kind of action. Some were quick to point out again the potential social consequences of the move: the former First Deputy Minister of Education, Vladimir Shadrikov, for example, warned that it could lead to further intensification of inequality, and he also cast doubts on the ability of Russia's banking system to cope with the complexities involved in such a scheme.[8] Supporters of the move, however, predicted that it could relieve the pressure on the overstretched regional and municipal budgets.

More stringent (and, one might suggest, socially unacceptable) proposals were also aired. According to Tikhonov, in certain ministries, such as the Ministry of Finances, the search for cost-cutting in education even went so far as suggestions to charge for the marking of pupils' work in their exercise books, while other ideas included the expansion of class sizes (i.e. the number of pupils per class) to 45 from the current goal of 25, and an increase in the teacher's contact hours (i.e. the base-rate *stavka*) from 18 to 27 hours (which would mean that salary costs would be cut, if teachers only received additional payment after 27, rather than 18 hours of work).[9] Although Tikhonov stated his opposition to any such changes, their mention could not have been welcomed by the already demoralised teaching force, whose problem of teachers' wage arrears still showed no signs of diminishing: although it was reported that the backlog of payments had more or less been resolved by December 1997,[10] the crisis had quickly re-emerged, leaving teachers in the middle of a bitter struggle, in the summer of 1998, for the right to receive the money they had earned.[11] By this point any lingering reputation the teaching force might have had for reluctance to engage in strike action had disappeared: according to Goskomstat (the State Committee responsible for collecting and disseminating statistical data), of all the strikes which took place in the Russian Federation in 1997, some 92 per cent were accounted for by teachers' strikes.[12]

Against this backdrop the decision to prioritise the stabilisation of the schools' socio-economic position may be seen to be prudent – if some of the measures proposed are not in themselves. This brings me back to the original goal of my research, which was to study the process of reform in the Russian school system. Perhaps my final conclusion should be that reform and innovation are not so important after all, that it does not matter that much if inertia is holding up the reforms, that the main – only? – priority should be to ensure that the school system survives the current turbulent period more or less intact.

In December 1995 I observed a lesson of English in a specialised English school in a large Russian city. The teacher was aged around 65, and the lesson followed, as one might expect, fairly 'traditional' lines: pupils were expected to regurgitate pre-learned material, were admonished if they forgot the 'right' answer, and were kept under tight control by the teacher. For the author, watching with his conditioned British view of the teaching process, the lesson had a number of shortcomings: the teacher failed to make sufficient cognitive demands on the pupils, did not encourage them to develop their skills of reasoning and enquiry, did not provide sufficient praise and encouragement, and so on. Yet when the pupils were questioned later by the author (without any teachers present), all professed to having a great deal of respect for this teacher, and did not even hint at any dissatisfaction with the methods she used. Indeed, as was later explained by the deputy headteacher, the pupils are grateful to this teacher for returning from retirement, for without her they would not have had a teacher of English, since the younger foreign language staff had left to take up jobs in the commercial sector. So much for reform.

One cannot escape the feeling that the school system is living on borrowed time, however. For a few more years, it will be able to survive on the inertia of the old system, with its old textbooks, old buildings, and existing, but increasingly ageing, teaching force. But what comes then?

Appendix 1: Educational Establishments Catering for the 6–17 Age-Band

Age (Grade)	Soviet model	'New' establishments
6–17 (I–XI)	Comprehensive school (*Obshcheobrazovatel'naya shkola*)	Gymnasium (*gimnaziya*) Lycée (*litsei*)
	Specialised school (in-depth study of particular discipline) (*Spetsializirovannaya shkola*)	
15–17 (IX–XI)	Evening school (*vechernyaya srednyaya shkola*)	
15–17 (IX–XI)	Professional-Technical College (*Professional'no-tekhnicheskoe uchilishche* – PTU)	College (*kolledzh*)
15–19	Technical college (*Tekhnikum*)	
	Pedagogical college (*Pedagogicheskoe uchilishche*)	

Appendix 2: Questionnaire for Teachers translated from Russian

Part 1: Personal and Professional Details

Sex F [ ] M [ ] Age
Position
Type of school
Length of service
Subject taught
Town/rural

Part 2: The Course of Reform

Change	*Level of necessity*	*Effect*
Decentralisation		
New types of school		
Democratisation		
Humanisation		
Humanitarisation		
Core curriculum		
State educational standards		
Private schools		
A teacher appraisal system		
Differentiation of education		
A national examinations system		
Selective entrance to the 10th grade		

1 With regard to the following please indicate

a) to what extent they are (were) necessary and b) what effect they have had, on the scale:
- a) necessity: 4–very nec. 3–nec. 2–not v. nec. 1–not at all nec. 0–do not know
- b) effect: 5–v. positive 4–positive 3–not noticeable 2–negative 1–v. negative 0–do not know

2 To what extent do the direction and content of reform reflect the opinions of practising teachers? (Circle the appropriate answer)

very quite not very not at all do not know

3 What level of influence do the following have on the course of reform? Give an assessment on the scale: 5–v. large 4–large 3–average 2–small 1–none 0–do not know

Headteacher . . . Municipal ed. authority . . . Ministry of Ed. . . . Regional ed. authority . . . District ed. auth. . . . Russian Academy of Education. . . . Teacher . . . Others . . .

Part 3: Teachers' Professional Activities

3a How do you view the issue of empowerment of teachers with greater freedom in the choice of the content of subjects taught and the methodology to be used?

[ ] v. positively [ ] pos. [ ] pos. and negative factors [ ] negatively
[ ] v. negatively [ ] do not know

4 What, in your opinion, are the 3 most important functions of a teacher? a) . . . b) . . . c) . . .

5 Will you still be working as a teacher in 5 years' time? [ ] Yes [ ] No [ ] Do not know

Part 4: Professional Development

6 In which type(s) of establishment did you train to be a teacher?

[ ] pedagogical institute/university [ ] pedagogical college [ ] university
[ ] pedagogical class

7 If you qualified as a teacher in the last 3 years, indicate how effectively you think your training prepared you for working in the modern Russian school

[ ] very well [ ] well [ ] satisfactorily [ ] unsatisfactorily [ ] do not know

8a How many in-service training courses have you attended in the last five years (indicate length)

i) ii) iii) iv) v) vi)

8b Where did these courses take place?

[ ] IUU/IPK [ ] *pedinstitut* [ ] your school [ ] another school
[ ] district ed. auth. [ ] private organisation [ ] others

8c To what extent have these courses helped you in the task of reform implementation?

[ ] very substantially [ ] substantially [ ] to some extent [ ] not at all
[ ] do not know

9 How often do you engage in the following forms of professional dialogue?

Form	*Never*	*Rarely*	*Monthly*	*Weekly*	*Daily*
Reading educational press					
Discussion with colleagues					
Reading ed. research literature					
Teachers' associations					
Reading official documents					
Attending lectures/seminars					
Research work					

Notes

Introduction

1 With regard to works published in the English language, the field of contemporary Soviet education studies was relatively strong in the UK for some time until the early 1990s, with scholars such as John Dunstan, Nigel Grant, James Muckle, Robert Pullin, James Riordan and others producing a considerable number of important publications, while in the USA such scholars as Ben Eklof, Larry Holmes, Mark Johnson, Anthony Jones and Stephen Kerr all continue to make valuable contributions. In the UK, however, this field of study has, unfortunately, declined in the 1990s, as the specialists mentioned have either retired or moved to other areas of research. It should be noted that German scholars such as Oskar Anweiler and Friedrich Kuebart have continued to produce a great deal of material on the subject of Soviet and Russian education, although such publications remain out of reach for the non-German-speaking student.

2 B. Eklof and E. Dneprov (eds), *Democracy in the Russian School: the Reform Movement in Education since 1984* (Boulder, CO: Westview, 1993).

3 B. Holmes, G. Read and N. Voskresenskaya, *Russian Education: Tradition and Transition* (London: Garland, 1995).

4 A. Jones (ed.), *Education and Society in the New Russia* (Armonk, NY: M.E. Sharpe, 1994).

5 For an evaluation of developments in Russian sociology, see V. Staroverov and C. Williams, 'Russian Sociology: Problems and Perspectives – Two Perspectives', in C. Williams, V. Chuprov and V. Staroverov (eds), *Russian Society in Transition* (Aldershot: Dartmouth, 1996), pp. 37–54.

6 I do not describe in detail the content of the school curriculum, or engage in an in-depth discussion of teaching methods and other matters concerning the learning process. For sources on curricular matters, the reader is advised to consult the bibliography of English-, French- and German-language works provided in the journal *Education in Russia, the Independent States and Eastern Europe.*

7 G. Thiesen and D. Adams, 'Comparative Education Research', in R. Murray Thomas (ed.) *International Comparative Education: Practices, Issues and Prospects* (Oxford: Pergamon, 1990), pp. 277–87.

8 I hope that the reader will allow me the adoption of the term 'comprehensive' school, common to readers in the UK but less so elsewhere, to refer to the Russian *obshcheobrazovatel'naya shkola*. This is justified, I feel, by the close similarity in function between the Russian and English models (although in the English system, of course, primary and secondary levels of education (roughly 4/5–11 and 11–16/18 respectively) are provided in separate establishments, while in the Russian system they are, on the whole, catered for in one establishment).

9 Specialised schools are to be found in most Russian cities, and have various 'profiles'. A school may, for example, be a foreign-language *spetsshkola* (usually English, German or French), while other profiles include mathematics, physics, music and sport.

10 See, for example, Geoffrey Walford's account of the difficulties which can confront researchers in the English school system, in G. Walford, 'Reflexive Accounts of Doing Educational Research' in G. Walford (ed.), *Doing Educational Research* (London: Routledge, 1991), pp. 1–18.

11 Various reasons can be suggested for such low levels of awareness. It reflects, for instance, the reluctance of many in Russia to assume responsibility for matters wider than those of immediate personal concern, a legacy of the Soviet era, in which the individual was discouraged from displaying initiative in the domain of societal development, but a trait also of life in the period of transition, with the pressures caused by economic and social crises causing a good number of people to focus on their 'micro-worlds' and withdraw from active social participation. For a discussion of the relationship between the individual and the 'system', and issues of personal agency in the Soviet Union and post-Soviet Russia, see V. Shlapentokh, *Public and Private Life of the Soviet People: Changing Values in Post-Stalin Russia* (Oxford: Oxford University Press, 1989) and V. Shlapentokh, 'Early Feudalism – the Best Parallel for Contemporary Russia?', *Europe-Asia Studies*, vol. 48, no. 3, 1996, pp. 393–411.

12 G. Men'shikova, 'Press-konferentsiya federal'nogo ministra obrazovaniya E.V. Tkachenko', *Narodnoe obrazovanie*, no. 7, 1995, p. 7.

1 What Does Russia Need from Its Schools?

1 See A. Jones, 'Problems in the Schools' in A. Jones, W. Connor and D. Powell (eds), *Soviet Social Problems* (Boulder, CO: Westview, 1991), p. 218.

2 On the perceived significance of 'vision' in educational change, see K. Louis and M. Miles, *Improving the Urban High School: What Works and Why* (New York: Teachers' College Press, 1990).

3 J. White, *The Aims of Education Revisited* (London: Routledge & Kegan Paul, 1982), pp. 2–3.

4 R. Jonathan, 'Education and "The Needs of Society"', in A. Hartnett and M. Nash (eds), *Education and Society Today* (London: Falmer Press, 1986), pp. 134–45.

5 P. Bourdieu and J. Passeron, *Reproduction in Education, Society and Culture* (London: Sage, 1977).

6 P. Willis, *Learning to Labour* (Farnborough: Saxon House, 1977).

7 On the case of the UK, for instance, see B. Troyna and J. Williams, *Racism, Education and the State* (London: Croom Helm, 1986).

8 L. Davies, 'The Management and Mismanagement of School Effectiveness', *Compare*, vol. 24, no. 3, 1994, p. 206.

9 On popular attitudes towards education in England, see J. McKenzie, *Education as a Political Issue* (Aldershot: Avebury, 1993).

10 T. Rigby, 'Russia in Search of Its Future', in A. Saikal and W. Maley

(eds), *Russia in Search of its Future* (Cambridge: Cambridge University Press, 1995), p. 217.

11 B. Yeltsin, 'Ukaz No. 1 prezidenta Rossiiskoi Sovetskoi Federativnoi Sotsialisticheskoi Respubliki: O pervoocherednykh merakh po razvitiyu obrazovaniya v RSFSR', *Uchitel'skaya gazeta*, no. 29, 16–23 July 1991, p. 2.

2 The Development of the Reform Agenda

1 M. Archer, *Social Origins of Educational Systems* (London: Sage, 1984), pp. 132–4.

2 For discussion of the role of 'negotiation' in the functioning of education systems, see Archer, *ibid.*, pp. 120–24 and 130–36.

3 E. Dneprov, 'Bureaucratic Tyranny (Must be Eliminated from the School)', in B. Eklof and E. Dneprov (eds), *Democracy in the Russian School: the Reform Movement since 1984* (Boulder, CO: Westview), p. 36.

4 W. Mitter, 'The Teacher and the Bureaucracy: Some Considerations Concluded from a Soviet Case', *Compare*, vol. 17, no. 1, 1987, pp. 47–60.

5 J. Muckle, *Portrait of a Soviet School under Glasnost'* (London: Macmillan, 1990), p. 74.

6 On this period, see L. Holmes, *The Kremlin and the Schoolhouse: Reforming Education in Soviet Russia, 1917–1931* (Bloomington, IN: Indiana University Press, 1991).

7 D. Shturman, *The Soviet Secondary School* (London: Routledge, 1988), pp. 63–4.

8 For a fascinating and revealing account of the pattern of relations between the Party authorities and the general public, see L. Holmes, 'Legitimizing the Soviet Regime: School No. 35, 1931–1937', in B. Eklof (ed.), *School and Society in Tsarist and Soviet Russia* (London: Macmillan, 1993), pp. 176–203.

9 On the 1958 reforms, see M. Matthews, *Education in the Soviet Union: Policies and Institutions since Stalin* (London: Allen and Unwin, 1982) and J. Schwartz and W. Keech, 'Group Influence and the Policy Process in the Soviet Union', *The American Political Science Review*, no. 62, 1968, p. 840.

10 A. Jones, 'Problems in the Schools', in A. Jones, W. Connor and D. Powell (eds), *Soviet Social Problems* (Boulder, CO: Westview, 1991), p. 216.

11 E. Jones, *Red Army and Society* (London: Allen & Unwin, 1985).

12 K. Shaw, 'Change in the Soviet School System: Some Factors Associated with the 1984 Reforms', University of Exeter: Unpublished PhD thesis, 1987.

13 See, for example, V. Sukhomlinskii, *Serdtse otdayu detyam* (Kiev: Radians'ka shkola, 1973).

14 For Russian-language accounts, see I. Bazhenova (ed.), *Pedagogicheskii poisk* (Moscow: Pedagogika, 1988); E. Dneprov, *Chetvertaya shkol'naya reforma v Rossii* (Moscow: Interfaks, 1994); A. Petrovskii (ed.), *Novoe pedagogicheskoe myshlenie* (Moscow: Pedagogika, 1989). For an English-language account, see B. Holmes, G. Read and N. Voskresenskaya, *Russian Education: Tradition and Transition* (London: Garland Publishing, 1995).

15 V. Shatalov, *Pedagogicheskaya proza* (Moscow: Pedagogika, 1980).

16 V. Shatalov, *Kuda i kak ischezli troiki?* (Moscow: Pedagogika, 1980).
17 In the Soviet school system pupils were assessed according to a five-point scale, with 1 as the lowest, 5 as the highest grade. The middle grade of 3, or a *troika*, was used more and more infrequently by Soviet teachers towards the 1980s, with grade inflation becoming a common feature of the system, as a result of pressure (from the educational authorities) for evidence of improvements in results.
18 Sh. Amonashvili, *Zdravstvuite deti!* (Moscow: Prosveshchenie, 1988).
19 Sh. Amonashvili, *Kak zhivete, deti?* (Moscow: Prosveshchenie, 1991).
20 See 'Pedagogika sotrudnichestva', *Uchitel'skaya gazeta*, October 18, 1986, p. 2; 'Demokratizatsiya lichnosti', *Uchitel'skaya gazeta*, October 17, 1987, p. 3; 'Metodika obnovleniya', *Uchitel'skaya gazeta*, March 19, 1988, pp. 2–3; 'Voidem v novuyu shkolu', *Uchitel'skaya gazeta*, October 18, 1988, p. 2.
21 J. Dunstan and A. Suddaby, 'The Progressive Tradition in Soviet Schooling to 1988', in J. Dunstan (ed.), *Soviet Education under Perestroika* (London: Routledge), p. 9.
22 N. Grant, 'Education in the Soviet Union: the Last Phase', *Compare*, vol. 22, no. 1, 1992, p. 74.
23 See, for example, the contributions to I. Bazhenova (ed.), *Pedagogicheskii poisk* (Moscow: Pedagogika, 1988).
24 A. Suddaby, 'An Evaluation of the Contribution of the Teacher-Innovators to Soviet Educational Reform', *Comparative Education*, vol. 25, no. 2, 1989, pp. 245–56.
25 *Tvorcheskii soyuz uchitelei SSSR* (Moscow: VNIK, 1989).
26 B. Yeltsin, 'School Reform: Ways to Accelerate It', *Soviet Education*, vol. 31, no. 2, 1989, pp. 76–90 (translated from *Uchitel'skaya gazeta*, July 3, 1986, pp. 1–2).
27 M. Gorbachev, 'Youth: A Creative Force for Revolutionary Renewal', *Soviet Education*, vol. 31, no. 3, 1989, pp. 3–4 (translated from *Uchitel'skaya gazeta*, April 18, 1987, pp. 1–2).
28 E. Ligachev, 'O khode perestroiki srednei i vysshei shkoly i zadachakh Partii po ee osushchestvleniyu', *Uchitel'skaya gazeta*, February 18, 1988, pp. 1–4.
29 Jones, *op cit.*, p. 217.
30 Yu. Rostovtsev, 'Demokratizatsiya. Glasnost'. Samostoyatel'nost'.', *Studencheskii meridian*, no. 3, 1988, pp. 24–9.
31 For an impression of the policies being proposed by Yagodin and Shadrikov, see G. Yagodin, 'Cherez gumanizatsiyu i demokratizatsiyu k novomu kachestvu obrazovaniya', *Uchitel'skaya gazeta*, April 11, 1988, p. 1; and V. Shadrikov, 'Shkola: Vremya obnovleniya', *Narodnoe obrazovanie*, no. 9, 1988, pp. 7–12.
32 Jones, *loc cit.*
33 See, for example, *VNIK–Shkola: Bibliografiya osnovnykh rabot* (Moscow: VNIK, 1989); *VNIK–Shkola: Promezhutochnye rezul'taty raboty* (Moscow: VNIK, 1990).
34 On this matter, see B. Gershunskii, 'Eto li doroga k khramu?', *Sovetskaya pedagogika*, no. 1, 1990, pp. 98–102 and I. Khankasaeva, 'Akademicheskii teatr pedagogicheskoi dramy', *Rossiiskaya gazeta*, December 14, 1991, p. 4.

35 'Proekt: Kontseptsiya obshchego srednego obrazovaniya kak bazovogo v edinoi sisteme nepreryvnogo obrazovaniya (tezisy)', *Uchitel'skaya gazeta*, August 25, 1988, p. 2.
36 *Proekt: Kontseptsiya obshchego srednego obrazovaniya* (Moscow: Gosudarstvennyi komitet po narodnomu obrazovaniyu / Vremennyi nauchno-issledovatel'skii kollektiv SHKOLA, 1988).
37 Muckle, *op cit.*, p. 78.
38 For discussion of the two concepts, see Muckle, *Portrait of a Soviet School under Glasnost'* (London: Macmillan, 1990).
39 'Zakon Rossiiskoi Sovetskoi Federativnoi Sotsialisticheskoi Respubliki ob obrazovanii. Proekt', *Uchitel'skaya gazeta*, no. 29, July 16–23, 1991, pp. 2 and 5.
40 O. Marinicheva, 'Power Was Dumped in Our Laps: What Happens to the Former Opposition When it Ends Up in the Corridors of Power', in B. Eklof and E. Dneprov (eds), *Democracy in the Russian School: the Reform Movement in Education since 1984* (Boulder, CO: Westview), p. 130.
41 'Zakon Rossiiskoi Federatsii ob obrazovanii', *Uchitel'skaya gazeta*, no. 28, August 4, 1992, pp. 10–15; 'O poryadke vvedeniya v deistvie zakona Rossiiskoi Federatsii "Ob obrazovanii"', *Vedemosti S"ezda Narodnykh Deputatov Rossiiskoi Federatsiii Verkhovnogo Soveta Rossiiskoi Federatsii*, no. 30, 1992, p. 1797.
42 J. de Groof, 'Analysis of the Legislation on Education of the Russian Federation, in J. De Groof (ed.), *Comments on the Law on Education of the Russian Federation* (Leuven: Acco, 1993) p. 31.
43 *Ibid.*
44 For one such critical, but constructive, appraisal, see M. Johnson, 'Russian Education Reform in the 1990s', *The Harriman Review*, vol. 9, no. 4, 1996, pp. 36–45.
45 J. Sutherland, '*Perestroika* in the Soviet General School: From Innovation to Independence?' in J. Dunstan (ed.), *Soviet Education Under Perestroika* (London: Routledge), pp. 14–29.
46 See the account of this struggle in B. Holmes, G. Read and N. Voskresenskaya, *Russian Education: Tradition and Transition* (London: Garland), pp. 296–7.
47 'Ofitsioz: Tul'skii pedsovet', *Uchitel'skaya gazeta*, no. 29, August 11, 1992, p. 20.
48 G. Semykina, 'Glavnoe – est' vybor', *Narodnoe obrazovanie*, no. 6, 1993, p. 14.

3 The Programme for Change

1 E. Dneprov, *Chetvertaya shkol'naya reforma v Rossii* (Moscow: Interfaks, 1994), p. 76.
2 For a summary of the programme of the 1984 reforms, see B. Szekeley, 'The New Soviet Educational Reform', *Comparative Education Review*, vol. 30, no. 3, 1986, pp. 321–43.
3 See, for example, 'Polozhenie o srednei obshcheobrazovatel'noi shkole', *Uchitel'skaya gazeta*, August 16, 1988, p. 2.
4 For Western critiques of the standard of Soviet school education, see

G. Avis (ed.), *The Making of the Soviet Citizen: Character Formation and Civic Training in Soviet Education* (London: Croom Helm, 1987); J. Dunstan (ed.) *Soviet under Scrutiny* (Glasgow: Jordanhill College, 1987); J. Muckle, *Portrait of a Soviet School under Glasnost'* (London: Macmillan, 1990).

5 B. Gershunskii and R. Pullin, 'Current Dilemmas for Soviet Secondary Education: An Anglo-Soviet Analysis', *Comparative Education*, 26, 2 and 3, 1990, pp. 310–11.

6 See for example, V. Sobkin and P. Pisarskii, *Sotsiokul'turnyi analiz obrazovatel'noi situatsii v megapolise* (Moscow: Tsentr sotsiologii obrazovaniya, 1992) (a study of teacher and parent opinion in Moscow). For a study of pupils' views on the education they received, see A. Ovsyannikov, 'Innovatsii v shkole: Kharakter i rezul'taty', *Narodnoe obrazovanie*, no. 6, 1993, pp. 16–27.

7 The essence of the 1992 Law, for instance, is evident in such documents as VNIK–Shkola's publication: V. Sobkin, A. Levinson and A. Grazhdankin, *Shkola – 1988: Problemy. Protivorechii. Perspektivy* (Moscow: Gosudarstvennyi komitet SSSR po narodnomu obrazovaniyu, 1988).

8 I. Khankasaeva, untitled article, *Rossiiskie vesti*, August 29, 1992, cited in B. Eklof, 'The Most Difficult Year in the History of Our Schools', *ISSE Newsletter*, vol. 2, no. 1, 1992, p. 1.

9 J. Coons, 'The New Russian Education Law: an Appreciation and Some Precautions', in J. de Groof (ed.) *Comments on the Law on Education of the Russian Federation* (Leuven: Acco, 1993), p. 87.

10 E. Rutkovskaya, 'Legko li vzroslet' segodnya?', *Pedagogika*, no. 4, 1995, pp. 111–13.

11 See, for example, Ya. Sokolov, 'O demagogii i demokratii', *Uchitel'skaya gazeta*, nos. 19–20, May 4, 1994, p. 11.

12 V. Bolotov, 'Political Education in Russia: the Rôle of Secondary Education', *Education in Russia, the Independent States and Eastern Europe*, vol. 14, no. 1, 1996, pp. 2–7.

13 V. Karakovskii, 'Vospitanie v obshchestve sotsial'nykh peremen', *Mir obrazovaniya*, no. 0 (special first number), 1995, pp. 24–5.

14 R. Kurbatov, 'Drugaya shkola', *Sem'ya i shkola*, no. 7, 1996, p. 3.

15 V. Bolotov, 'The Challenge of Educational Reform in Russia', *ISRE Newsletter*, vol. 3, nos. 1 and 2, 1994, p. 3.

16 For an account of an interview with Yagodin on these matters, see L. Pleshakov, 'Vek zhivi, vek uchis'', *Ogonek*, vol. 36, nos. 1–2, 1990, p. 31.

17 By 1992 there were more than 100 non-state educational establishments across the Russian Federation, with 31 of these in Moscow, 9 in St Petersburg (A. Kuzyakin, 'Negosudarstvennym shkolam–gosudarstvennuyu podderzhku', *Vospitanie shkol'nikov*, nos. 5–6, 1992, p. 8).

18 'Specialised' schools, in which certain subjects (e.g. mathematics and physics, a foreign language, or sport) were studied intensively had been a feature of Soviet education since the late 1950s. (See J. Dunstan, *Paths to Excellence and the Soviet School* (Windsor: NFER Publishing, 1978)).

19 At the start of the 1991–92 school year there were 303 gymnasia and 195 lycées in Russia, compared with the figures of 100 and 77 respectively a year before (D. Savel'ev, 'Chto pridet na smenu pedagogicheskomu romantizmu?', *Narodnoe obrazovanie*, no. 8, 1994, p. 16).

20 V. Bibler, *Shkola dialoga kul'tur: Osnovy programmy* (Kemerovo: ALEF gumanitarnyi tsentr, 1992).
21 See, for example, A. Adamskii, 'Gde uchit' detei?', *Ogonek*, nos. 20–21, 1992, pp. 1–2 and A. Baiduzhii, 'V shkolakh Rossii poyavyatstya vauchery', *Nezavisimaya gazeta*, February 3, 1995, p. 5.
22 V. Zhukov, 'Chastnye shkoly kak obshchestvennoe yavlenie', *Vospitanie shkol'nikov*, nos. 3–4, 1992, pp. 21–5.
23 A. Kuzyakin, 'Negosudarstvennym shkolam – gosudarstvennuyu podderzhku', *Vospitanie shkol'nikov*, nos. 5–6, 1992, pp. 8–9.
24 See, for example, L. Rybakova, E. Moroz and E. Panova, 'Trudnosti uchitel'skoi professii', *Pedagogika*, no. 2, 1993, pp. 59–63.
25 See Dunstan, *loc cit.*
26 L. Denisova, 'Problemy malokomplektnoi', *Narodnoe obrazovanie*, no. 5, 1989, pp. 46–51.
27 See, for example, R. Vendrovskaya, 'Lessons of Differentiated Instruction', *Russian Education and Society*, vol. 34, no. 1, 1992, pp. 73–94 (translated from *Sovetskaya pedagogika*, no. 11, 1990, pp. 78–86).
28 E. Belova, 'Odarennyi rebenok na poroge shkoly', *Sem'ya i shkola*, no. 3, 1994, pp. 10–13.
29 J. Dunstan, 'Clever Children and Curriculum Reform', in A. Jones (ed.), *Education and Society in the New Russia* (Armonk, NY: M.E. Sharpe, 1994), p. 96.
30 'The Law on Education of the Russian Federation', in J. De Groof (ed.), *Comments on the Law on Education of the Russian Federation* (Leuven: Acco, 1993), p. 118.
31 See, for example, G. Yagodin, 'Tol'ko svobodnaya shkola vospitaet svobodnogo cheloveka', *Sem'ya*, no. 5, February 11, 1990, pp. 8–9.
32 V. Serikov, 'Lichnostno-orientirovannoe obrazovanie', *Pedagogika*, no. 4, 1994, pp. 101–2.
33 O. Stepunina, 'Pedagogicheskaya kontseptsiya P.P. Blonskogo i sovremennost'', *Pedagogika*, no. 3, 1995, pp. 108–10.
34 For Western analyses of the introduction of the policy of humanisation in the Russian school, see H. Daniels, N. Lucas, M. Totterdell and O. Fromina, 'Humanisation in Russian Education: a Transition Between State Determinism and Individualism', *Educational Studies*, vol. 21, no. 1, 1995, pp. 29–39; W. Kohli, 'Humanising Education in the Soviet Union: A Plea for Caution in these Postmodern Times', *Studies in Philosophy and Education*, vol. 11, no. 2, 1991, pp. 51–63.
35 E. Dneprov, *Reform of Education in Russia and State Policy in the Educational System* (Moscow: Ministry of Education of the Russian Federation, 1992), p. 4.
36 Ovsyannikov, *op cit.*, p. 20.
37 See, for example, K. Ivanov, 'Shkola glazami uchashchikhsya', *Vospitanie shkol'nikov*, no. 2, 1991, pp. 26–8; A. Ovsyannikov, V. Shuvalova and O. Shinyaeva, 'Mikroklimat v shkole i samochuvstvie shkol'nikov i uchitelei', *Narodnoe obrazovanie*, nos. 7–8, 1993, pp. 27–36.
38 L. Davies, *Beyond Authoritarian School Management* (Ticknell: Education Now Books, 1994).
39 C. Rogers, *Freedom to Learn for the Eighties* (Columbus, OH: Merrill, 1983).

40 See, for example, L. Aizerman, 'Gumanizm – protiv tekhnokratizma', *Narodnoe obrazovanie*, no. 7, 1989, pp. 76–81; V. Ermolaev, 'Na minnykh polyakh gumanitarizatsii', *Uchitel'skaya gazeta*, no. 44, November 14, 1995, p. 9.
41 R. Lewis, M. Newitt and A. Sokolov, *Reform of History Teaching and Research in Russia* (University of Exeter: Report to Nuffield Foundation, 1993).
42 *Russia: Education in the Transition* (Washington, DC: World Bank, 1995) p. 23.
43 M. Levitskii, L. van den Brook and G. Andre (eds), *Ekonomicheskoe obrazovanie v shkole: Materialy mezhdunarodnogo seminara* (St Petersburg: Obrazovanie, 1995).
44 See, for example, Beare and Slaughter, *op cit.*
45 A. Sandi, 'Why Is It So Difficult? Misconceptions about East European Education in Transition', *International Review of Education*, vol. 38, no. 6, 1992, p. 638.
46 See, for example, M. Jennings and R. Niemi (eds), *The Political Character of Adolescence: the Influence of Families and Schools* (Princeton, NJ: Princeton University Press, 1974).
47 M. Hepburn (ed.), *Education in Democratic Schools and Classrooms* (Washington, DC: National Council for the Social Sciences, 1983).
48 P. Szebenyi, 'Change in the Systems of Public Education in East Central Europe', *Comparative Education*, vol. 28, no. 1, 1992, p. 19.
49 J. Kotásek, 'Visions of Educational Development in the Post-Socialist Era', *International Review of Education*, vol. 39, no. 6, 1993, pp. 473–87; N. Paustovič, 'Problems of Reforming Educational Systems in Post-Communist Countries', *International Review of Education*, vol. 39, no. 5, 1993, pp. 405–18.
50 C. Bîrzea, *Educational Policies of the Countries in Transition* (Strasbourg: Council of Europe Press, 1994); M. Kozakiewicz, 'The Difficult Road to Educational Pluralism in Central and Eastern Europe', *Prospects*, vol. 22, no. 2, 1992, pp. 207–15.

Introduction to Part II

1 E. Tkachenko, 'Education Reform in Russia', *ISRE Newsletter*, vol. 3, nos 1–2, 1994, p. 14.
2 P. Shchedrovitskii, 'Zhizn' vzaimy', *Uchitel'skaya gazeta*, no. 31, August 15, 1995, p. 6.
3 'Ob itogakh raboty Ministerstva obrazovaniya Rossiiskoi Federatsii v 1994 godu i osnovnykh zadachakh razvitiya obrazovaniya na 1995 god', *Vestnik obrazovaniya*, no. 6, 1995, p. 63.
4 S. Hord, *Evaluating Educational Innovation* (London: Croom Helm, 1987); S. Sarason, *Revisiting 'The Culture of the School and the Problem of Change'* (New York: Teachers' College Columbia University, 1996), pp. 69–93.
5 See, for example, M. Fullan, *The New Meaning of Educational Change* (London: Cassell, 1991); J. Goodlad, *The Dynamics of Educational Change* (Toronto: McGraw-Hill, 1975).
6 S. Sarason, *The Predictable Failure of Educational Reform* (San Francisco, CA: Jossey-Bass 1990).

7 E. Tkachenko, 'Vystuplenie ministra obrazovaniya RF Evgeniya Tkachenko na mezhdunarodnoi konferentsii po obrazovaniyu "K kul'ture mira, pravam cheloveka, demokratii"', *Narodnoe obrazovanie*, nos. 9–10, 1994, p. 5.

8 M. Raywid, 'The Evolving Effort to Improve Schools: Pseudo-Reforms, Incremental Reform, and Restructuring', *Phi Delta Kappan*, vol. 72, no. 2, 1990, pp. 139–43.

9 M. Sashkin and J. Egermeier, 'School Change Models and Processes: a Review of Research and Practice', Paper presented at the Annual Meeting of the American Educational Research Association, San Francisco, 1992.

4 The Challenge of Devolution

1 M. Fullan, *Change Forces* (London: Falmer Press, 1993).

2 Yu. Gromyko, N. Alekseev and V. Slobodchikov, 'Chetvertaya reforma obrazovaniya v Rossii proizoshla! (No ob etom znayut tol'ko v apparate Filatova i chleny VAKa iz Prezidiuma Rossiiskoi akademii obrazovaniya', *Rossiya 2010*, no. 5, 1994, pp. 112–13.

3 V. Molodtsova, 'A v ostal'nom, prekrasnaya markiza, vse khorosho. Vse – khorosho?', *Uchitel'skaya gazeta*, no. 2, January 11, 1994, p. 4.

4 Dneprov had served as a naval officer, and had subsequently worked as an historian in the Academy of Pedagogical Sciences.

5 V. Molodtsova, 'Vse tainoe kogda-to stanet yavnym', *Uchitel'skaya gazeta*, no. 36, September 14, 1993, p. 16.

6 In contradiction of this point, Kinelev resigned in February 1998, as the final draft of the present manuscript was being prepared. He was replaced by Aleksandr Nikolaevich Tikhonov, the former first deputy minister under Kinelev. An appraisal of this development is given in the epilogue. See 'Kinelevym stal Tikhonov', *Uchitel'skaya gazeta*, no. 9, March 10, 1998, p. 3.

7 'Poltora goda: Lyusinovskaya – Chistye prudy', *Uchitel'skaya gazeta*, no. 8, March 3, 1998, p. 2.

8 G. Semykina, 'Glavnoe – est' vybor', *Narodnoe obrazovanie*, no. 6, 1993, pp. 6–13.

9 'Polozhenie o Ministerstve obrazovaniya RSFSR', *Vestnik obrazovaniya*, no. 3, 1991, pp. 16–23.

10 See, for example, E. Tkachenko, 'Ne zhdut ukazov, prikazanii i direktiv', *Uchitel'skaya gazeta*, nos. 27–9, July 6, 1993, p. 2.

11 V. Kinelev, the future Minister of Education, in an interview with O. Ogorodnikova, 'O tom, kak possorilis' Evgenii Viktorovich i Vladimir Georgievich', *Uchitel'skaya gazeta*, no. 6, February 6, 1996, p. 10.

12 H. Corbett and B. Wilson, *Testing, Reform and Rebellion* (Norwood, NY: Ablex, 1990).

13 M. Archer, *Social Origins of Educational Systems* (London: Sage, 1984), p. 179.

14 M. Fullan, *The New Meaning of Educational Change* (London: Cassell, 1991).

15 Archer, *op cit.*

16 C. Glenn, 'Organizing the Russian Educational System for Freedom and Accountability', in J. de Groof (ed.), *Comments on the Law on Education*

of the Russian Federation (Leuven: Acco, 1993) pp. 95–104. See also V. Shaulin, 'The Law on Education of the Russian Federation', *ISRE Newsletter*, vol. 4, no. 2, 1995 pp. 2–11.

17 V. Petrulenkov, 'Nash orientir: "Ne otstupat'"', *Uchitel'skaya gazeta*, no. 6, February 8, 1994, p. 7.

18 The text of the amendments is provided in 'O vnesenii izmenenii i dopolnenii v Zakon Rossiiskoi Federatsii "Ob obrazovanii"', *Uchitel'skaya gazeta*, no. 5, January 31, 1996, pp. 1–4 (supplement 'Iz pervykh ruk') and no. 6, February 6, 1996, pp. 1–4 (supplement 'Iz pervykh ruk'). For a commentary by the Ministry of Education official responsible for overseeing the preparation of the amendments, see Z. Dashchinskaya, 'Nashu zhizn' izmenili i dopolnili', *Uchitel'skaya gazeta*, no. 6, February 6, 1996, p. 15.

19 See, for example, D. Dmitriev, 'Struktura razvitiya obrazovaniya', *Uchitel'skaya gazeta*, no. 4, February 2, 1993, p. 23; B. Gershunskii, *Federal'naya programma razvitiya obrazovaniya v Rossii-kontseptsiya* (Moscow: Institut teoreticheskoi pedagogiki i mezhdunarodnykh issledovanii v obrazovanii, 1993).

20 *Federal'naya programma razvitiya obrazovaniya v Rossii: Proekt* (Moscow: Ministerstvo obrazovaniya Rossiiskoi Federatsii, 1994).

21 E. Podosenova, 'Federal'naya programma: Kak ee vypolnyat'?', *Narodnoe obrazovanie*, nos. 9–10, 1994, pp. 7–9.

22 E. Tkachenko, 'Deti i shkola: Problemy i perspektivy', *Mir obrazovaniya*, no. 1, 1996, p. 4.

23 'Den'gi, den'gi. Nichego, krome deneg', *Uchitel'skaya gazeta*, no. 25, June 6, 1995, pp. 16–17.

24 Yu. Koveshnikov and P. Polozhevets, 'Nishchii uchitel' – ne opora gosudarstvu', *Uchitel'skaya gazeta*, no. 4, February 7, 1996, p. 24.

25 *Federal'naya programma*, *loc cit.*, p. 39.

26 'Proekt: Prilozhenie k Federal'nomu zakonu "O realizatsii Federal'noi programmy razvitiya obrazovaniya"', *Uchitel'skaya gazeta*, no. 14, April 15, 1997, pp. 11–14 (supplement 'Iz pervykh ruk') and no. 15, April 22, 1997, pp. 11 and 14 (supplement 'Iz pervykh ruk').

27 'Kommentarii redaktsii', *Uchitel'skaya gazeta*, no. 14, April 15, 1997, p. 14 (supplement 'Iz pervykh ruk').

28 See, for example, the regional plan developed in Vladimir: Yu. Istratov and V. Popov, *Regional'naya programma razvitiya obrazovaniya Vladimirskoi oblasti* (Vladimir: Vladimirskii gosudarstvennyi pedagogicheskii institut, 1993).

29 See, for example, V. Koshkina and S. Raschetina, 'Regional'naya programma: Put' k novomu kachestvu', *Narodnoe obrazovanie*, no. 7, 1994, pp. 2–10.

30 'O sisteme soglashenii mezhdu Ministerstvom obrazovaniya Rossiiskoi Federatsii i pravitel'stvami (administratsiyami) sub"ektov Rossiiskoi Federatsii o sotrudnichestve v sfere obrazovaniya (i ikh realizatsii)', *Narodnoe obrazovanie*, no. 2, 1995, pp. 118–23.

31 Tkachenko, *op cit.*, p. 7.

32 See, for example, T. Klyusova, 'Surgut: Fokus upravleniya – obrazovatel'nyi', *Rossiya 2010*, no. 5, 1994, pp. 80–81.

33 L. Dorokhova, 'Sverdlovskii variant', *Uchitel'skaya gazeta*, no. 33, August 24, 1993, p. 4.
34 In St Petersburg, for instance, an ambitious programme has been conducted to encourage school pupils to learn more about the heritage of their city. See 'Nasledniki velikogo goroda: Orientiry deyatel'nosti uchastnikov kul'turno-patrioticheskogo molodezhnogo dvizheniya "Yunye za vozrozhdenie Peterburga" na 1995–1996 uchebnyi god' (St Petersburg: Sankt-Peterburgskii gorodskoi dvorets tvorchestva yunykh, 1995).
35 G. Men'shikova, 'Press-konferentsiya federal'nogo ministra obrazovaniya E.V. Tkachenko', *Narodnoe obrazovanie*, no. 7, 1995, p. 5.
36 S. Tsaregorodtseva, 'Obshchestvennaya ekspertiza. Kakova tsel'?', *Uchitel'skaya gazeta*, no. 46, November 23, 1993, p. 17.
37 Istratov and Popov, *op cit.*, pp. 149–50.
38 V. Zaitsev, 'Rukovoditel' poluchaet otmetki', *Uchitel'skaya gazeta*, nos. 22–23, May 23, 1995, p. 16.
39 In a survey of headteachers conducted in 1994 for the World Bank, for instance, only 30 per cent apparently were able to name correctly which level of the administrative system was responsible for funding the schools (D. Mann and V. Briller, 'Russian School Directors: Problems and Proposals' (Washington, DC: World Bank, 1994) p. 5).
40 Petrulenkov, *loc cit.*
41 V. Molodtsova, 'Boites' Dneprovykh, dary prinosyashchikh', *Uchitel'skaya gazeta*, no. 23, May 24, 1994, p. 12.
42 V. Bolotov, 'The Challenge of Educational Reform in Russia', *ISRE Newsletter*, vol. 3, nos. 1–2, 1994, p. 3.
43 See, for instance, an account of corruption in educational administration in V. Molodtsova, 'Razvod po-krasnodarskii', *Uchitel'skaya gazeta*, no. 41, October 19, 1993, p. 15.
44 See V. Surkov, 'Mamigonov protiv Tkachenko. Kto kogo?', *Uchitel'skaya gazeta*, nos. 22–23, May 23, 1995, p. 19. On this subject, Russian colleagues, sociologists working in a leading research institute in Moscow, attempted to find out, on my behalf, exactly how many kindergartens and PTU had been privatised by the end of 1997. The initial response in the Ministry of Education was that privatisation was prohibited, and thus no establishments had been affected; when my colleagues pointed out that the practice on the ground is to ignore legal barriers, and to engage in privatisation anyway, the ministry officials agreed, but admitted that although they knew such 'sales' were taking place, it was impossible to provide exact figures for the number of privatisations.
45 T. Mazzoni, 'Politics of Education at the Federal Level', in J. Scribner and D. Layton (eds), *The Study of Educational Politics* (London: Falmer Press, 1994), pp. 53–73.
46 'The Law on Education of the Russian Federation', in J. de Groof (ed.), *Comments on the Law on Education of the Russian Federation* (Leuven: Acco, 1993), p. 149.
47 Figures for the 1970s, 1991–92 and 1994 are from *Russia: Education in the Transition* (Washington, DC: World Bank, 1995) p. 15; for 1995, from *Finansy v Rossii: Statisticheskii sbornik* (Moscow: Goskomstat Rossii, 1996), p. 18.

48 *Russia: Education in the Transition, op cit.*, p. 15.
49 C. Williams, 'Economic Reform and Political Change in Russia, 1991–1996', in C. Williams, V. Chuprov and V. Staroverov (eds), *Russian Society in Transition* (Aldershot: Dartmouth, 1996), p. 13.
50 *Russia: Education in the Transition, loc cit.*
51 'Den'gi, den'gi', *op cit.*, p. 16.
52 *Russia: Education in the Transition, op cit.*, p. 26.
53 V. Nesterov, 'Mezhdu ognom i skovorodkoi', *Uchitel'skaya gazeta*, no. 33, August 24, 1993, pp. 12–13.
54 Yu. Rogovskii, '89 regionov – 89 ekonomiki obrazovaniya', *Uchitel'skaya gazeta*, nos. 19–20, May 11, 1995, p. 6.
55 'Deneg net', *op cit.*, p. 2.
56 E. Zhirkov, 'Den'gi, den'gi. Nichego, krome deneg', *Uchitel'skaya gazeta*, no. 25, June 6, 1995, p. 17.
57 *Ibid.*
58 E. Tkachenko, 'Deti i shkola: Problemy i perspektivy', *Mir obrazovaniya*, no. 1, 1996, p. 7.
59 E. Tkachenko, 'Den'gi, den'gi. Nichego, krome deneg', *Uchitel'skaya gazeta*, no. 25, June 6, 1995, p. 16.
60 A. Shpeko, 'Imen v pedagogike ne pribavilos'', *Uchitel'skaya gazeta*, no. 46, November 23, 1993, p. 17.
61 Molodtsova, *loc cit.*
62 G. Zhuravlev, O. Kuchmaeva, B. Mel'nikov and I. Orlova, 'The Socio-Demographic Situation' in C. Williams, V. Chuprov and V. Staroverov (eds), *Russian Society in Transition* (Aldershot: Dartmouth, 1996), pp. 58–60. Over the 5-year period from 1991 to 1996, for instance, the number of children (ages 0–16) in Russia decreased by 2 200 000 (E. Rybinskii, 'Sirotlivoe detstvo', *Uchitel'skaya gazeta*, no. 45, November 12, 1996, p. 6).
63 According to some forecasts, in the early years of the 21st century half of Russia's schools will not be required, as a result of falling rolls. Indeed, some demographers (cited by the chairman of the state *Duma*'s committee on health) predict that by 2015 Russia's population will have fallen to 137 million persons (from approximately 147 million in 1997), and thence to 40–45 million by the end of the century. Even if such figures prove to be alarmist, the trends are still extremely worrying, thus placing any respite for beleaguered educational administrators, searching for extra capacity in the system, into stark perspective. See S. Rykov, 'Rossiya stanovitsya stranoi vdov', *Uchitel'skaya gazeta*, no. 14, April 15, 1997, p. 15.
64 See, for example, V. Eroshin, 'Kto zashchitit shkolu?', *Narodnoe obrazovanie*, no. 2, 1995, pp. 2–4; N. Gurbatov, 'Cherez "Zolotye vorota" v rynok', *Uchitel'skaya gazeta*, nos. 19–20, May 11, 1995, p. 10; M. Musarskii, 'V usloviyakh ogranichennykh resursov', *Uchitel'skaya gazeta*, nos. 19–20, May 11, 1995, p. 6.
65 V. Eroshin, 'Istochniki finansirovaniya obrazovaniya', *Pedagogika*, no. 2, 1995, pp. 10–14.
66 A. Baiduzhii, 'V shkolakh Rossii poyavyatsya vauchery', *Nezavisimaya gazeta*, February 3, 1995, p. 5.
67 'Deneg – net', *loc cit.*

68 'Osnovnye napravleniya i itogi deyatel'nosti Ministerstva obshchego i professional'nogo obrazovaniya Rossiiskoi Federatsii v 1997 godu i pervoocherednye zadachi na 1998 god', *Uchitel'skaya gazeta*, no. 11, March 24, 1998, p. 11.
69 *Ibid.*, p. 1.
70 'Ob itogakh raboty Ministerstva obrazovaniya Rossiiskoi Federatsii v 1994 godu i osnovnykh zadachakh razvitiya obrazovaniya na 1995 god', *Vestnik obrazovaniya*, no. 6, 1995, p. 82.
71 'Deneg – net', *loc cit.*
72 V. Tkachenko, 'Deti i shkola: Problemy i perspektivy', *Mir obrazovaniya*, no. 1, 1996, p. 5.
73 I am grateful to Dr John Dunstan of CREES for drawing my attention to this point.
74 V. Eroshin, 'Istochniki finansirovaniya obrazovaniya', *Pedagogika*, no. 2, 1995, pp. 10–14.
75 *Ibid.*
76 N. Bunyakina, 'Plata za eksperiment', *Uchitel'skaya gazeta*, no. 11, March 21, 1995, p. 17.
77 See, for example, V. Kuznetsov, 'Lichnost' direktora shkoly', *Narodnoe obrazovanie*, nos. 9–10, 1993, pp. 19–23; E. Rozanova, 'Kak udovletvorit' obrazovatel'nyi zakaz', *Narodnoe obrazovanie*, no. 1, 1995, pp. 45–7; R. Shakurov, 'Odin na odin s uchitelem', *Narodnoe obrazovanie*, no. 1, 1995, pp. 48–9.
78 G. Suvorova, 'Demokratizatsiya shkol', *Nachal'naya shkola*, vol. 71, no. 2, 1989, pp. 59–61.
79 While the inclusion of pupils can be seen as an innovative and, I would argue, progressive measure, which offers much potential with regard to the democratisation of the Russian school (and is a development which many English schools could learn from, one might suggest) it has led to problems in some cases where the principle of democratisation has been taken too far. As the first Deputy Minister of Education observed, in some schools the subjects of mathematics and science were actually removed from the curriculum, after being voted down in the school council, with pupils giving preference to 'lighter' subjects such as Russian literature. (See V. Bolotov, 'The Challenge of Educational Reform in Russia', *ISRE Newsletter*, vol. 3, nos. 1 and 2, 1994, p. 4).
80 G. Men'shikova, 'Press-konferentsiya federal'nogo ministra obrazovaniya E.V. Tkachenko', *Narodnoe obrazovanie*, no. 7, 1995, pp. 4–11.
81 *Sbornik po materialam Inspektsii Komiteta po obrazovaniyu Sankt-Peterburga* (St Petersburg: Tsentr pedagogicheskoi informatsii, 1995).

5 The Culture of the Russian School and the Teaching Profession

1 See, for example, P. Dalin and H.-G. Rolff, *Changing the School Culture* (London: Cassell, 1993); S. Sarason, *The Culture of the School and the Problem of Change* (Boston: Allyn & Bacon, 1971).
2 Dalin and Rolff, *ibid.*, p. 18.
3 To complete Dalin and Rolff's typology, at the lowest level of innovative capacity is the 'fragmented' school, in which a culture of change

is said to be absent; then comes the 'project' school, which is engaged in change but which appears to lack a strong strategic vision; leaving the 'organic' school as the learning organisation, which is 'open' to improvement. *Ibid.*, pp. 15–20.

4 M. Fullan, *Change Forces* (London: Falmer Press, 1993), p. 42.

5 S. Hord, *Evaluating Educational Innovation* (London: Croom Helm, 1987) p. 15.

6 S. Rosenholtz, *Teacher's Workplace: the Social Organization of Schools* (New York: Longman, 1989).

7 D. Lortie, 'Built-in Tendencies toward Stabilizing the Principal's Rôle', *Journal of Research and Development in Education*, vol. 22, no. 1, 1987, pp. 80–90.

8 As one headteacher commented to me: 'I am supposed to provide leadership among the pedagogical collective [i.e. the teaching staff of the school), yet I find that such a task is extremely difficult to tackle, as I too am in need of the skills I am supposed to be encouraging my teachers to develop' (interview with the author, April 1996).

9 The title *metodist* (i.e. expert in teaching methods) is conferred on experienced teachers with a successful teaching record. Often a *metodist* will continue to work in a particular school, but will also be engaged in working as an adviser in a group of local schools, offering support on teaching methods and curriculum content to classroom teachers.

10 V. Kuznetsov, 'Lichnost' direktora shkoly', *Narodnoe obrazovanie*, nos. 9–10, 1993, pp. 19–23.

11 See, for example, L. Rybakova, E. Moroz and E. Panova, 'Trudnosti uchitel'skoi professii', *Pedagogika*, no. 2, 1993, pp. 59–63.

12 A. Orlov, 'Professional'noe myshlenie uchitelya kak tsennost'', *Pedagogika*, no. 6, 1995, p. 64.

13 For one example of many articles dealing with such issues, see V. Postavalova, 'Avtoritet uchitelya vysok, no polozhenie ego uzhasno', *Uchitel'skaya gazeta*, no. 35, September 2, 1997, p. 7.

14 For an interesting discussion of a study of the amount of time devoted to professionally related activities by a sample of teachers from Moscow, see 'A poutru oni prosnulis' "kontorskimi krysami"', *Uchitel'skaya gazeta*, nos. 14–15, April 14, 1998, p. 7.

15 The legal framework concerning the workload of educationalists in the Russian Federation is described by N. Tumova, 'Za chto nam ne platyat', *Uchitel'skaya gazeta*, nos. 14–15, April 14, 1998, p. 6.

16 D. Lawton, 'The National Curriculum in England since 1988', in D. Carter and M. O'Neill (eds), *International Perspectives on Educational Reform and Policy Implementation* (London: Falmer Press, 1995), pp. 45–51.

17 See, for example, A. Dworkin, *Teacher Burnout in the Public Schools: Structural Causes and the Consequences for Children* (Albany, NY: State University of New York Press, 1986).

18 M. Johnson, 'Russian Education Reform in the 1990s', *The Harriman Review*, vol. 9, no. 4, 1996, p. 37. In his analysis Johnson draws on other English-language sources on the subject of professionalism in the USSR and Russia, which the reader may wish to consult. See: A. Jones, 'Teachers in the Soviet Union', in A. Jones and E. Krause (eds), *Professions*

and the State: Expertise and Autonomy in the Soviet Union and Eastern Europe (Philadelphia: Temple University Press, 1991), pp. 152–66; H. Balzer (ed.), *Russia's Missing Middle Class: The Professions in Russian History* (Armonk, NY: M.E. Sharpe, 1996).

19 Johnson, *ibid.*, p. 44.

20 For analyses of the question of civil society in Russia, see, for example: A. Chernykh. 'Dolgii put' k grazhdanskomu obshchestvu', *Sotsiologicheskie issledovaniya*, nos. 8–9, 1994, pp. 173–81; Yu. Reznik, 'Formirovaniya institutov grazhdanskogo obshchestva', *Sotsiologicheskie issledovaniya*, no. 10, 1994, pp. 21–30.

21 P. Shchedrovitskii, 'Chto budet so shkoloi?', *Pervoe sentyabrya*, no. 12, February 1, 1994, p. 1.

22 V. Tumalev, 'The Teaching Profession in a Situation of Social and Political Change: Part 1 – The Teaching Profession as a Socio-Occupational Stratum', *Russian Education and Society*, vol. 39, no. 3, March 1997, pp. 41–2 (translated from *Uchitel'stvo v situatsii sotsial'no-politicheskikh peremen* (St Petersburg: Izdatel'stvo Sankt-Peterburgskogo universiteta ekonomiki i finansov, 1995). One can also note that St Petersburg may not be a typical example here, as the large size of the city, and the relatively prosperous living standards enjoyed by its inhabitants may well make it easier for teachers of the city to move jobs.

23 Unfortunately it did not prove possible to find statistical evidence to support this hypothesis which, nonetheless, was endorsed by all Russian contacts whom I questioned.

24 The credit for this analogy (and the chain of thoughts it set off in my research) is due to Edward Neather of the School of Education, University of Exeter.

25 S. Webber and T. Webber, 'Restructuring Initial Teacher Education in Russia', *Education in Russia, the Independent States and Eastern Europe*, vol. 12, no. 1, 1994, pp. 4–5.

26 I am grateful to Arfon Rees for reminding me of this point.

27 See, for example, J. Goodlad, *A Place Called School: Prospects for the Future* (New York: McGraw-Hill, 1984).

28 Dalin and Rolff, *op cit.*, p. 101.

29 See, Jones, *op cit.*; L. Panina, 'Gosudarstvo ravnodushno k uchitelyu', *Narodnoe obrazovanie*, no. 1, 1995, pp. 10–16.

30 See Shturman, *op cit.*

31 Tumalev, *op cit.*, p. 27.

32 *Ibid.*

33 S. Kerr, 'Teachers' Continuing Education and Russian School Reform', Paper delivered at the Conference of the American Association for the Advancement of Slavic Studies, October 28, 1995, p. 6.

34 See, for example, V. Yakovlev, 'Tak zhit' nel'zya!', *Uchitel'skaya gazeta*, no. 38, September 24, 1996, p. 4.

35 'Bastovat'? Ne bastovat'?', *Uchitel'skaya gazeta*, no. 35, September 12, 1995, p. 2.

36 S. Heyneman, 'Education and Social Stability in Russia: an Essay', *Compare*, vol. 27, no. 1, 1997, p. 7.

37 'Zabastovka zakonchilas'. Zabastovka prodolzhaetsya?', *Uchitel'skaya gazeta*, no. 38, October 3, 1995, p. 2.
38 G. Tarasevich, 'Den' uchitelya stal dnem zabastovki', *Uchitel'skaya gazeta*, no. 40, October 8, 1996, p. 4.
39 L. Sycheva, 'Otchayanie otchayavshikhsya', *Uchitel'skaya gazeta*, no. 42, October 31, 1995, p. 7.
40 'Osnovnye napravleniya i itogi deyatel'nosti Ministerstva' (1998), *op cit.*, p. 13.
41 *Ibid.*
42 O. Rodionova, 'Plany ministerstva – nashi plany?', *Uchitel'skaya gazeta*, no. 13, April 7, 1998, p. 2.
43 'Ne khotim rabotat' besplatno', *Uchitel'skaya gazeta*, nos. 14–15, April 14, 1998, p. 5.
44 See, for example, N. Bunyakina, 'Tak skol'ko zhe vse-taki deneg vydelili uchitelyam?', *Uchitel'skaya gazeta*, no. 25, June 18, 1996, p. 4.

6 Signs of Change?

1 Ovsyannikov, *op cit.*
2 Tumalev, *op cit.*, p. 7.
3 See, for example, N. Shirokova, 'Retsept "bul'ona" u kazhdogo svoi', *Uchitel'skaya gazeta*, nos. 22–3, May 23, 1995, p. 9.
4 A. Tubel'skii, 'Assotsiatsiya innovatsionnykh shkol i tsentrov predlagaet otmenit' "Polozhenie ob attestatsii", i ne tol'ko eto', *Uchitel'skaya gazeta*, no. 14, April 5, 1994, p. 16.
5 M. Fisher, 'Preodelenie neopredelennosti v rossiiskom obrazovanii', *Pedagogika*, no. 6, 1993, p. 18.
6 E. Yamburg, 'Kazhdoe vremya rozhdaet svoi nadezhdy. Ono zhe ikh i ispytivaet', *Uchitel'skaya gazeta*, no. 41, October 19, 1993, pp. 12–13.
7 Ovsyannikov, *op cit.*, p. 17.
8 'Osnovnye napravleniya i itogi deyatel'nosti Ministerstva' (1998), *op cit.*, p. 11.
9 *Ibid.*
10 *Ibid.*
11 V. Bolotov, 'The Reform of Education in New Russia: a Background Report for the OECD Review of Russian Education', *ISRE Newsletter*, vol. 6, no. 2, 1997, p. 9.
12 N. Bunyakina, 'Tak skol'ko zhe vse-taki deneg vydelili uchitelyam?', *Uchitel'skaya gazeta*, no. 25, June 18, 1996, p. 4.
13 By way of example, I can refer to the case of one alternative school in Moscow, called 'Kovcheg' (the Ark), which was established to cater for children with 'special educational needs,' providing them with a level of care which the Soviet system could rarely, if ever, have matched.
14 For examples of such guidelines for parents, see A. Glebova, N. Zolotova and S. Sokolov, 'Doroga v shkolu', *Domovoi*, March 3, 1995, pp. 138–43; 100 luchshikh shkol Rossii', *Ogonek*, no. 15, 1995, pp. 32–3.
15 Tubel'skii, *loc cit.*
16 See, for example, V. Zhukov, 'Chestno o chastnoi shkole', *Sem'ya i shkola*, no. 5, 1996, pp. 2–5.

17 See, for example, V. Zaitsev, 'Elitarnaya shkola i sud'ba strany', *Narodnoe obrazovanie*, nos. 2–3, 1994, pp. 5–18.
18 For examples of the character of the discussion of alternative and non-state schools in the early 1990s, see A. Anatol'ev, 'Protsent geniev vyshe v negosudarstvennykh shkolakh', *Nezavisimaya gazeta*, January 10, 1992, p. 6; A. Baiduzhii, 'Private Schools Teach Shooting and Praying', *Current Digest of the Post-Soviet Press*, vol. 44, no. 28, p. 27 (translated from *Nezavisimaya gazeta*, July 16, 1992, p. 6).
19 E.g. Zaitsev, *loc cit.*
20 E. Tkachenko, 'Deti i shkola: Problemy i perspektivy', 1996, p. 5.
21 O. Kutasova, 'Ne chastnyi vopros o chastnoi shkole', *Uchitel'skaya gazeta*, no. 36, September 27, 1994, p. 8.
22 'Kontseptsiya razvitiya negosudarstvennogo obrazovaniya v Rossii', *Uchitel'skaya gazeta*, no. 51, December 20, 1994, pp. 6–7.
23 See, for example, I. Pastukhova, 'Vsekh pod odnu grebenku?', *Uchitel'skaya gazeta*, no. 11, March 21, 1995, p. 14; T. Zgorzhel'skaya, '"Chastniki" zvonyat i sprashivayut', *Uchitel'skaya gazeta*, no. 9, March 7, 1995, p. 9.
24 K. Louis and M. Miles, *Improving the Urban High School: What Works and Why* (New York: Teachers' College Press, 1990).
25 Ovsyannikov, *loc cit.*
26 M. Fullan, *The New Meaning of Educational Change* (London: Cassell, 1991), p. 127.
27 On the reaction to the 1988 reforms in England, see N. Bennett and C. Carré, 'Teachers' Early Experiences of the Implementation of the British National Curriculum', in D. Carter and M. O'Neill (eds), *Case Studies in International Change: An International Perspective* (London: Falmer Press, 1995), pp. 184–98.
28 M. Westbrook, 'St Petersburg's Independent Schools', in A. Jones (ed.), *Education and Society in the New Russia* (Armonk, NY: M.E. Sharpe, 1994), pp. 103–17.
29 See, for example, I. Aref'ev, 'Proforientatsiya: uchenik, uchitel', vuz', *Pedagogika*, no. 3, 1995, pp. 65–8.
30 See, for example, S. Aleshenok, V. Chuprov and Yu. Zubok, 'Will It Be Possible to Integrate Young People in a Society Undergoing Transformation?', *Prospects*, vol. 25, no. 3, 1995, pp. 439–49.
31 V. Sobkin and P. Pisarskii, *Sotsiokul'turnyi analiz obrazovatel'noi situatsii v megapolise* (Moscow: Rossiiskaya Akademiya Obrazovaniya – Respublikanskii tsentr sotsiologii obrazovaniya, 1992), p. 88.
32 Ovsyannikov, *op cit.*, p. 22.
33 On the question of uniforms, a mixed pattern has developed since 1991, with some schools abandoning uniforms altogether, others doing so but then reintroducing them, either in the traditional design or in a more flexible format, in which, for example, male and female pupils wear a school sweatshirt, similar to the practice adopted by many schools in England in recent years.
34 See, for example, C. Hull and J. Rudduck, *Introducing Innovation to Pupils* (Norwich: Centre for Applied Research in Education, 1980).
35 G. Men'shikova, 'Press-konferentsiya federal'nogo ministra obrazovaniya E.V. Tkachenko', *Narodnoe obrazovanie*, no. 7, 1995, pp. 4–11.

36 See, for example, R. Davies, *Soviet History in the Yeltsin Era* (London: Macmillan, 1997), pp. 119–26.
37 A. Abramov, 'U semi vedomstv ditiya bez uchebnikov', *Uchitel'skaya gazeta*, nos. 22–3, 1995, p. 17.
38 O. Kutasova, 'Uchit'sya pridetsya bez uchebnikov', *Uchitel'skaya gazeta*, no. 26, June 14, 1995, p. 6.
39 'Ekspress-rassledovanie', *Uchitel'skaya gazeta*, no. 13, April 4, 1994, p. 2.
40 S. Kerr, 'Lessons Learned: Western Aid to Russian Education', *ISRE Newsletter*, vol. 5, no. 1, 1996, pp. 1–2.
41 B. Holmes, G. Read and N. Voskresenskaya, *Russian Education: Tradition and Transition* (London: Garland, 1995), p. 319.
42 'Bastovat'? Ne bastovat'?', *Uchitel'skaya gazeta*, no. 35, September 12, 1995, p. 2.
43 V. Molodtsova, 'Kto daet sovety Prezidentu?', *Uchitel'skaya gazeta*, no. 15, April 18, 1995, p. 19.
44 N. Tselishcheva, 'Otchet pered vsei stranoi', *Narodnoe obrazovanie*, no. 1, 1995, p. 3.
45 M. Levitskii and T. Goryunova, 'Uchitelem stat' legko. Trudnee im ostat'sya', *Uchitel'skaya gazeta*, no. 31, June 30, 1996, p. 3 (supplement 'Iz pervykh ruk').
46 'Deneg – net. Rezul'taty est'!', *op cit.*, p. 1.
47 'Osnovnye napravleniya i itogi deyatel'nosti Ministerstva', (1998), *loc cit.*
48 M. Kostikova, *K avgustovskim pedagogicheskim chteniyam* (Moscow: Ministerstvo obrazovaniya Rossiiskoi Federatsii, 1995), p. 1.
49 Tselishcheva, *op cit.*, p. 8.
50 Levitskii and Goryunova, *loc cit.*
51 'Osnovnye napravleniya i itogi deyatel'nosti Ministerstva', (1998), *loc cit.*
52 G. Berger, 'The Morale of Teachers in Crisis: Russia 1992', *Journal of Research and Development in Education*, vol. 27, no. 1, 1993, pp. 24–7.
53 Levitskii and Goryunova, *loc cit.*
54 'Ob itogakh raboty Ministerstva', (1995), *op cit.*, pp. 72–3.
55 E. Rybinskii, 'Polozhenie detei v Rossii', *Pedagogika*, no. 6, 1994, p. 5.
56 E. Val'kova, 'Klyuch ne beri!', *Uchitel'skaya gazeta*, no. 1, January 10, 1995, p. 18.
57 Rybinskii, *loc cit.*
58 Rybinskii, *op cit.*, p. 6.
59 V. Molodtsova, 'Znakomo li pravitel'stvo s Pasterom?', *Uchitel'skaya gazeta*, nos. 19–20, May 11, 1995, p. 7.
60 Aleshenok, Chuprov and Zubok, *loc cit.*
61 See, for example, V. Karakovskii, 'Obshchechelovecheskie tsennosti – osnova uchebno-vospitatel'nogo protsessa', *Vospitanie shkol'nikov*, no. 2, 1993, pp. 4–7.
62 Rybinskii, *op cit.*, p. 9.
63 'Deneg – net', *loc cit.*
64 See A. Markova, 'Sotrudnichestvo uchitelya i shkol'nogo psikhologa', *Pedagogika*, no. 6, 1994, pp. 43–51.

7 Mechanisms of Cohesion and Support

1 'Poyasnitel'naya zapiska k Bazisnomu uchebnomu planu obshcheobrazovatel'nykh uchrezhdenii Rossiiskoi Federatsii', *Uchitel'skaya gazeta,* nos. 27–9, July 6, 1993, pp. 18–19.

2 There are two versions of the curriculum for the primary-level classes (I to III) to cater for the needs of so-called 'profile' (*profil'nye*) schools or classes, in which pupils study additional subjects or a more intensive programme of core subjects (i.e. with a total of 26 as opposed to 22 hours load per week for the 1st form).

3 *Federal Components of the State Educational Standard for Primary, Secondary (Incomplete) and Secondary (Complete) Schools: General Provisions* (Moscow: Ministerstvo obrazovaniya Rossiiskoi Federatsii, 1995).

4 L. Vanyushkina, 'Nam nado ponimat' drug druga s poluslova', *Uchitel'skaya gazeta*, nos. 47–8, November 29, 1994, p. 14.

5 I. Yakimanskaya, 'My ne gotovy k vvedeniyu standarta', *Uchitel'skaya gazeta*, no. 1, January 4, 1994, p. 12.

6 See, for example, D. Dmitriev, 'Nestandartnye standarty', *Uchitel'skaya gazeta*, no. 31, September 22, 1992, p. 8–9; V. Simonov and E. Chernenko, 'Obrazovatel'nyi minimum: Izmerenie, dostovernost', nadezhnost'', *Pedagogika*, no. 4, 1994, pp. 30–4.

7 L. Sycheva, 'Regional'nyi komponent: Ot Moskvy do samykh do okrain', *Uchitel'skaya gazeta*, no. 8, February 20, 1996, p. 6.

8 'Bazisnyi uchebnyi plan: uspekhi i problemy', *Uchitel'skaya gazeta*, no. 31, September 30, 1996, p. 1.

9 See V. Mekhedov, 'Attestatsiya uchrezhdeniya: kak ee provodit', *Narodnoe obrazovanie*, no. 7, 1994, pp. 23–9.

10 'Polozhenie o poryadke litsenzirovaniya obrazovatel'nykh uchrezhdenii', *Uchitel'skaya gazeta*, no. 1, January 10, 1995, p. 14.

11 M. Rutkevich, 'Reforma shkoly i ee posledstviya', *Svobodnaya mysl'*, nos. 12–18, 1994, p. 53.

12 I am grateful to Dr John Dunstan of CREES for information supplied on the issue of appraisal in the Soviet system.

13 *Attestatsiya pedagogicheskikh i rukovodyashchikh rabotnikov gosudarstvennykh, munitsipal'nykh uchrezhdenii i organizatsii obrazovaniya Rossiiskoi Federatsii: Sbornik dokumentov Ministerstva obrazovaniya Rossiiskoi Federatsii – vypusk 1* (Moscow: Ministerstvo obrazovaniya Rossiiskoi Federatsii, 1994) and *Attestatsiya pedagogicheskikh i rukovodyashchikh rabotnikov gosudarstvennykh, munitsipal'nykh uchrezhdenii i organizatsii obrazovaniya Rossiiskoi Federatsii: Sbornik dokumentov Ministerstva obrazovaniya Rossiiskoi Federatsii – vypusk 2* (Moscow: Ministerstvo obrazovaniya Rossiiskoi Federatsii, 1994).

14 A. Alisova, 'Nam nado ponimat' drug druga s poluslova', *Uchitel'skaya gazeta*, nos. 47–8, November 29, 1994, p. 14.

15 V. Vershinin, 'Attestatsiya: dokazatel'stvo aksiomy', *Narodnoe obrazovanie*, no. 8, 1994, pp. 35–7.

16 In the town of Elets, for instance, among other problems it was reported that in some schools up to a quarter of the staff were awarded the second category, while elsewhere headteachers felt that none of their staff had shown their teaching skills to be of a sufficient standard to warrant assessment (Alisova, *loc cit.*).

17 *Ibid.*
18 I. Noskov, 'Bez pessimizma', *Uchitel'skaya gazeta*, no. 26, June 25, 1996, p. 13.
19 E. Nikitin, 'Posle kvalifikatsii – attestatsiya', *Uchitel'skaya gazeta*, no. 37, September 17, 1996, p. 10.
20 O. Ogorodnikova and P. Polozhevets, 'Fundamental'nost', preemstvennost', edinstvo', *Uchitel'skaya gazeta*, no. 7, February 16, 1996, p. 24.
21 M. Leont'eva, 'Rekomendatsii po provedeniyu vypusknykh ekzamenov v IX, XI (XII) klassakh obshcheobrazovatel'nykh uchrezhdenii Rossiiskoi Federatsii', *Uchitel'skaya gazeta*, no. 17, May 6, 1997, p. 7.
22 V. Khlebnikov, '"A ty gotov k testirovaniyu?"', *Uchitel'skaya gazeta*, no. 11, March 24, 1998, p. 10.
23 L. Aizerman, '"Ibo ot izbytka serdtsa govoryat usta"', *Uchitel'skaya gazeta*, no. 10, March 17, 1998, p. 9.
24 L. Kezina, 'Uchenye RAO – shkolam stolitsy', *Pedagogika*, no. 3, 1994, pp. 69–71.
25 I. Noskov, 'Bez pessimizma', *Uchitel'skaya gazeta*, no. 26, June 25, 1996, p. 13.
26 Webber and Webber, *loc cit.*; S. Webber, 'Demand and Supply: Meeting the Need for Teachers in the New Russian School', *Journal of Education for Teaching*, vol. 22, no. 1, 1996, pp. 9–26.

8 Teacher Education: Questions of Quality and Quantity

1 Among the extensive body of research conducted on this issue in the West, see, for example, J. Goodlad, *Teachers for Our Nation's Schools* (San Francisco, CA: Jossey-Bass, 1990).
2 See, for example, K. Howey and N. Zimphner. *Profiles of Preservice Teacher Education* (Albany, NY: SUNY Press, 1989).
3 The problem of neglect had a long tradition in the USSR. G. Mikhalev, for instance, in his article 'Sovershenstvovat' podgotovku uchitel'skikh kadrov', *Sovetskaya pedagogika*, no. 6, 1965, pp. 104–9, describes the problems caused by underfunding by the mid-1960s. For an account of the state of the system by the early 1990s, see S. Webber and T. Webber, 'Issues in Teacher Education', in A. Jones (ed.), *Education and Society in the New Russia* (Armonk, NY: M.E. Sharpe, 1994), pp. 231–59.
4 B. Gershunskii and R. Pullin, 'Current Dilemmas for Soviet Secondary Education: An Anglo-Soviet Analysis', *Comparative Education*, vol. 25, nos. 2 and 3, 1990, p. 311.
5 'Kafedra: Statfakt', *Uchitel'skaya gazeta*, September 8, 1992, p. 22.
6 P. Poppleton, R. Bolton, R. Pullin and G. Riseborough, '*Perestroika* and the Soviet Teachers', *New Era in Education*, vol. 71, no. 3, 1990, pp. 92–7.
7 See, for example, A. Marinin, 'My – storonniki otkrytosti', *Narodnoe obrazovanie*, no. 3, 1996, pp. 106–10.
8 For an analysis of developments in provision, see S. Kerr, 'Diversification in Russian Education', in A. Jones (ed.), *Education and Society in the New Russia* (Armonk, NY: M.E. Sharpe, 1944), pp. 47–74.
9 I. Noskov, 'Bez pessimizma', *Uchitel'skaya gazeta*, no. 26, June 25, 1996, p. 13.

10 'Ob itogakh raboty Ministerstva', (1995), *op cit.*, pp. 77–8.
11 Webber and Webber, *op cit.*, p. 246.
12 V. Men'shikov, 'Are We Teaching Any Old Thing, Any Old Way?', *Soviet Education*, vol. 33, no. 3, 1991, pp. 39–40.
13 E. Belozertsev, 'Pedagogicheskoe obrazovanie: Realii i perspektivy', *Pedagogika*, nos. 1–2, 1992, pp. 61–5; Yu. Kruglov, 'Podgotovka uchitelei: Problemy, problemy', *Sovetskaya pedagogika*, no. 4, 1991, pp. 87–92.
14 J. Higgins, 'Problems of the Selection and Professional Orientation of Soviet Pedagogical Students', *Comparative Education*, vol. 12, no. 2, 1976, pp. 157–62.
15 L. Dzhilavian, 'The Professional Attitude of Teacher Training Graduates in the Armenian SSR Toward Their Profession', *Soviet Education*, vol. 21, no. 6, 1981, pp. 92–6 (translated from *Sotsiologicheskie issledovaniya*, no. 4, 1978, pp. 141–43).
16 *Nepreryvnoe pedagogicheskoe obrazovanie* (St Petersburg: Rossiiskii gosudarstvennyi pedagogicheskii universitet imeni A.I. Gertsena, 1993).
17 See, for example, P. Reshetnikov, 'Podgotovka uchitelei v komplekse "peduchilishche-pedinstitut"', *Sovetskaya pedagogika*, no. 5, 1991, pp. 93–6; I. Zyazun, *Uchitel', kotorogo zhdut* (Moscow: Pedagogika, 1988).
18 A. Shpeko, 'Problemy obrazovaniya – eto problemy natsional'noi bezopasnosti', *Uchitel'skaya gazeta*, no. 47, November 30, 1993, p. 8.
19 Kostikova, *op cit.*, p. 4.
20 Webber, *op cit.*, pp. 18–19.
21 *Polozhenie o podgotovke magistra obrazovaniya: Proekt Vladimirskogo gosudarstvennogo pedagogicheskogo universiteta* (Vladimir: Vladimirskii gosudarstvennyi pedagogicheskii universitet, 1993).
22 G. Sarantsev, 'Poznavatel'naya samostoyatel'nost' budushchego uchitelya', *Pedagogika*, no. 4, 1995, pp. 63–6; G. Zhelezovskaya, 'Formirovanie pedagogicheskoi intellektual'noi kul'tury', *Pedagogika*, no. 2, 1995, pp. 55–60.
23 Z. Malobitskaya, 'Psikhologicheskaya perestroika uchitel'ya', *Narodnoe obrazovanie*, nos. 9–10, 1993, pp. 84–7.
24 N. Mel'nikova and N. Moreva, 'Gotovim pedagoga-novatora', *Narodnoe obrazovanie*, nos. 4–5, 1996, pp. 56–8.
25 I. Nekhames, 'V sentyabre zarplaty iz Moskvy mozhet i ne byt', *Uchitel'skaya gazeta*, no. 28, July 14, 1998, p. 8.

10 The Vulnerability of the School

1 J. Cook, *The Soviet Social Contract and Why It Failed* (Cambridge, MA: Harvard University Press, 1993). See also B. Silverman and M. Yanowitch, *New Rich, New Poor, New Russia: Winners and Losers on the Road to Capitalism* (Armonk, NY: M.E. Sharpe, 1997).
2 For a useful overview of the education 'policies' of the leading political parties before the December 1995 *Duma* elections, see 'Vybiraem dostoinykh. Ne agitiruem ni za kogo', *Uchitel'skaya gazeta*, no. 47, November 30, 1995, pp. 12–13.
3. See, for example, I. Afanas'ev, 'Boisya togo, kto skazhet "Ya znayu vse"', *Uchitel'skaya gazeta*, no. 47, November 30, 1993, pp. 14–15.

4 Television interview with V. Yakovlev, 21 December 1995, interview witnessed by the author.
5 T. Zarorina, 'Likvidatsiya budushchego?', *Molodezh'*, no. 1, 1995, pp. 63–6.
6 See, for example, P. Kulakov, 'Uchashchayasya molodezh' i religiya', *Sotsiologicheskie issledovaniya*, no. 11, 1995, pp. 91–9.
7 See, for example, question L64 in the monthly survey report *Ekonomicheskie i sotsial'nye peremeny*, no. 2, 1996, p. 70.
8 N. Nikandrov, 'Russian Education After *Perestroika*: the Search for New Values?', *International Review of Education*, vol. 41, nos. 1–2, 1995, pp. 47–57.
9 See, for example, question B1, *Ekonomicheskie i sotsial'nye peremeny*, no. 1, 1996, p. 96.
10 S. Kerr, 'Teachers' Continuing Education and Russian School Reform', Paper delivered at the Conference of the American Association for the Advancement of Slavic Studies, October 28, 1995.
11 V. Molodtsova, 'Esli kto-to mozhet vam pomoch' – eto profsoyuz', *Uchitel'skaya gazeta*, no. 13, April 4, 1995, p. 1 (supplement 'Iz pervykh ruk').
12 S. Vishnikina, 'Byt' ryadom so shkoloi', *Narodnoe obrazovanie*, no. 7, 1996, p. 38.
13 '"Obrazovanie i budushchee" – novoe obshchestvenno-politicheskoe dvizhenie', *Pedagogika*, no. 2, 1994, pp. 3–9.
14 'Speshite delat' "DOBRO"', *Uchitel'skaya gazeta*, no. 30, August 8, 1995, pp. 18–19.
15 '"DOBRO" sozdaet fraktsiyu', *Uchitel'skaya gazeta*, no. 25, June 6, 1995, p. 3.
16 O. Ogorodnikova and A. Emelin, 'Kazhdyi uchitel' mozhet stat' chlenom parlamenta. Pedagogicheskogo', *Uchitel'skaya gazeta*, no. 25, June 18, 1996, p. 5.
17 Yu. Gromyko, N. Alekseev, L. Babukh, Yu. Krupnov, V. Rubtsov and V. Slobodchikov, 'Natsional'naya doktrina razvitiya Rossiiskogo obrazovaniya, *Narodnoe obrazovanie*, no. 7, 1996, p. 12.
18 'The Law on Education of the Russian Federation', 1993, p. 117.
19 I. Prelovskaya, 'Kto vybiraet?', *Semya i shkola*, no. 4, 1996, pp. 2–4.
20 L. Sycheva, 'Dobro pozhalovat', ili postoronnym vkhod vospreshchen', *Uchitel'skaya gazeta*, no. 37, September 26, 1995, p. 10.
21 G. Krylova, 'Ne zakrivat', a razvivat' i sovershenstvovat', *Narodnoe obrazovanie*, no. 7, 1994, pp. 11–12.
22 G. Frolova, 'Nesostoyavshiesya?', *Uchitel'skaya gazeta*, no. 44, November 9, 1993, p. 18.
23 *Ibid.*
24 I. Afanas'ev, 'Ministr oborony pogoryachilsya', *Uchitel'skaya gazeta*, no. 17, April 28, 1998, p. 15.
25 G. Gleizer, 'Vash rebenok "ne sootvetsvuet" shkole?', *Narodnoe obrazovanie*, no. 8, 1996, p. 13.
26 *Ibid.*
27 S. Tsymbalenko and S. Shcheglova, 'Kakie oni, podrostki devyanostykh?', *Vospitanie shkol'nikov*, no. 1, 1996, pp. 2–5.

28 G. Slobodchikova, 'Podrostka nel'zya ostavit' na ulitse', *Pervoe sentyabrya*, July 2, 1994, p. 1.
29 *Konstitutsiya Rossiiskoi Federatsii* (Moscow: Yuridicheskaya literatura, 1995), p. 17.
30 N. Vasil'eva, 'A kak dumayut v nashem ministerstve?', *Vechernyaya srednyaya shkola*, no. 2, 1994, p. 3.
31 V. Molodtsova, 'A v ostal'nom, prekrasnaya markiza, vse khorosho. Vse – khorosho?', *Uchitel'skaya gazeta*, no. 2, January 11, 1994, p. 4.
32 A. Asmolov, 'Svoboda ne uchit'sya', *Uchitel'skaya gazeta*, no. 34, August 31, 1993, p. 12.
33 V. Shadrikov, 'Otkrytoe pis'mo Prezidentu Rossii', *Uchitel'skaya gazeta*, no. 46, November 23, 1993, p. 12.
34 A. Shpeko, 'Problemy obrazovaniya – eto problemy natsional'noi bezopasnosti', *Uchitel'skaya gazeta*, no. 47, November 30, 1993, p. 8.
35 See, for example, 'Kuda podat'sya "15-letnim kapitanam?"', *Vechernyaya srednyaya shkola*, no. 1, 1994, p. 3.
36 V. Myskin, Letter to editor, *Uchitel'skaya gazeta*, no. 46, November 23, 1993, p. 13.
37 'O garantiyakh prav grazhdan Rossiiskoi Federatsii na poluchenie obrazovaniya' (Ukaz Prezidenta Rossiiskoi Federatsii), *Sobranie zakonodatel'stva Rossiiskoi Federatsii*, no. 11, 1994 p. 1662.
38 '28 aprelia – nasha vzyala!', *Uchitel'skaya gazeta*, nos. 19–20, May 4, 1994, p. 2.
39 'Vozvrashchaemsya k vseobshchemu srednemu obrazovaniyu', *Rossiiskie vesti*, July 12, 1994, p. 1.
40 'Nam nado ponimat' drug druga s poluslova', *Uchitel'skaya gazeta*, nos. 47–8, November 29, 1994, p. 14.
41 T. Mamedova, 'V shkolakh prokhodit "chistka" neugodnykh uchashchikhsya', *Rossiiskie vesti*, June 30, 1994, p. 4.
42 D. Orlov, 'Molodezh predostavlena sama sebe', *Rossiiskie vesti*, July 1, 1994, p. 2.
43 T. Kolysko, 'V desyatom uchit'sya ty ne budesh'!', *Rossiiskie vesti*, July 14, 1994, p. 8.
44 G. Frolova, 'Otchislen za neuspevaemost'', *Uchitel'skaya gazeta*, no. 52, December 27, 1994, p. 10.
45 Gleizer, *loc cit*.
46 F. Kekhlerov, 'Zakon na storone rebenka', *Pervoe sentyabrya*, June 25, 1994, p. 1.
47 Gleizer, *loc cit*.; Kolysko, *loc cit*.
48 See, for example, Slobodchikova, *loc cit*.
49 See, for example, I. Lushagina, 'Molodezh na rynke truda', *Uchitel'skaya gazeta*, no. 12, March 29, 1994, p. 5.
50 N. Ivanova, 'Obrazovaniyu – gosudarstvennyi prioritet', *Narodnoe obrazovanie*, no. 7, 1996, p. 123.
51 N. Tselishcheva, 'Otchet pered vsei stranoi', *Narodnoe obrazovanie*, no. 1, 1995, pp. 6–7.
52 'Deneg – net. Rezul'taty est'!', *Uchitel'skaya gazeta*, no. 27, July 2, 1996, p. 1.
53 Gleizer, *op cit*., p. 14.

54 Anatolii Borisovich Chubais, who was the head of *Goskomimushchestvo* at that time (1994).

55 'Zakon Rossiiskoi Federatsii "O razgosudarstvlenii i demonopolizatsii v obrazovatel'noi sfere – Proekt', *Uchitel'skaya gazeta*, no. 34, September 13, 1994, pp. 14–16. For a summary of the bill in English see J. Sutherland, 'The Law of the Russian Federation on Denationalization and Demonopolization in the Educational Sphere: A Summary', *Education in Russia, the Independent States and Eastern Europe*, vol. 13, no. 2, 1995, pp. 92–4.

56 'Kontseptsiya razvitiya negosudarstvennogo obrazovaniya v Rossii', *Uchitel'skaya gazeta*, no. 51, December 20, 1994, pp. 6–7.

57 See, for example, P. Gornostaev, 'Deputaty, skazhite net!', *Uchitel'skaya gazeta*, nos. 43–4, November 15, 1994, p. 11; 'Privatizatsiya shkol: mif, real'nost', budushchee?', *Uchitel'skaya gazeta*, nos. 17–18, April 26, 1994, pp. 18–19.

58 G. Yavlinskii, 'Fraktsiya "YABLOKO" o probleme privatizatsii obrazovatel'nykh uchrezhdenii', *Uchitel'skaya gazeta*, nos. 43–4, November 15, 1994, p. 10.

59 'O proekte federal' nogo zakona "O sokhranenii statusa gosudarstvennykh i munitsipal'nykh obrazovatel'nykh uchrezhdenii i moratorii na ikh razgosudarstvlenie i privatizatsiyu"', *Sobranie zakonodatel'stva Rossiiskoi Federatsii*, no. 35, 1994, p. 5204.

60 V. Molodtsova, 'S chego nachinaetsya demokratiya v shkole?', *Uchitel'skaya gazeta*, no. 3, January 24, 1995, p. 9.

61 A. Baiduzhii, 'V shkolakh Rossii poyavyatsya vauchery', *Nezavisimaya gazeta*, February 3, 1995, p. 5.

62 See, for example, B. Golovachev and L. Kosova, 'Vysokostatusnye gruppy: Shtrikhi k sotsial'nomu portretu', *Sotsiologicheskie issledovaniya*, no. 1, 1996, pp. 45–51; Yu. Levada, 'Sotsial'nye tipy perekhodnogo perioda: Popytka kharakteristiki', *Ekonomicheskie i sotsial'nye peremeny*, no. 2, 1997, pp. 9–14.

63 According to figures produced by the Russian government, in the first quarter of 1996 some 33 200 000 people, or 22.4 per cent of the population, were living on an income which was below the official poverty line (*prozhitochnyi minimum*) ('Sotsial'no-ekonomicheskoe polozhenie v Rossii', *Voprosy statistiki*, no. 8, 1996, p. 51).

64 For a review of the problems of studying the issue of stratification *per se* in contemporary Russia, see O. Ourja, 'Problems of Social Stratification Research in Russia', in A. Kapto, V. Kultygin, V. Chuprov, V. Sukmodeev (eds), *Social Knowledge in Russia: Heritage, Challenges, Perspectives* (Moscow: Institute for Social and Political Research, 1998), pp. 43–6.

65 Readers wishing to read around the subject of education and stratification can consult R. Morrow and C. Torres, *Social Theory and Education* (Albany, NY: SUNY Press, 1995); R. Rogers (ed.), *Education and Social Class* (London: Falmer Press, 1986).

66 V. Molodtsova, 'Znakomo li pravitel'stvo s Pasterom?', *Uchitel'skaya gazeta*, nos. 19–20, May 11, 1995, p. 7.

67 *Ekonomicheskie i sotsial'nye peremeny*, no. 2, 1996, p. 70 (question L64).

Epilogue

1 'Zvonok na peremenu iz Belogo doma', *Uchitel'skaya gazeta*, no. 30, July 29, 1997, p. 3.
2 L. Sycheva, 'Chto budet, nikto ne znaet', *Uchitel'skaya gazeta*, no. 46, November 18, 1997, p. 7.
3 V. Kinelev, E. Dneprov and A. Adamskii, 'Kak reformirovat' obrazovanie?', *Uchitel'skaya gazeta*, nos. 33–4, August 26, 1997, pp. 3–7.
4 A. Asmolov, M. Dmitriev, T. Klyachko, Ya. Kuz'minov and A. Tikhonov, 'Vse reshaet kapital. Chelovecheskii', *Uchitel'skaya gazeta*, no. 36, September 9, 1997, pp. 11–14.
5 P. Polozhevets, 'Uiti ot vzyatok mozhno', *Uchitel'skaya gazeta*, no. 10, March 17, 1998, p. 3.
6 *Ibid.*
7 Rodionova, *loc cit.* See also Baiduzhii, 'V shkolakh Rossii poyavyatsya vauchery', *loc cit.*
8 O. Ogorodnikova, 'Dogonyat li den'gi rebenka?', *Uchitel'skaya gazeta*, no. 46, November 18, 1997, p. 6.
9 A. Tikhonov, 'Govoryat, chto', *Uchitel'skaya gazeta*, no. 26, June 30, 1998, p. 4.
10 Polozhevets, *loc cit.*
11 I. Nekhames, 'Pyat'desyat na pyat'desyat? Ne poluchaetsya', *Uchitel'skaya gazeta*, no. 28, July 14, 1998, p. 3.
12 Rodionova, *loc cit.*

Bibliography

1. Newspapers and journals

Russian-language

Direktor shkoly
Domovoi
Ekonomicheskie i sotsial'nye peremeny: Monitoring obshchestvennogo mneniya
Izvestiya
Mir obrazovaniya
Molodezh'
Moskovskaya pravda
Nachal'naya shkola
Narodnaya mysl'
Narodnoe obrazovanie
Nezavisimaya gazeta
Ogonek
Pedagogicheskii kaleidoskop
Pedagogika (formerly *Sovetskaya pedagogika*)
Pervoe sentyabrya
Pravda
Rossiya 2010
Rossiiskie vesti
Sem'ya
Sem'ya i shkola
Sobranie zakonodatel'stva Rossiiskoi Federatsii
Sotsiologicheskie issledovaniya
Statisticheskoe obozrenie
Studencheskii meridian
Svobodnaya mysl'
Uchitel'skaya gazeta
V edinom stroyu
Vechernyaya srednyaya shkola
Vedomosti Rossiiskoi Federatsii
Vestnik obrazovaniya
Voprosy statistiki
Vospitanie shkol'nikov

English-language

Britain–Russia
Comparative Education
Comparative Education Review
Compare
Current Digest of the Post-Soviet Press (formerly *Current Digest of the Soviet Press*)

Education in Russia, the Independent States and Eastern Europe (formerly *Soviet Education Study Bulletin*)
Educational Evaluation and Policy Analysis
Educational Studies
International Review of Education
ISRE Newsletter (formerly *ISSE Newsletter*)
Journal of Education for Teaching
Journal of Research and Development in Education
Journal of Russian Studies
Moral Education Forum
New Era in Education
Phi Delta Kappan
Prospects
Russian Education and Society (formerly *Soviet Education*)
Studies in Philosophy and Education
The Elementary School Journal
Times Educational Supplement

2. Russian-language sources

'A poutru oni prosnulis' "kontorskimi krysami"', *Uchitel'skaya gazeta*, nos. 14–15, 14 April 1998, p. 7
Abramov, A., 'U semi vedomstv ditiya bez uchebnikov', *Uchitel'skaya gazeta*, nos. 22–3, 1995, p. 17
Adamskii, A., 'Gde uchit' detei?', *Ogonek*, nos. 20–21, 1992, pp. 1–2
Afanas'ev, I., 'Boisya togo, kto skazhet "Ya znayu vse"', *Uchitel'skaya gazeta*, no. 47, November 30, 1993, pp. 14–15
Aizerman, L., 'Gumanizm protiv tekhnokratizma', *Narodnoe obrazovanie*, no. 7, 1989, pp. 76–81
Aizerman, L., '"Ibo ot izbytka serdtsa govoryat usta"', *Uchitel'skaya gazeta*, no. 10, March 17, 1998, p. 9
Alisova, A., 'Nam nado ponimat' drug druga s poluslova', *Uchitel'skaya gazeta*, nos. 47–8, November 29, 1994, p. 14
Amonashvili, Sh., *Kak zhivete, deti?* (Moscow: Prosveshchenie, 1991)
Amonashvili, Sh., *Zdravstvuite deti!* (Moscow: Prosveshchenie, 1988)
Anatol'ev, A., 'Protsent geniev vyshe v negosudarstvennykh shkolakh', *Nezavisimaya gazeta*, January 10, 1992, p. 6
Arefev, I., 'Proforientatsiya: uchenik, uchitel', vuz', *Pedagogika*, no. 3, 1995, pp. 65–8
Asmolov, A., 'Svoboda ne uchit'sya', *Uchitel'skaya gazeta*, no. 34, August 31, 1993, pp. 12–13
Asmolov, A., Dmitriev, M., Klyachko, T., Kuz'minov, Ya. and Tikhonov, A., 'Vse reshaet kapital. Chelovecheskii', *Uchitel'skaya gazeta*, no. 36, September 9, 1997, pp. 11–14
Attestatsiya pedagogicheskikh i rukovodyashchikh rabotnikov gosudarstvennykh, munitsipal'nykh uchrezhdenii i organizatsii obrazovaniya Rossiiskoi Federatsii: Sbornik dokumentov Ministerstva obrazovaniya Rossiiskoi Federatsii: vypusk 1 (Moscow: Ministerstvo obrazovaniya Rossiiskoi Federatsii, 1994)

Attestatsiya pedagogicheskikh i rukovodyashchikh rabotnikov gosudarstvennykh, munitsipal'nykh uchrezhdenii i organizatsii obrazovaniya Rossiiskoi Federatsii: Sbornik dokumentov Ministerstva obrazovaniya Rossiiskoi Federatsii: vypusk 2 (Moscow: Ministerstvo obrazovaniya Rossiiskoi Federatsii, 1994)

Baiduzhii, A., 'V shkolakh Rossii poyavyatsya vauchery', *Nezavisimaya gazeta,* February 3, 1995, p. 5

'Bastovat'? Ne bastovat'?', *Uchitel'skaya gazeta,* no 35, September 12, 1995, p. 2

Bazhenova, I. (ed.), *Pedagogicheskii poisk* (Moscow: Pedagogika, 1988)

'Bazisnyi uchebnyi plan: uspekhi i problemy', *Uchitel'skaya gazeta,* no. 31, September 20, 1996, p. 1

Belova, E., 'Odarennyi rebenok na poroge shkoly', *Sem'ya i shkola,* no. 3, 1994, pp. 10–13

Belozertsev, E., 'Pedagogicheskoe obrazovanie: Realii i perspektivy', *Pedagogika,* nos. 1–2, 1992, pp. 61–5

Bibler, V., *Shkola dialoga kul'tur: Osnovy programmy* (Kemerovo: ALEF gumanitarnyi tsentr, 1992)

Bunyakina, N., 'Plata za eksperiment', *Uchitel'skaya gazeta,* no. 11, March 21, 1995, p. 17

Bunyakina, N., 'Tak skol'ko zhe vse-taki deneg vydelili uchitelyam?', *Uchitel'skaya gazeta,* no. 25, June 18, 1996, p. 4

Chernykh, A., 'Dolgii put' k grazhdanskomu obshchestvu', *Sotsiologicheskie issledovaniya,* nos. 8–9, 1994, pp. 173–8

Dashchinskaya, Z., 'Nashu zhizn' izmenili i dopolnili', *Uchitel'skaya gazeta,* no. 6, February 6, 1996, p. 15

'Demokratizatsiya lichnosti', *Uchitel'skaya gazeta,* October 17, 1987, p. 3

'Den'gi, den'gi. Nichego, krome deneg', *Uchitel'skaya gazeta,* no. 25, June 6, 1995, pp. 16–17

Denisova, L., 'Problemy malokomplektnoi', *Narodnoe obrazovanie,* no. 5, 1989, pp. 46–51

Dmitriev, D., 'Nestandartnye standarty', *Uchitel'skaya gazeta,* no. 31, September 22, 1992, pp. 8–9

Dmitriev, D., 'Struktura razvitiya obrazovaniya', *Uchitel'skaya gazeta,* no. 4, February 2, 1993, p. 23

Dneprov, E., *Chetvertaya shkol'naya reforma v Rossii* (Moscow: Interfaks, 1994)

'"DOBRO" sozdaet fraktsiyu', *Uchitel'skaya gazeta,* no. 25, June 6, 1995, p. 3

Dorokhova, L., 'Sverdlovskii variant', *Uchitel'skaya gazeta,* no. 33, August 24, 1993, p. 4

'Ekspress-rassledovanie', *Uchitel'skaya gazeta,* no. 13, April 4, 1994, p. 2

Ermolaev, V., 'Na minnykh polyakh gumanitarizatsii', *Uchitel'skaya gazeta,* no. 44, November 14, 1995, p. 9

Eroshin, V., 'Istochniki finansirovaniya obrazovaniya', *Pedagogika,* no. 2, 1995, pp. 10–14

Eroshin, V., 'Kto zashchitit shkolu?', *Narodnoe obrazovanie,* no. 2, 1995, pp. 2–4

Federal'naya programma razvitiya obrazovaniya v Rossii: Proekt (Moscow: Ministerstvo obrazovaniya Rossiiskoi Federatsii, 1994)

Finansy v Rossii: Statisticheskii sbornik (Moscow: Goskomstat Rossii, 1996)

Fisher, M., 'Preodelenie neopredelennosti v rossiiskom obrazovanii', *Pedagogika,* no. 6, 1993, pp. 18–28

Frolova, G., 'Nesostoyavshiesya?', *Uchitel'skaya gazeta*, no. 44, November 9, 1993, p. 18

Frolova, G., 'Otchislen za neuspevaemost'', *Uchitel'skaya gazeta*, no. 52, December 27, 1994, p. 10

Gershunskii, B., *Federal'naya programma razvitiya obrazovaniya v Rossii: kontseptsiya* (Moscow: Institut teoreticheskoi pedagogiki i mezhdunarodnykh issledovanii v obrazovanii, 1993)

Gershunskii, B., 'Eto li doroga k khramu?', *Sovetskaya pedagogika*, no. 1, 1990, pp. 98–102

Glebova, A., Zolotova, N. and Sokolov, S., 'Doroga v shkolu', *Domovoi*, March 3, 1995, pp. 138–43

Gleizer, G., 'Vash rebenok "ne sootvetsvuet" shkole?', *Narodnoe obrazovanie*, no. 8, 1996, pp. 12–15

Golovachev, B. and Kosova, V., 'Vysokostatusnye gruppy: Shtrikhi k sotsial'nomu portretu', *Sotsiologicheskie issledovaniya*, no. 1, 1996, pp. 45–51

Gornostaev, P., 'Deputaty, skazhite net!', *Uchitel'skaya gazeta*, nos. 43–4, November 15, 1994, p. 11

Gromkova, M., 'Pedagogika zdes' i teper', *Narodnoe obrazovanie*, nos. 9–10, 1993, pp. 89–92

Gromyko, Yu., Alekseev, N., Babukh, L., Krupnov, Yu., Rubtsov, V. and Slobodchikov, V., 'Natsional'naya doktrina razvitiya Rossiiskogo obrazovaniya', *Narodnoe obrazovanie*, no. 7, 1996, pp. 10–13

Gromyko, Yu., Alekseev, N. and Slobodchikov, V., 'Chetvertaya reforma obrazovaniya v Rossii proizoshla! (No ob etom znayut tol'ko v apparate Filatova i chleny VAKa iz Prezidiuma Rossiiskoi akademii obrazovaniya', *Rossiya 2010*, no. 5, 1994, pp. 112–13

Gurbatov, N., 'Cherez "Zolotye vorota" v rynok', *Uchitel'skaya gazeta*, nos. 19–20, May 11, 1995, p. 10

Istratov, Yu. and Popov, V., *Regional'naya programma razvitiya obrazovaniya Vladimirskoi oblasti* (Vladimir: Vladimirskii gosudarstvennyi pedagogicheskii institut, 1993)

Ivanov, K., 'Shkola glazami uchashchikhsya', *Vospitanie shkol'nikov*, no. 2, 1991, pp. 26–8

Ivanova, N., 'Obrazovaniyu – gosudarstvennyi prioritet', *Narodnoe obrazovanie*, no. 7, 1996, pp. 123–7

'Kafedra: Statfakt', *Uchitel'skaya gazeta*, September 8, 1992, p. 22

Karakovskii, V., 'Obshchechelovecheskie tsennosti – osnova uchebno-vospitatel'nogo protsessa', *Vospitanie shkol'nikov*, no. 2, 1993, pp. 4–7

Karakovskii, V., 'Vospitanie v obshchestve sotsial'nykh peremen', *Mir obrazovaniya*, no. 0, 1995, pp. 24–5

Kekhlerov, F., 'Zakon na storone rebenka', *Pervoe sentyabrya*, June 25, 1994, p. 1

Kezina, L., 'Uchenye RAO – shkolam stolitsy', *Pedagogika*, no. 3, 1994, pp. 69–71

Khankasaeva, I., 'Akademicheskii teatr pedagogicheskoi dramy', *Rossiiskaya gazeta*, December 14, 1991, p. 4

Khlebnikov, V., '"A ty gotov k testirovaniyu?"', *Uchitel'skaya gazeta*, no. 11, March 24, 1998, p. 10

Kinelev, V., Dneprov, E. and Adamskii, A., 'Kak reformirovat' obrazovanie?', *Uchitel'skaya gazeta*, nos. 33–4, August 26, 1997, pp. 3–7

'Kinelevym stal Tikhonov', *Uchitel'skaya gazeta*, no. 9, March 10, 1998, p. 3
Klyusova, T., 'Surgut: Fokus upravleniya obrazovatel'nyi, *Rossiya 2010*, no. 5, 1994, pp. 80–81
Kolysko, T., 'V desyatom uchit'sya ty ne budesh'!', *Rossiiskie vesti*, July 14, 1994, p. 8
'Kommentarii redaktsii', *Uchitel'skaya gazeta*, no. 14, April 15, 1997, p. 14 (supplement 'Iz pervykh ruk')
Konstitutsiya Rossiiskoi Federatsii (Moscow: Yuridicheskaya literatura, 1995)
'Kontseptsiya razvitiya negosudarstvennogo obrazovaniya v Rossii', *Uchitel'skaya gazeta*, no. 51, December 20, 1994, pp. 6–7
Koshkina, V. and Raschetina, S., 'Regional'naya programma: Put' k novomu kachestvu', *Narodnoe obrazovanie*, no. 7, 1994, pp. 2–10
Kostikova, M., *K avgustovskim pedagogicheskim chteniyam* (Moscow: Ministerstvo obrazovaniya Rossiiskoi Federatsii, 1995)
Koveshnikov, Yu. and Polozhevets, P., 'Nishchii uchitel' ne opora gosudarstvu', *Uchitel'skaya gazeta*, no. 4, February 7, 1996, p. 24
Kruglov, Yu., 'Podgotovka uchitelei: Problemy, problemy', *Sovetskaya pedagogika*, no. 4, 1991, pp. 87–92
Krylova, G., 'Ne zakrivat', a razvivat' i sovershenstvovat', *Narodnoe obrazovanie*, no. 7, 1994, pp. 11–12
'Kuda podat'sya "15-letnim kapitanam?"', *Vechernyaya srednyaya shkola*, no. 1, 1994, pp. 1 and 3
Kulakov, P., 'Uchashchayasya molodezh' i religiya', *Sotsiologicheskie issledovaniya*, no. 11, 1995, pp. 91–9
Kurbatov, R., 'Drugaya shkola', *Sem'ya i shkola*, no. 7, 1996, pp. 3–5
Kutasova, O., 'Ne chastnyi vopros o chastnoi shkole', *Uchitel'skaya gazeta*, no. 36, September 27, 1994, p. 8
Kutasova, O., 'Uchit'sya pridetsya bez uchebnikov', *Uchitel'skaya gazeta*, no. 26, June 14, 1995, p. 6
Kuznetsov, V., 'Lichnost' direktora shkoly', *Narodnoe obrazovanie*, nos. 9–10, 1993, pp. 19–23
Kuzyakin, A., 'Negosudarstvennym shkolam – gosudarstvennuyu podderzhku', *Vospitanie shkol'nikov*, nos. 5–6, 1992, pp. 8–9
Leont'eva, M. 'Rekomendatsii po provedeniyu vypusknykh ekzamenov v IX, XI (XII) klassakh obshcheobrazovatel'nykh uchrezhdenii Rossiiskoi Federatsii', *Uchitel'skaya gazeta*, no. 17, May 6, 1997, p. 7
Levada, Yu., 'Sotsial'nye tipy perekhodnogo perioda: Popytka kharakteristiki', *Ekonomicheskie i sotsial'nye peremeny*, no. 2, 1997, pp. 9–14
Levitskii, M., van den Brook, L. and Andre, G. (eds), *Ekonomicheskoe obrazovanie v shkole: Materialy mezhdunarodnogo seminara* (St Petersburg: Obrazovanie, 1995)
Levitskii, M. and Goryunova, T., 'Uchitelem stat' legko. Trudnee im ostat'sya', *Uchitel'skaya gazeta*, no. 31, June 30, 1996, p. 3 (supplement 'Iz pervykh ruk')
Ligachev, E., 'O khode perestroiki srednei i vysshei shkoly i zadachakh Partii po ee osushchestvleniyu', *Uchitel'skaya gazeta*, February 18, 1988, pp. 1–4
Lushagina, I., 'Molodezh' na rynke truda', *Uchitel'skaya gazeta*, no. 12, March 29, 1994, p. 5
Malobitskaya, Z., 'Psikhologicheskaya perestroika uchitel'ya', *Narodnoe obrazovanie*, nos. 9–10, 1993, pp. 84–7

Mamedova, T., 'V shkolakh prokhodit "chistka" neugodnykh uchashchikhsya', *Rossiiskie vesti*, June 30, 1994, p. 4
Marinin, A., 'My storonniki otkrytosti', *Narodnoe obrazovanie*, no. 3, 1996, pp. 106–10
Markova, A., 'Sotrudnichestvo uchitelya i shkol'nogo psikhologa', *Pedagogika*, no. 6, 1994, pp. 43–51
Mekhedov, V., 'Attestatsiya uchrezhdeniya: kak ee provodit', *Narodnoe obrazovanie*, no. 7, 1994, pp. 23–9
Mel'nikova, N. and Moreva, N. 'Gotovim pedagoga-novatora', *Narodnoe obrazovanie*, nos. 4–5, 1996, pp. 56–8
Men'shikova, G., 'Press-konferentsiya federal'nogo ministra obrazovaniya E.V. Tkachenko', *Narodnoe obrazovanie*, no. 7, 1995, pp. 4–11
'Metodika obnovleniya', *Uchitel'skaya gazeta*, March 19, 1988, pp. 2–3
Mikhalev, G., 'Sovershenstvovat' podgotovku uchitel'skikh kadrov', *Sovetskaya pedagogika*, no. 6, 1965, pp. 104–9
Molodtsova, V., 'A v ostal'nom, prekrasnaya markiza, vse khorosho. Vse – khorosho?', *Uchitel'skaya gazeta*, no. 2, January 11, 1994, p. 4
Molodtsova, V., 'Boites' Dneprovykh, dary prinosyashchikh', *Uchitel'skaya gazeta*, no. 23, May 24, 1994, pp. 2 and 11
Molodtsova, V., 'Esli kto-to mozhet vam pomoch' – eto profsoyuz', *Uchitel'skaya gazeta*, no. 13, April 4, 1995, p. 1 (supplement 'Iz pervykh ruk')
Molodtsova, V., 'Kto daet sovety Prezidentu?', *Uchitel'skaya gazeta*, no. 15, April 18, 1995, p. 19
Molodtsova, V., 'Razvod po-krasnodarskii', *Uchitel'skaya gazeta*, no. 41, October 19, 1993, p. 15
Molodtsova, V., 'S chego nachinaetsya demokratiya v shkole?', *Uchitel'skaya gazeta*, no. 3, January 24, 1995, p. 9
Molodtsova, V., 'Vse tainoe kogda-to stanet yavnym', *Uchitel'skaya gazeta*, no. 36, September 14, 1993, p. 16
Molodtsova, V., 'Znakomo li pravitel'stvo s Pasterom?', *Uchitel'skaya gazeta*, nos. 19–20, May 11, 1995, p. 7
Musarskii, M., 'V usloviyakh ogranichennykh resursov', *Uchitel'skaya gazeta*, nos. 19–20, May 11, 1995, p. 6
Myskin, V., Letter to editor, *Uchitel'skaya gazeta*, no. 46, November 23, 1993, p. 13
'Nam nado ponimat' drug druga s poluslova', *Uchitel'skaya gazeta*, nos. 47–8, November 29, 1994, p. 14
Nasledniki velikogo goroda: Orientiry deyatel'nosti uchastnikov kul'turno-patrioticheskogo molodezhnogo dvizheniya 'Yunye za vozrozhdenie Peterburga' na 1995–1996 uchebnyi god (St Petersburg: Sankt Peterburgskii gorodskoi dvorets tvorchestva yunykh, 1995)
Nekhames, I., 'Pyat'desyat na pyat'desyat? Ne poluchaetsya', *Uchitel'skaya gazeta*, no. 28, July 14, 1998, p. 3
Nekhames, I. 'V sentyabre zarplaty iz Moskvy mozhet i ne byt', *Uchitel'skaya gazeta*, no. 28, July 14, 1998, p. 8
'Ne khotim rabotat' besplatno', *Uchitel'skaya gazeta*, nos. 14–15, April 14, 1998, p. 5
Nepreryvnoe pedagogicheskoe obrazovanie (St Petersburg: Rossiiskii gosudarstvennyi pedagogicheskii universitet imeni A.I. Gertsena, 1993)

Nesterov, V., 'Mezhdu ognom i skovorodkoi', *Uchitel'skaya gazeta*, no. 33, August 24, 1993. pp. 12–13

Nikitin, E., 'Posle kvalifikatsii – attestatsiya', *Uchitel'skaya gazeta*, no. 37 September 17, 1996, p. 10

Noskov, I., 'Bez pessimizma', *Uchitel'skaya gazeta*, no. 26, June 25, 1996, p. 13

'O garantiyakh prav grazhdan Rossiiskoi Federatsii na poluchenie obrazovaniya (Ukaz Prezidenta Rossiiskoi Federatsii)', *Sobranie zakonodatel'stva Rossiiskoi Federatsii*, no. 11, 1994, p. 1662

'O proekte federal'nogo zakona "O sokhranenii statusa gosudarstvennykh i munitsipal'nykh obrazovatel'nykh uchrezhdenii i moratorii na ikh razgosudarstvlenie i privatizatsiyu', *Sobranie zakonodatel'stva Rossiiskoi Federatsii*, no. 35, 1994, p. 5204

'O sisteme soglashenii mezhdu Ministerstvom obrazovaniya Rossiiskoi Federatsii i pravitel'stvami (administratsiyami) sub"ektov Rossiiskoi Federatsii o sotrudnichestve v sfere obrazovaniya (i ikh realizatsii)', *Narodnoe obrazovanie*, no. 2, 1995, pp. 118–23

'O vnesenii izmenenii i dopolnenii v Zakon Rossiiskoi Federatsii "Ob obrazovanii"', *Uchitel'skaya gazeta*, no. 5, January 31, 1996, pp. 1–4 (supplement 'Iz pervykh ruk')

'O vnesenii izmenenii i dopolnenii v Zakon Rossiiskoi Federatsii "Ob obrazovanii"', *Uchitel'skaya gazeta*, no. 6, February 6, 1996, pp. 1–4 (supplement 'Iz pervykh ruk')

'Ob itogakh raboty Ministerstva obrazovaniya Rossiiskoi Federatsii v 1994 godu i osnovnykh zadachakh razvitiya obrazovaniya na 1995 god', *Vestnik obrazovaniya*, no. 6, 1995, p. 82

'"Obrazovanie i budushchee:" novoe obshchestvenno-politicheskoe dvizhenie', *Pedagogika*, no. 2, 1994, pp. 3–9

'Ofitsioz: Tul'skii pedsovet', *Uchitel'skaya gazeta*, no. 29, August 11, 1992, p. 20

Ogorodnikova, O., 'Dogonyat li den'gi rebenka?', *Uchitel'skaya gazeta*, no. 46, November 18, 1997, p. 6

Ogorodnikova, O., 'O tom, kak possorilis' Evgenii Viktorovich i Vladimir Georgievich', *Uchitel'skaya gazeta*, no. 6, February 6, 1996, p. 10

Ogorodnikova, O. and Emelin, A., 'Kazhdyi uchitel' mozhet stat' chlenom parlamenta. Pedagogicheskogo', *Uchitel'skaya gazeta*, no. 25, June 18, 1996, p. 5

Ogorodnikova, O. and Polozhevets, P., 'Fundamental'nost', preemstvennost', edinstvo', *Uchitel'skaya gazeta*, no. 7, February 16, 1996, p. 24

Orlov, A., 'Professional'noe myshlenie uchitelya kak tsennost"', *Pedagogika*, no. 6, 1995, p. 64

Orlov, D., 'Molodezh' predostavlena sama sebe', *Rossiiskie vesti*, July 1, 1994, p. 2

'Osnovnye napravleniya i itogi deyatel'nosti Ministerstva obshchego i professional'nogo obrazovaniya Rossiiskoi Federatsii v 1997 godu i pervoocherednye zadachi na 1998 god', *Uchitel'skaya gazeta*, no. 11, March 24, 1998, p. 11

Ovsyannikov, A., Shuvalova, V. and Shinyaeva, O., 'Mikroklimat v shkole: samochuvstvie shkol'nikov i uchitelei', *Narodnoe obrazovanie*, nos. 7–8, 1993, pp. 27–36

Ovsyannikov, A., 'Innovatsii v shkole: Kharakter i rezul'taty', *Narodnoe obrazovanie*, no. 6, 1993, pp. 16–27
Pastukhova, I., 'Vsekh pod odnu grebenku?', *Uchitel'skaya gazeta*, no. 11, March 21, 1995, p. 14
'Pedagogika sotrudnichestva', *Uchitel'skaya gazeta*, October 18, 1986, p. 2
Petrovskii, A. (ed.), *Novoe pedagogicheskoe myshlenie* (Moscow: Pedagogika, 1989)
Petrulenkov, V., 'Nash orientir: "Ne otstupat", *Uchitel'skaya gazeta*, no. 6, February 8, 1994, p. 7
Pleshakov, L., 'Vek zhivi, vek uchis", *Ogonek*, vol. 36, nos. 1–2, 1990, p. 31
Podosenova, E., 'Federal'naya programma: Kak ee vypolnyat'?', *Narodnoe obrazovanie*, nos. 9–10, 1994, pp. 7–9
'Polozhenie o Ministerstve obrazovaniya RSFSR', *Vestnik obrazovaniya*, no. 3, 1991, pp. 16–23
Polozhenie o podgotovke magistra obrazovaniya: Proekt Vladimirskogo gosudarstvennogo pedagogicheskogo universiteta (Vladimir: Vladimirskii gosudarstvennyi pedagogicheskii universitet, 1993)
'Polozhenie o poryadke litsenzirovaniya obrazovatel'nykh uchrezhdenii', *Uchitel'skaya gazeta*, no. 1, January 10, 1995, p. 14
'Polozhenie o srednei obshcheobrazovatel'noi shkole', *Uchitel'skaya gazeta*, August 16, 1988, p. 2
Polozhevets, P. 'Uiti ot vzyatok mozhno', *Uchitel'skaya gazeta*, no. 10, March 17, 1998, pp. 3 and 8
'Poltora goda: Lyusinovskaya – Chistye prudy', *Uchitel'skaya gazeta*, no. 8, March 3, 1998, p. 2
Postavalova, V., 'Avtoritet uchitelya vysok, no polozhenie ego uzhasno', *Uchitel'skaya gazeta*, no. 35, September 2, 1997, p. 7
'Poyasnitel'naya zapiska k Bazisnomu uchebnomu planu obshcheobrazovatel'nykh uchrezhdenii Rossiiskoi Federatsii', *Uchitel'skaya gazeta*, nos. 27–9, July 6, 1993, pp. 18–19
Prelovskaya, I., 'Kto vybiraet?', *Sem'ya i shkola*, no. 4, 1996, pp. 2–4
'Privatizatsiya shkol: mif, real'nost', budushchee?', *Uchitel'skaya gazeta*, nos. 17–18, April 26, 1994, pp. 18–19
Proekt: Kontseptsiya obshchego srednego obrazovaniya (Moscow: Gosudarstvennyi komitet po narodnomu obrazovaniyu/Vremennyi naucho-issledovatel'skii kollektiv SHKOLA, 1988)
'Proekt: Kontseptsiya obshchego srednego obrazovaniya kak bazovogo v edinoi sisteme nepreryvnogo obrazovaniya (tezisy)', *Uchitel'skaya gazeta*, August 25, 1988, p. 2
'Proekt: Prilozhenie k Federal'nomu zakonu "O realizatsii Federal'noi programmy razvitiya obrazovaniya"', *Uchitel'skaya gazeta*, no. 14, April 15, 1997, pp. 11–14 (supplement 'Iz pervykh ruk')
'Proekt: Prilozhenie k Federal'nomu zakonu "O realizatsii Federal'noi programmy razvitiya obrazovaniya"', *Uchitel'skaya gazeta*, no. 15, April 22, 1997, pp. 11 and 14 (supplement 'Iz pervykh ruk')
Reshetnikov, P., 'Podgotovka uchitelei v komplekse "peduchilishche-pedinstitut"', *Sovetskaya pedagogika*, no. 5, 1991, pp. 93–6
Reznik, Yu., 'Formirovaniya institutov grazhdanskogo obshchestva', *Sotsiologicheskie issledovaniya*, no. 10, 1994, pp. 21–30
Rodionova, O., 'Plany ministerstva – nashi plany?', *Uchitel'skaya gazeta*, no. 13, April 7, 1998, p. 2

Rogovskii, Yu., '89 regionov. 89 ekonomiki obrazovaniya', *Uchitel'skaya gazeta*, nos. 19–20, May 11, 1995, p. 6

Rostovtsev, Yu., 'Demokratizatsiya. Glasnost'. Samostoyatel'nost", *Studencheskii meridian*, no. 3, 1988, pp. 24–9

Rozanova, B., 'Kak udovletvorit' obrazovatel'nyi zakaz', *Narodnoe obrazovanie*, no. 1, 1995, pp. 5–7

Rutkevich, M., 'Reforma shkoly i ee posledstviya', *Svobodnaya mysl'*, nos. 12–18, 1994, p. 53

Rutkovskaya, E., 'Legko li vzroslet' segodnya?', *Pedagogika*, no. 4, 1995, pp. 111–13

Rybakova, L., Moroz, E. and Panova, E., 'Trudnosti uchitel'skoi professii', *Pedagogika*, no. 2, 1993, pp. 59–63

Rybinskii, E., 'Polozhenie detei v Rossii', *Pedagogika*, no. 6, 1994, p. 5

Rybinskii, E., 'Sirotlivoe detstvo', *Uchitel'skaya gazeta*, no. 45, November 12, 1996, p. 6

Rykov, S., 'Rossiya stanovitsya stranoi vdov', *Uchitel'skaya gazeta*, no. 14, April 15, 1997, p. 15

Sarantsev, G., 'Poznavatel'naya samostoyatel'nost' budushchego uchitelya', *Pedagogika*, no. 4, 1995, pp. 63–6

Savel'ev, D., 'Chto pridet na smenu pedagogicheskomu romantizmu?', *Narodnoe obrazovanie*, no. 8, 1994, pp. 16–19

Sbornik po materialam Inspektsii Komiteta po obrazovaniyu Sankt-Peterburga (St Petersburg: Tsentr pedagogicheskoi informatsii, 1995)

Semykina, G., 'Glavnoe – est' vybor', *Narodnoe obrazovanie*, no. 6, 1993, pp. 6–14

Serivok, V., 'Lichnostno-orientirovannoe obrazovanie', *Pedagogika*, no. 4, 1994, pp. 101–2

Shadrikov, V., 'Otkrytoe pis'mo Prezidentu Rossii', *Uchitel'skaya gazeta*, no. 46, November 23, 1993, p. 12

Shadrikov, V., 'Shkola: Vremya obnovleniya', *Narodnoe obrazovanie*, no. 9, 1998, pp. 7–12

Shakurov, R., 'Odin na odin s uchitelem', *Narodnoe obrazovanie*, no. 1, 1995, pp. 48–9

Shatalov, V., *Kuda i kak ischezli troiki?* (Moscow: Pedagogika, 1980)

Shatalov, V., *Pedagogicheskaya proza* (Moscow: Pedagogika, 1980)

Shchedrovitskii, P., 'Chto budet so shkoloi?', *Pervoe sentyabrya*, no. 12, February 1, 1994, p. 1

Shchedrovitskii, P., 'Zhizn' vzaimy', *Uchitel'skaya gazeta*, no. 31, August 15, 1995, p. 6

Shirokova, N., 'Retsept "bul'ona" u kazhdogo svoi', *Uchitel'skaya gazeta*, nos. 22–3, May 23, 1995, p. 9

Shpeko, A., 'Imen v pedagogike ne pribavilos', *Uchitel'skaya gazeta*, no. 46, November 23, 1993, p. 17

Shpeko, A., 'Problemy obrazovaniya – eto problemy natsional'noi bezopasnosti', *Uchitel'skaya gazeta*, no. 47, November 30, 1993, p. 8

Simonov, V. and Chernenko, E., 'Obrazovatel'nyi minimum: Izmerenie, dostovernost', nadezhnost', *Pedagogika*, no. 4, 1994, pp. 30–34

Slobodchikova, G., 'Podrostka nel'zya ostavit' na ulitse', *Pervoe sentyabrya*, July 2, 1994, p. 1

Sobkin, V., Levinson, A. and Grazhdankin, A., *Shkola 1988: Problemy.*

Protivorechii. Perspektivy (Moscow: Gosudarstvennyi komitet SSSR po narodnomu obrazovaniyu, 1988)

Sobkin, V. and Pisarskii, P., *Sotsiokul'turnyi analiz obrazovatel'noi situatsii v megapolise* (Moscow: Rossiiskaya Akademiya Obrazovaniya, Respublikanskii tsentr sotsiologii obrazovaniya, 1992)

Sokolov, Ya., 'O demagogii i demokratii', *Uchitel'skaya gazeta*, nos. 19–20, May 4, 1994, p. 11

'Speshite delat' "DOBRO"', *Uchitel'skaya gazeta*, no. 30, August 8, 1995, pp. 18–19

'Statfakt', *Uchitel'skaya gazeta*, no. 30, July 19, 1997, p. 3

Stepunina, O., 'Pedagogicheskaya kontseptsiya P.P. Blonskogo i sovremennost'', *Pedagogika*, no. 3, 1995, pp. 108–10

Sukhomlinskii, V., *Serdtse otdayu detyam* (Kiev: Radians'ka shkola, 1973)

Surkov, V., 'Mamigonov protiv Tkachenko. Kto kogo?', *Uchitel'skaya gazeta*, nos. 22–3, May 23, 1995, p. 19

Suvorova, G., 'Demokratizatsiya shkol', *Nachal'naya shkola*, vol. 71, no. 2, 1989, pp. 59–61

Sycheva, L., 'Chto budet, nikto ne znaet', *Uchitel'skaya gazeta*, no. 46, November 18, 1997, p. 7

Sycheva, L., 'Dobro pozhalovat', ili postoronnym vkhod vospreshchen', *Uchitel'skaya gazeta*, no. 37, September 26, 1995, p. 10

Sycheva, L., 'Otchayanie otchayavshikhsya', *Uchitel'skaya gazeta*, no. 42, October 31, 1995, p. 7

Sycheva, L., 'Regional'nyi komponent: Ot Moskvy do samykh do okrain', *Uchitel'skaya gazeta*, no. 8, February 20, 1996, p. 6

Tarasevich, G., 'Den' uchitelya stal dnem zabastovki', *Uchitel'skaya gazeta*, no. 40, October 8, 1996, p. 4

Tikhonov, A., 'Govoryat, chto', *Uchitel'skaya gazeta*, no. 26, June 30, 1998, p. 4

Tkachenko, E., 'Vystuplenie ministra obrazovaniya RF Evgeniya Tkachenko na mezhdunarodnoi konferentsii po obrazovaniyu "K kul'ture mira, pravam cheloveka, demoktratii"', *Narodnoe obrazovanie*, nos. 9–10, 1994, pp. 4–6.

Tkachenko, E., 'Den'gi, den'gi. Nichego, krome deneg', *Uchitel'skaya gazeta*, no. 25, June 6, 1995, p. 16

Tkachenko, E., 'Deti i shkola: Problemy i perspektivy', *Mir obrazovaniya*, no. 1, 1996, pp. 4–7

Tkachenko, E., 'Ne zhdut ukazov, prikazanii i direktiv', *Uchitel'skaya gazeta*, nos. 27–9, July 6, 1993, p. 2

Tsaregorodtseva, S., 'Obshchestvennaya ekspertiza. Kakova tsel'?', *Uchitel'skaya gazeta*, no. 46, November 23, 1993, p. 17

Tselishcheva, N., 'Otchet pered vsei stranoi', *Narodnoe obrazovanie*, no. 1, 1995, pp. 3–10

Tsymbalenko, S. and Shcheglova, S., 'Kakie oni, podrostki devyanostykh?', *Vospitanie shkol'nikov*, no. 1, 1996, pp. 2–5

Tubel'skii, A., 'Assotsiatsiya innovatsionnykh shkol i tsentrov predlagaet otmenit' "Polozhenie ob attestatsii", i ne tol'ko eto', *Uchitel'skaya gazeta*, no. 14, April 5, 1994, p. 16

Tumova, N., 'Za chto nam ne platyat', *Uchitel'skaya gazeta*, nos. 14–15, April 14, 1998, p. 6

Tvorcheskii soyuz uchitelei SSSR (Moscow: VNIK, 1989)
Val'kova, E., 'Klyuch ne beri!', *Uchitel'skaya gazeta*, no. 1, January 10, 1995, p. 18
Vanyushkina, L., 'Nam nado ponimat' drug druga s poluslova', *Uchitel'skaya gazeta*, nos. 47–8, November 29, 1994, p. 14
Vasil'eva, N., 'A kak dumayut v nashem ministerstve?', *Vechernyaya srednyaya shkola*, no. 2, 1994, pp. 3–5
Vershinin, V., 'Attestatsiya: dokazatel'stvo aksiomy', *Narodnoe obrazovanie*, no. 8, 1994, pp. 35–7
Vishnikina, I., 'Byt' ryadom so shkoloi', *Narodnoe obrazovanie*, no. 7, 1996, pp. 38–40
VNIK – Shkola: Bibliografiya osnovnykh rabot (Moscow: VNIK, 1989)
VNIK – Shkola: Promezhutochnye rezul'taty raboty (Moscow: VNIK, 1990)
'Voidem v novuyu shkolu', *Uchitel'skaya gazeta*, October 18, 1988, p. 2
'Vozvrashchaemsya k vseobshchemu srednemu obrazovaniyu', *Rossiiskie vesti*, July 12, 1994, p. 1
'Vybiraem dostoinykh. Ne agitiruem ni za kogo', *Uchitel'skaya gazeta*, 47, November 30, 1995, pp. 12–13
Yagodin, G., 'Tol'ko svobodnaya shkola vospitaet svobodnogo cheloveka', *Sem'ya*, no. 5, February 11, 1990, pp. 8–9
Yagodin, G., 'Cherez gumanizatsiyu i demokratizatsiyu k novomu kachestvu obrazovaniya', *Uchitel'skaya gazeta*, April 11, 1988, p. 1
Yakimanskaya, I., 'My ne gotovy k vvedeniyu standarta', *Uchitel'skaya gazeta*, no. 1, January 4, 1994, p. 12
Yakovlev, V., 'Tak zhit' nel'zya!', *Uchitel'skaya gazeta*, no. 38, September 24, 1996, p. 4
Yamburg, E., 'Kazhdoe vremya rozhdaet svoi nadezhdy. Ono zhe ikh i ispytivaet', *Uchitel'skaya gazeta*, no. 41, October 19, 1993, pp. 12–13
Yavlinskii, G., 'Fraktsiya "YABLOKO" o probleme privatizatsii obrazovatel'nykh uchrezhdenii', *Uchitel'skaya gazeta*, nos. 43–4, November 15, 1994, p. 10
Yel'tsin, B., 'Ukaz No. 1 prezidenta Rossiiskoi Sovetskoi Federativnoi Sotsialisticheskoi Respubliki: O pervoocherednykh merakh po razvitiyu obrazovaniya v RSFSR', *Uchitel'skaya gazeta*, no. 29, July 16–23, 1991, p. 2
'Zabastovka zakonchilas'. Zabastovka prodolzhaetsya?', *Uchitel'skaya gazeta*, no. 38, October 3, 1995, p. 2
'Zakon Rossiiskoi Federatsii "O razgosudarstvlenii i demonopolizatsii v obrazovatel'noi sfere – Proekt', *Uchitel'skaya gazeta*, no. 34, September 13, 1994, pp. 14–16
'Zakon Rossiiskoi Federatsii ob obrazovanii', Uchitel'skaya gazeta, no. 28, August 4, 1992, *Vedemosti S"ezda Narodnykh Deputatov Rossiiskoi Federatsiii Verkhovnogo Soveta Rossiiskoi Federatsii*, no. 30, 1992, p. 1797
'Zakon Rossiiskoi Sovetskoi Federativnoi Sotsialisticheskoi Respubliki ob obrazovanii. Proekt', *Uchitel'skaya gazeta*, no. 29, July 16–23, 1991, pp. 2 and 5
Zaitsev, V., 'Rukovoditel' poluchaet otmetki', *Uchitel'skaya gazeta*, nos. 22–3, May 23, 1995, p. 16
Zaitsev, V. 'Elitarnaya shkola i sud'ba strany', *Narodnoe obrazovanie*, nos. 2–3, 1994, pp. 5–18
Zazorina, T., 'Likvidatsiya budushchego?', *Molodezh'*, no. 1, 1995, pp. 63–6

Zgorzhel'skaya, T., '"Chastniki" zvonyat i sprashivayut', *Uchitel'skaya gazeta*, no. 9, March 7, 1995, p. 9
Zhelezovskaya, G., 'Formirovanie pedagogicheskoi intellektual'noi kul'tury', *Pedagogika*, no. 2, 1995, pp. 55–60
Zhirkov, E., 'Den'gi, den'gi. Nichego, krome deneg', *Uchitel'skaya gazeta*, no. 25, June 6, 1995, p. 17
Zhukov, V., 'Chestno o chastnoi shkole', *Sem'ya i shkola*, no. 5, 1996, pp. 2–5
Zhukov, V., 'Chastnye shkoly kak obshchestvennoe yavlenie', *Vospitanie shkol'nikov*, nos. 3–4, 1992, pp. 21–5
'Zvonok na peremenu iz Belogo doma', *Uchitel'skaya gazeta*, no. 30, July 29, 1997, p. 3
Zyazun, I., *Uchitel', kotorogo zhdut* (Moscow: Pedagogika, 1988)
'28 aprelya – nasha vzyala!', *Uchitel'skaya gazeta*, nos. 19–20, May 4, 1994, p. 2
'100 luchshikh shkol Rossii', *Ogonek*, no. 15, 1995, pp. 32–3

3. English-language sources

Aleshenok, S., Chuprov, V. and Zubok, Yu., 'Will It Be Possible To Integrate Young People in a Society Undergoing Transformation?', *Prospects*, vol. 25, no. 3, 1995, pp. 439–49
Archer, M., *Social Origins of Educational Systems* (London: Sage, 1984)
Aspin, D., 'The Conception of Democracy: A Philosophy for Democratic Education', in J. Chapman, I. Froumin and D. Aspin (eds), *Creating and Managing the Democratic School* (London: Falmer Press, 1995), pp. 30–59
Avis, G. (ed.), *The Making of the Soviet Citizen: Character Formation and Civic Training in Soviet Education* (London: Croom Helm, 1987)
Baiduzhii, A., 'Private Schools Teach Shooting and Praying', *Current Digest of the Post-Soviet Press*, vol. 44, no. 28, p. 27 (translated from *Nezavisimaya gazeta*, July 16, 1992, p. 6)
Balzer, H. (ed.), *Russia's Missing Middle Class: The Professions in Russian History* (Armonk, NY: M.E. Sharpe, 1996)
Beare, H. and Slaughter, R., *Education for the Twenty-First Century* (London: Routledge, 1993)
Bennett, N. and Carr, C., 'Teachers' Early Experiences of the Implementation of the British National Curriculum', in D. Carter and M. O'Neill (eds), *Case Studies in International Change: an International Perspective* (London: Falmer Press, 1995), pp. 184–98
Berger, G., 'The Morale of Teachers in Crisis: Russia 1992', *Journal of Research and Development in Education*, vol. 27, no. 1, 1993, pp. 24–7
Birzea, C., *Educational Policies of the Countries in Transition* (Strasbourg: Council of Europe Press, 1994)
Bolotov, V., 'The Challenge of Educational Reform in Russia', *ISRE Newsletter*, vol. 3, nos. 1–2, 1994, pp. 2–7
Bolotov, V., 'Political Education in Russia: The Role of Secondary Education', *Education in Russia, the Independent States and Eastern Europe*, vol. 14, no. 1, 1996, pp. 2–7

Bolotov, V., 'The Reform of Education in New Russia: A Background Report for the OECD Review of Russian Education', *ISRE Newsletter*, vol. 6, no. 2, 1997, p. 9

Bourdieu, P. and Passeron, J., *Reproduction in Education, Society and Culture* (London: Sage, 1977)

Buckley, M., *Redefining Russian Society and Polity* (Boulder, CO: Westview Press, 1993)

Cook, J., *The Soviet Social Contract and Why It Failed* (Cambridge: Harvard University Press, 1993)

Coons, J., 'The New Russian Education Law: an Appreciation and Some Precautions', in J. de Groof (ed.), *Comments on the Law on Education of the Russian Federation* (Leuven: Acco, 1993), pp. 87–94

Corbett, H. and Wilson, B., *Testing, Reform and Rebellion* (Norwood, NY: Ablex, 1990)

Dalin, P. and Rolff, H.-G., *Changing the School Culture* (London: Cassell, 1993)

Daniels, H., Lucas, N., Totterdell, M. and Fromina, O., 'Humanisation in Russian Education: a Transition Between State Determinism and Individualism', *Educational Studies*, vol. 21, no. 1, 1995, pp. 29–39

Davies, L., *Beyond Authoritarian School Management* (Ticknell: Education Now Books, 1994)

Davies, L., 'The Management and Mismanagement of School Effectiveness', *Compare*, vol. 24, no. 3, 1994, p. 205–16

de Groof, J. (ed.), *Comments on the Law on Education of the Russian Federation* (Leuven, Acco, 1993)

de Groof, J., 'Analysis of the "Legislation on Education of the Russian Federation"', in J. de Groof (ed.), *Comments on the Law on Education of the Russian Federation* (Leuven: Acco, 1993) pp. 31–59

Dneprov, E., 'Bureaucratic Tyranny (Must Be Eliminated from the School)', in B. Eklof and E. Dneprov (eds), *Democracy in the Russian School: the Reform Movement since 1984* (Boulder, CO: Westview), pp. 36–41

Dneprov, E., *Reform of Education in Russia and State Policy in the Educational System* (Moscow: Ministry of Education of the Russian Federation, 1992)

Dunstan, J. (ed.), *Soviet Education Under Scrutiny* (Glasgow: Jordanhill College, 1987)

Dunstan, J. and Suddaby, A., 'The Progressive Tradition in Soviet Schooling to 1988', in J. Dunstan (ed.), *Soviet Education under Perestroika* (London: Routledge, 1992), pp. 1–13

Dunstan, J., 'Clever Children and Curriculum Reform', in A Jones (ed.), *Education and Society in the New Russia* (Armonk, NY: M.E. Sharpe), pp. 75–101

Dunstan, J., *Paths to Excellence and the Soviet School* (Windsor: NFER Publishing, 1978)

Dworkin, A., *Teacher Burnout in the Public Schools: Structural Causes and the Consequences for Children* (Albany, NY: State University of New York Press, 1986)

Dzhilavian, L., 'The Professional Attitude of Teacher Training Graduates in the Armenian SSR Toward Their Profession', *Soviet Education*, vol. 21, no. 6, 1981, pp. 92–6 (translated from *Sotsiologicheskie issledovaniya*, no. 4, 1978, pp. 141–3)

Eklof, B. and Dneprov. E. (eds), *Democracy in the Russian School: the Reform Movement in Education since 1984* (Boulder, CO: Westview, 1993)

Federal Components of the State Educational Standard for Primary, Secondary (Incomplete) and Secondary (Complete) Schools: General Provisions (Moscow: Ministerstvo obrazovaniya Rossiiskoi Federatsii, 1995)

Fullan, M., *The New Meaning of Educational Change* (London: Cassell, 1991)

Gershunskii, B. and Pullin, R., 'Current Dilemmas for Soviet Secondary Education: an Anglo-Soviet Analysis', *Comparative Education*, vol. 26, nos 2 and 3, 1990, pp. 307–18

Glenn, C., 'Organizing the Russian Educational System for Freedom and Accountability', in J. de Groof (ed.), *Comments on the Law on Education of the Russian Federation* (Leuven: Acco, 1993), pp. 95–104

Goodlad, J., *Teachers for Our Nation's Schools* (San Francisco: Jossey-Bass, 1990)

Goodlad, J., *A Place Called School: Prospects for the Future* (New York: McGraw-Hill, 1984)

Goodlad, J., *The Dynamics of Educational Change* (Toronto: McGraw-Hill, 1975)

Gorbachev, M., 'Youth: a Creative Force for Revolutionary Renewal', *Soviet Education*, vol. 31, no. 3, 1989, pp. 3–4 (translated from *Uchitel'skaya gazeta*, April 18, 1987, pp. 1–2)

Grant, N., 'Education in the Soviet Union: the Last Phase', *Compare*, vol. 22, no. 1, 1992, pp. 69–80

Hepburn, M. (ed.), *Education in Democratic Schools and Classrooms* (Washington, DC: National Council for the Social Sciences, 1983)

Heyneman, S., 'Education and Social Stability in Russia: an Essay', *Compare*, vol. 27, no. 1, 1997, pp. 5–18

Higgins, J., 'Problems of the Selection and Professional Orientation of Soviet Pedagogical Students', *Comparative Education*, vol. 12, no. 2, 1976, pp. 157–62

Holmes, L., 'Legitimizing the Soviet Regime: School No. 35, 1931–1937', in B. Eklof (ed.), *School and Society in Tsarist and Soviet Russia* (London: Macmillan, 1993), pp. 176–203

Holmes, L., *The Kremlin and the Schoolhouse: Reforming Education in Soviet Russia*, 1917–1933 (Bloomington: Indiana University Press, 1991)

Holmes, B., Read, G. and Voskresenskaya, N., *Russian Education: Tradition and Transition* (London: Garland Publishing, 1995)

Hord, S., *Evaluating Educational Innovation* (London: Croom Helm, 1987)

Howey, K. and Zimphner, N., *Profiles of Preservice Teacher Education* (Albany: SUNY Press, 1989)

Hull, C. and Rudduck, J., *Introducing Innovation to Pupils* (Norwich: Centre for Applied Research in Education, 1980)

Jennings, M. and Niemi, R. (eds), *The Political Character of Adolescence: the Influence of Families and Schools* (Princeton: Princeton University Press, 1974)

Johnson, M., 'Russian Education Reform in the 1990s', *The Harriman Review*, vol. 9, no. 4, 1996, pp. 36–45

Jonathan, R. 'Education and "The Needs of Society"', in A. Hartnett and M. Nash (eds), *Education and Society Today* (London: Falmer Press, 1986), pp. 134–45

Jones, A. (ed.) *Education and Society in the New Russia* (Armonk, NY: M.E. Sharpe, 1994)

Jones, A., 'Teachers in the Soviet Union', in A. Jones (ed.), *Professions and the State: Expertise and Autonomy in the Soviet Union and Eastern Europe* (Philadelphia: Temple University Press, 1991), pp. 152–66

Jones, A., 'Problems in the Schools', in A. Jones, W. Connor and D. Powell (eds), *Soviet Social Problems* (Boulder, CO: Westview, 1991), pp. 213–26

Jones, E., *Red Army and Society* (London: Allen & Unwin, 1985)

Kapto, A., Kultygin, V. and Sukmodeev, V. (eds), *Social Knowledge in Russia: Heritage, Challenges, Perspectives* (Moscow: Institute for Social and Political Research, 1998)

Kerr, S., 'Diversification in Russian Education', in A. Jones (ed.), *Education and Society in the New Russia*, pp. 47–74

Kerr, S., 'Lessons Learned: Western Aid to Russian Education', *ISRE Newsletter*, vol. 5, no. 1, 1996, pp. 1–2

Kerr, S., 'Teachers' Continuing Education and Russian School Reform', Paper delivered at the Conference of the American Association for the Advancement of Slavic Studies, October 28, 1995

Khankasaeva, I., untitled article, *Rossiiskie vesti*, August 29, 1992, cited in B. Eklof, 'The Most Difficult Year in the History of Our Schools', *ISSE Newsletter*, vol. 2, no. 1, 1992, p. 1

Kohli, W., 'Humanising Education in the Soviet Union: a Plea for Caution in these Postmodern Times', *Studies in Philosophy and Education*, vol. 11, no. 2, 1991, pp. 51–63

Kotasek, J., 'Visions of Educational Development in the Post-Socialist Era', *International Review of Education*, vol. 39, no. 6, 1993, pp. 473–87

Kozakiewicz, M., 'The Difficult Road to Educational Pluralism in Central and Eastern Europe', *Prospects*, vol. 22, no. 2, 1992, pp. 207–15

Lawton, D., 'The National Curriculum in England Since 1988', in D. Carter and M. O'Neill (eds), *International Perspectives on Educational Reform and Policy Implementation* (London: Falmer Press, 1995), pp. 44–51

Lewis, R., Newitt, M. and Sokolov, A., *Reform of History Teaching and Research in Russia* (University of Exeter: Report to Nuffield Foundation, 1993)

Lortie, D., 'Built-in Tendencies Toward Stabilizing the Principal's Role', *Journal of Research and Development in Education*, vol. 22, no. 1, 1987, pp. 80–90

Louis, K. and Miles, M., *Improving the Urban High School: What Works and Why* (New York: Teachers' College Press, 1990)

Mann, D. and Briller, V., *Russian School Directors: Problems and Proposals* (Washington, DC: World Bank, 1994)

Marinicheva, O., 'Power Was Dumped in Our Laps: What Happens to the Former Opposition When it Ends Up in the Corridors of Power', in B. Eklof and E. Dneprov (eds) *Democracy in the Russian School: The Reform Movement in Education Since 1984* (Boulder, CO: Westview, 1993), pp. 128–33

Matthews, M., *Education in the Soviet Union: Policies and Institutions since Stalin* (London: Allen & Unwin, 1982)

Mazzoni, T., 'Politics of Education at the Federal Level', in J. Scribner and D. Layton (eds), *The Study of Educational Politics* (London: Falmer Press, 1994), pp. 53–73

McKenzie, J., *Education as a Political Issue* (Aldershot: Avebury, 1993)

Men'shikov, V., 'Are We Teaching Any Old Thing, Any Old Way?', *Soviet Education*, vol. 33, no. 3, 1991, pp. 39–40
Mitter, W., 'The Teacher and the Bureaucracy: Some Considerations Concluded from a Soviet Case', *Compare*, vol. 17, no. 1, 1987, pp. 47–60
Morrow, R. and C. Torres, *Social Theory and Education* (Albany, NY: SUNY Press, 1995)
Muckle, J., *Portrait of a Soviet School Under Glasnost'* (London: Macmillan, 1990)
Nikandrov, N., 'Russian Education After Perestroika: The Search for New Values?', *International Review of Education*, vol. 41, nos. 1–2, 1995, pp. 47–57
Ourja, O., 'Problems of Social Stratification Research in Russia', in A. Kapto *et al.* (eds), *Social Knowledge in Russia: Heritage, Challenges, Perspectives* (Moscow: Institute for Social and Political Research, 1998), pp. 43–6
Paustovic, N. 'Problems of Reforming Educational Systems in Post-Communist Countries', *International Review of Education*, vol. 39, no. 5, 1993, pp. 405–18
Poppleton, P., Bolton, R. Pullin, R. and Riseborough, G., '*Perestroika* and the Soviet Teachers', *New Era in Education*, vol. 71, no. 3, 1990, pp. 92–7
Raywid, M., 'The Evolving Effort to Improve Schools: Pseudo-Reforms, Incremental Reform, and Restructuring', *Phi Delta Kappan*, vol. 72, no. 2, 1990, pp. 139–43
Rigby, T., 'Russia in Search of Its Future', in A. Saikal and W. Maley (eds), *Russia in Search of its Future* (Cambridge: Cambridge University Press, 1995), pp. 207–25
Rogers, C., *Freedom to Learn for the Eighties* (Columbus, OH: Merrill, 1983)
Rogers, R., (ed.), *Education and Social Class* (London: Falmer Press, 1986)
Rosenholtz, S., *Teacher's Workplace: the Social Organization of Schools* (New York: Longman, 1989)
Russia: Education in the Transition (Washington, DC: World Bank, 1995)
Sandi, A., 'Why Is It So Difficult? Misconceptions about East European Education in Transition', *International Review of Education*, vol. 38, no. 6, 1992, pp. 629–39
Sarason, S., *The Culture of the School and the Problem of Change* (Boston: Allyn & Bacon, 1971)
Sarason, S., *The Predictable Failure of Educational Reform* (San Francisco, CA: Jossey-Bass, 1990)
Sarason, S., *Revisiting 'The Culture of the School and the Problem of Change'* (New York: Teachers' College Columbia University, 1996)
Sashkin, M. and Egermeier, J., 'School Change Models and Processes: a Review of Research and Practice', Paper presented at the Annual Meeting of the American Educational Research Association, San Francisco, 1992
Shaulin, V., 'The Law on Education of the Russian Federation', *ISRE Newsletter*, vol. 4, no. 2, 1995 pp. 2–11
Shaw, K., 'Change in the Soviet School System: Some Factors Associated with the 1984 Reforms', University of Exeter: Unpublished PhD thesis, 1987
Shlapentokh, V. 'Early Feudalism – the Best Parallel for Contemporary Russia?', *Europe–Asia Studies*, vol. 48, no. 3 1996, pp. 393–411
Shlapentokh, V., *Public and Private Life of the Soviet People: Changing Values in Post-Stalin Russia* (Oxford: Oxford University Press, 1989)

Shturman, D., *The Soviet Secondary School* (London: Routledge, 1988)

Silverman, B. and Yanowitch, M., *New Rich, New Poor, New Russia: Winners and Losers on the Road to Capitalism* (Armonk, NY: M.E. Sharpe, 1997)

Staroverov, V. and Williams, C., 'Russian Sociology: Problems and Perspectives – Two Perspectives', in C. Williams, V. Chuprov and V. Staroverov (eds), *Russian Society in Transition* (Aldershot: Dartmouth, 1996), pp. 37–54

Suddaby, A., 'An Evaluation of the Contribution of the Teacher-Innovators to Soviet Educational Reform', *Comparative Education*, vol. 25, no. 2, 1989, pp. 245–56

Sutherland, J., 'The Law of the Russian Federation on Denationalization and Demonopolization in the Educational Sphere: a Summary', *Education in Russia, the Independent States and Eastern Europe*, vol. 13, no. 2, 1995, pp. 92–4

Sutherland, J., '*Perestroika* in the Soviet General School: from Innovation to Independence?', in J. Dunstan (ed.), *Soviet Education Under Perestroika* (London: Routledge, 1992), pp. 14–29

Szebenyi, P., 'Change in the Systems of Public Education in East Central Europe', *Comparative Education*, vol. 28, no. 1, 1992, pp. 19–31

Szekeley, B., 'The New Soviet Educational Reform', *Comparative Education Review*, vol. 30, no. 3, 1986, pp. 321–43

Thiesen, G. and Adams, D., 'Comparative Education Research', in R. Murray Thomas (ed.), *International Comparative Education: Practices, Issues and Prospects* (Oxford: Pergamon, 1990), pp. 277–87

Tkachenko, E., 'Education Reform in Russia', *ISRE Newsletter*, vol. 3, nos. 1–2, 1994, pp. 14–17

Troyna, B. and Williams, J., *Racism Education and the State* (London: Croom Helm, 1986)

Tumalev, V., 'The Teaching Profession in a Situation of Social and Political Change: Part 1 The Teaching Profession as a Socio-Occupational Stratum', *Russian Education and Society*, vol. 39, no. 3, March 1997, pp. 4–90 (translated from *Uchitel'stvo v situatsii sotsial'no politicheskikh peremen* (St Petersburg: Izdatel'stvo Sankt-Peterburgskogo universiteta ekonomiki i finansov, 1995)

Vendrovskaya, R., 'Lessons of Differentiated Instruction', *Russian Education and Society*, vol. 34, no. 1, 1992, pp. 73–94 (translated from *Sovetskaya pedagogika*, no. 11, 1990, pp. 78–86)

Walford, G. 'Reflexive Accounts of Doing Educational Research' in G. Walford (ed.), *Doing Educational Research* (London: Routledge, 1991), pp. 1–18

Webber, S., 'Demand and Supply: Meeting the Need for Teachers in the New Russian School', *Journal of Education for Teaching*, vol. 22, no. 1, 1996, pp. 9–26

Webber, S. and Webber, T., 'Issues in Teacher Education', in A. Jones (ed.), *Education and Society in the New Russia* (Armonk, NY: M.E. Sharpe, 1994), pp. 231–59

Webber, S. and Webber, T., 'Restructuring Initial Teacher and Education in Russia', *Education in Russia, the Independent States and Eastern Europe*, vol. 12, no. 1, 1994, pp. 4–5

Westbrook, M., 'St Petersburg's Independent Schools', in A. Jones (ed.), *Education and Society in the New Russia* (Armonk, NY: M.E. Sharpe, 1994), pp. 103–17

White, J., *The Aims of Education Revisited* (London: Routledge & Kegan Paul, 1982), pp. 2–3

Williams, C., 'Economic Reform and Political Change in Russia, 1991–1996', in C. Williams, V. Chuprov and V. Staroverov (eds), *Russian Society in Transition* (Aldershot: Dartmouth, 1996), pp. 9–36

Willis, P., *Learning to Labour* (Famborough: Saxon House, 1977)

Yel'tsin, B., 'School Reform: Ways to Accelerate It', *Soviet Education*, vol. 31, no. 2, 1989, pp. 76–90 (translated from *Uchitel'skaya gazeta*, July 3, 1986, pp. 1–2)

Shuravlev, G., Kuchmaeva, O., Mel'nikov, B. and Orlova, I., 'The Socio-Demographic Situation' in C. Williams, V. Chuprov and V. Staroverov (eds), *Russian Society in Transition* (Aldershot: Dartmouth, 1996), pp. 58–60

Index of Names

Index of Subjects